KILT
IN THE
CLOSET

JIMMY TOLMIE

Tellwell Talent
www.tellwell.ca

ISBN
978-0-2288-2253-0 (Hardcover)
978-0-2288-2252-3 (Paperback)
978-0-2288-2254-7 (eBook)

For Irene, Alison and Grant whose courage,
grit and determination are an example to us all.

PART I

LITTLE STEPS

"It's the steady, quiet, plodding ones who win in the lifelong race."
- Robert Service

CHAPTER 1

LONDON

"It's too hot for Luca to stand on the sun!"

"And there's no air up there, Luca won't be able to breathe."

"How would we know that Luca turned on his torch at that time?"

Gregor Mitchell MacCrimmon took a deep breath and surveyed the mess of his mathematics class. Somehow he had found himself sucked into a red herring during his lesson on multiplication. The twelve year olds before him had asked about the speed of sound. They had moved onto the speed of light. He had explained that the light from the sun takes eight minutes to travel from the sun to the Earth's surface. Luca was sat at the back of the class, rocking on his chair with his arms folded and an impish grin on his face. Gregor had resolved to get him engaged in the topic.

"Imagine that Luca is sat on the surface of the sun with a torch. At midday, he turns it on. Eight minutes later we who are waiting here look up and see Luca's light. 186,000 miles per second multiplied by 60 multiplied by 8, that is the distance from the sun to the Earth."

The lesson had ceased to be mathematical. The centre of attention, the focus of concern, was now Luca. Luca was soon to be sent to sit on the sun, soon to be dismissed from his comfortable classroom setting in the London Borough of Hounslow and sent to an alien world equipped with nothing but a puny little flashlight.

The year was 1976. It was the first teaching post for young MacCrimmon. He had been trained to teach history and English but instead found himself teaching mathematics and the occasional Latin lesson. He was grateful for the job. He had been welcomed by kindly colleagues who wished him well. He had been allocated a supervisor teacher, a kindly Welsh woman named Ms. Brynna Thomas. Legend had it that Ms. Thomas' first excursion outside of Wales had been in hot pursuit of an American airman. She had followed him to London with Celtic ardour only to discover that his equal passion for her was sadly not exclusive. Too ashamed to admit her failure, she had stayed in London and found herself training to be a teacher. Now she was in her mid-fifties. Her family were her colleagues, her children were her pupils. Kindly or not, Gregor was grateful that she had not witnessed his mathematical misdemeanours.

Gregor Mitchell MacCrimmon had grown to like London. He had been born in a city but really that was where his connection with cities ended. Aberdeen was his place of birth but his early upbringing had been in rural Aberdeenshire until his parents exchanged the far northeast for the gentler climes of the southwest of England. So, his growing up had continued in rural Somerset. But he liked London. He liked the anonymity. He liked the bustle. He liked that he could disappear in the crowd. He liked that so many people did not know of his existence and, as a result, couldn't care less about him.

He had found himself living in an upstairs flat with Paul from Manchester and Les from North Wales. Paul was an avid Manchester United fan who worked for the British Oxygen Company (BOC) and Les was a P.E. teacher in his school. They had an easy relationship with each other. They had had the occasional weekend of alcoholic excess when they had "gone up West" to *really* sample London. The West End of London was the centre of the universe. But really Les, Paul and Gregor had not made the most of it. There was no talk of West End plays, no forays into musicals, no film shows, it was all about pubs and clubs. There were Yates' Wine Lodges for a bit of culture but then yoghurt left out of the fridge develops more culture than a Yates' Wine Lodge. No, they were young and naïve. They might as well have been in the pubs and clubs of their home towns for all that there was a difference. London was not Carnaby Street in the sixties, but it was still cool.

The flat had a spare bedroom. So, to save money the boys had decided to sublet it and line their pockets with a little bit extra. Accordingly, a young, attractive Primary School teacher had arrived to be interviewed by the three of them to see if she could fit in. Indeed, they had spent a hilarious midweek evening at the local German Bierkeller preparing questions that they would ask Jean in the interview. "What did Jean expect from her flatmates?" "Was she a tidy freak?" "Was she likely to spend hours in the bathroom?"

Jean positioned herself on the edge of the threadbare sofa and rested her feet on the careworn carpet. The tables were quickly turned. The interviewers quickly became the interviewees. It was Jean who conducted the interview. She had a list of expectations, a plethora of requirements, a myriad of unacceptable behaviours. If Jean was going to become part of their community it was obvious that it was going to be on Jean's terms.

"What do you think?" asked Gregor after she had left.

"There is absolutely **NO** way that I can live in the same place as *that* woman," Paul stated emphatically.

Les nodded with subdued agreement.

Jean moved in during the next week. In the week after that Paul moved into her room with her, And suddenly, again there was a spare room.

Dick had married too young, he claimed, and was now separated from his wife. He was determined to be a single man, forthright in his wish to make up for lost time. Dick did not have to go through the interview process, the interrogation that Jean had faced. The guys accepted him with relish. Jean, being new to the flat, was not consulted. He arrived with a car load of boxes, ready to move in.

"We have a dustbin already," observed Gregor as Dick dragged his massive rubbish bin up the stairs.

"This is for our homebrew, Gregor," was the enthusiastic reply.

"Oh goody," muttered Paul with the sarcasm of a man who was in love and had left those irresponsible days behind him, too mature now for a bit of daft carry-on with his flatmates of a weekend.

The brewing kit was left in the corner of the living room and soon "Dick's Demon," for so the beer was to be called, was frothing and bubbling away in its own inimical, ill-disciplined manner.

Gregor had long ago decided that midweek drinking was not for him. The "morning after" in the classroom with children to educate and to placate really was a "mourning after" with the fatigue and banging head of a hangover. It might have been different if one was Paul and could sit in one's cubicle at BOC nursing one's self-infliction into a new day with a pretence of work. No hiding place for pretence in the classroom. Dick was a math teacher. He knew the stupidity of midweek alcoholic carry-ons but he was newly single and tempted and simply didn't care.

"It's ready," Dick announced to all and sundry one Wednesday night. Gregor was still distracted by an incident he had had with young Maurice Bellknap during the working day.

"What's ready?" he asked quizzically.

"'Dick's Demon' is ready. I can feel it. I can sense it. Let me show you."

All five of them trekked off to the living room as Dick grinningly and proudly drew back the cover on his creation.

"What do you think?"

Jean turned her nose up. "Very cloudy."

"Looks like the sewage outflow in Bangor after the boys have had a night out on the beer and curry," said Les Welshly. North Wales had never seemed less attractive.

Dick rubbed his hands with glee. "Let's get some glasses."

They all took a taster.

"What's the verdict?" Dick licked his lips, proud to be the father of the brew.

"Soapy," Paul wrinkled his nose.

"Not an award winner," exclaimed Gregor who had avidly embraced the ideas of microbreweries but the "Campaign for Real Ale" (CAMRA) was still some years in the future.

"Good enough for London," ventured Les with a sudden exclamation of hometown jingoism.

"I have marking and prep to do." Jean took herself off, leaving her flatmates to ponder a vast vat of festering froth that nobody other than Dick was really rapt about.

All was quiet as Jean settled herself at the desk in her bedroom, which now doubled as their work place. It was well organized and neat. She settled before her marking and moved fluidly into the flow of tick and cross. Occasionally she muttered something in frustration at errors on the page, frequently there was a little squeal of joy as she read the work of the student who had an unexpectedly delightful turn of phrase. After an hour, Jean wondered at the quiet, indeed wondered **why** the quiet. She thought if her colleagues and her lover were trying and testing the evil looking brew, there would have been noise and high jinks but there were none. Maybe they had gone out. Jean stretched her hunched shoulders and stood up. She decided to go and investigate. At that moment, there was the crash of a door and a yell.

Jean dashed from her room and walked briskly to the sitting room. On entering she found the men poring over the innards of a shoebox. Each was offering advice about what to do with the contents.

"Mouth to mouth."

"It's dead I tell you."

"I think it is breathing."

Jean pushed her way to the shoebox to find a baby sparrow lying still, flat on its back, looking more dead than alive. The poor wee beast had obviously suffered a severe bout of vomiting and diarrhea. Les retreated to the sofa and put his head in his hands, obviously upset. Offers of more beer were made. Slurred noises of commiseration.

"You did your best, mate".

"Poor wee thing never had a chance."

"Looks like he shat himself to death," exclaimed Paul with all the sensitivity of a rock.

Jean sat down next to Les and placed a maternal arm around his hunched shoulders.

"Tell us what you did."

Les composed himself. "Well, I came home early from work one day. There was nobody else here. I made myself a cuppa tea and came and sat here in the living room. I noticed some movement in the fireplace and found this little character lying helpless in the ashes. I made him a home in a shoebox and hand fed him milk."

"This looks a little bit more than milk," observed Paul with quizzical, yet confident, scatology.

"Well, we had run out of milk, he looked hungry so I rummaged around for something else to feed him. I stumbled on a tin of Gregor's sardines, mashed them up and fed them gently to him."

Silence in the room. Jaws dropped open. All the others looked at each other aghast and agape. Eventually the silence was broken by Jean.

"Let's get this straight, Les, you fed a newborn nestling a tin of sardines because we had run out of milk?"

"Yes, I couldn't see the harm."

Dick could control himself no longer.

"You force fed the poor bastard sardines, Les. Les, you killed him."

"Were they spicy sardines, Les? You know the ones with hot peppers added?" said Paul.

"I don't know," mumbled Les.

Jean shook her head and went off to the kitchen. The men heard the fridge door open, the bustled clatter of dishes and, suddenly a loud shriek. Jean appeared at the door, holding the butter dish at arms length and with undisguised disgust.

"Ahhh, that's where they are!" exclaimed Gregor sheepishly.

He reached forward and removed his two false teeth from the slab of butter. He looked at them tersely as if he was about to scold them for taking themselves off without asking. He was blissfully unaware of the disgusted look on Jean's face.

The manslaughter of the bird and the finding of the teeth caused more beer to be drunk. Midnight came and went. The morning dawned with pale faces, red eyes, noxious fumes and the terrible realization that today was a work day.

Somehow ties and jackets were found. Water was drunk, coffee was consumed. Dick and Gregor were set for school together in the latter's Morris 1300. Hounslow High Street was not quite traffic gridlock but it was grid with a touch of lock and lock with a smidge of grid. There certainly was nowhere to pull off the road.

"Stop the car!" was the desperate plea from the passenger seat.

Such emphasis brooked no refusal as the door was already flung open. Dick delivered a technicolour yawn all over the kerb and closed the door quickly. A hundred yards down the road, the car was halted again and the driver's door was flung open and Gregor dumped his load on the bonnet of a polished looking red Mercedes crawling in the opposite direction. The immaculately dressed driver of this luxury car was forcefully loquacious and honest with his thoughts at the mess. Sadly, neither could stop and remonstrate for long. Gregor reflected that he was not overly impressed by the vocabulary of his new-found protagonist.

Dick and Gregor held things together until the school car park when both doors were flung open and further deposits were spread over the London Borough of Hounslow, a messy baptism of their place of work. Dick disappeared to where all good math teachers go to die. As he left, Gregor expressed the heartfelt wish that he wanted never to see Dick or his Demon Drink ever again. Then, piteously, he made his sorry way to the staffroom and collapsed on a chair. He felt like death and hoped that it would come to him soon.

There is a disease that hits upon certain school teachers after they have been in the profession for far too long. As far as Gregor knew there was no medical term for it, but the symptoms manifested themselves clearly enough. Gregor looked up and saw the shadow of Miss Arabella Mastiff, the Deputy Head of the Middle School, leaning over him.

"You don't look well, Gregor. Maybe you have the flu. Shall I send you home?"

All delivered as if to a child of five who suffered from a language deficit. Gregor had often wondered if Ms. Mastiff had always talked to everybody like that and wondered how that went down when she was having a Sunday afternoon's sherry with her close friends. However, wonder was a luxury at this moment of pale, frail existence. It was a thought too far. His aching head reminded him not to wonder anymore; wonder was a dwarf mining his way through a frontal lobe with his pick.

Gregor wanted nothing more but to go home and nurse his humiliating sorry state in the privacy of his own bed and own toilet. A disembodied voice, which he strangely recognized as his own, suddenly burst forth.

"No, no, I'll be fine. No problem."

Gregor could not believe what he had just said but what was done was done. He relapsed into a miserable silence, stared wretchedly at a spot on the far wall and swore miserably private oaths of temperance. If his life was spared this day no drop of alcohol would ever again pass his lips. He was done with the evils of drink. Dick's Demon was the last straw.

Gerry Napper appeared in his vision and sat down opposite him with a smile on his face. Gerry had retired from teaching some years before, but boredom had set in after he had completed his bucket list a couple of years previously. Now he hung about the staffroom, chain smoking his cigarettes and peering wisely over the florid bulbous rosiness of his nose. Gerry looked for moments in the day when he could help out a colleague in some way. Gerry had earned the right to be a law and a lore unto himself. He smiled knowingly across at Gregor's pale face and glanced briefly at his shaking right hand.

"I know what's wrong with you."

"Flu?" Gregor suggested pathetically.

"This is what I'll do for you. You sit here and nurse your *flu* for the morning and I will take your classes, OK?" Gerry's grin was knowing, he shook his head with a benign understanding.

"OK," conceded Gregor as the remnants of his pride and fight slumped into cowardly flight.

Midday arrived and with it the end of morning school. A caffeinated Gregor was now rampaging around the staffroom, laughing and bantering with his colleagues as they arrived for their lunch break. He observed Gerry entering the staffroom with his unlit cigarette in his mouth.

"Sooo?" questioned Gregor as Gerry sat down next to him, "How did it go?"

"Swimmingly. Only problem was Tina Barrett. I set the work and she said, 'I'm not f!@$#-ing doing that!'"

"What did you say?"

"I looked her in the eye and told her that she was f!@$%-ing going to do it otherwise there was no f!@#%-ing break time for her. She got on with it."

Gregor reflected that a retired Gerry could say what he wanted, he could iterate the thoughts of the first-year teacher with colourful honesty and bluntness, whereas Gregor was hidebound by his youth and first-year status and the looming presence of his mentor teacher, Ms. Thomas.

"Many, many years," he thought to himself, "until I can tell the Tina Barretts of this world what they really need to hear."

Gregor found Dick later in the day. He looked and sounded worse than Gregor. Gregor was now perky and ready for anything. Dick was down in the mouth. Gregor couldn't resist rubbing it in. He rested his arm on his shoulder.

"I want you to know, Dick, that I forgive you." He smiled, turned on his heel and left.

It was always interesting living with Dick. Gregor was trying to be a good and conscientious teacher. It became almost all consuming. He was not becoming a danger in traffic or anything like that but he was overthinking things, becoming distracted and missing cues. Dick had deserted those qualities when he had deserted his wife.

Carol Stable was a stunningly beautiful teacher. The men in the staffroom were frequently noisy and boisterous, but it all seemed to go quiet when Carol entered the room. To add to her attractiveness she was blissfully unaware of the effect she had. She was shy and retiring and deeply committed to her art teaching. She was totally oblivious of the many male heads that followed her every move when she entered a room.

One day, Gregor had the last period of the day free so decided to go home early. He escaped the car park and avoided the rush hour so was home far quicker than he had expected. He was desperate for the toilet so unlocked the door, dashed up the stairs through the kitchen and found the toilet door locked. This was a surprise. Nobody else should be home. He rattled the door knob.

"Is anybody in there?"

"Just a minute." A woman's voice.

Gregor stepped back. Eventually he heard the toilet flush, the door being unlocked and out came Carol Stable. Her head was bowed, her face was crimson with embarrassment. She raised a hand in greeting, grabbed a coat and bag from a chair and Gregor heard her running down the stairs and out of the front door.

Gregor had not moved. He was stunned. Eventually he heard a door close behind him and Dick appeared in the kitchen.

"What was Carol Stable doing in our toilet?"

"Hmmm, I guess she needed to go."

"OK. What was she doing in our flat?"

"Oh, she lost her key so I took pity on her and let her hang out here while she phoned her flatmate."

"That was nice of you, Dick."

"Yes, it was, wasn't it?"

He turned to go back to his room.

"Hey Dick, it's 4:00 p.m. Why are you in your dressing gown?"

"I was tired so I went for a nap."

"Carol was hanging around the flat and you went for a nap?"

"Yep, that's about the size of it." He grinned and winked impishly.

With that, Dick gave Gregor a wave, turned on his heel and disappeared into his room. Gregor thought nothing more of it, poured himself a glass of milk, changed into his running gear and went for a jog. He was running on the spot waiting for a traffic light to change when a light bulb exploded in his head. He was so, so naïve, it took him so, so long to read a situation and understand it. How could he hope to be effective in his job and help children and understand them if he could not read between the lines? He was going to have to learn to step back, to take a breath, not to be focused always on what he was going to teach and how he was going to teach it.

He thought back through what he had just witnessed in the flat. He thought about Carol's embarrassment, Dick's dressing gown, Dick's smirk and Dick's explanation. Most people would have understood the situation immediately and not questioned and quizzed. Had he gone into school the following day and blurted out something untoward in the staffroom to Carol about losing her keys or, generally to all, that Carol had dropped by their flat yesterday then he would have embarrassed Dick, actually that was probably not possible, and mortified Carol. He would have set tongues wagging.

Gregor was not a fool. He realized that his innocence was an endearing quality and gained him lots of friendships. People liked him for it. But he was going to have to learn wisdom, have to walk in on situations and watch and read and not say anything. A simple biting of his lip, a focused time lapse would help stop him blundering in with bull in a china shop vigour. "Why use a teaspoon when a hammer will do?" This had been a state of being for Gregor for a long time. He was resolved from now on to reach for the teaspoon more often.

So, life in the top flat near Hounslow Railway Station resumed a steady rhythm of comings and goings. Dick's Demon still throbbed away in the corner. Jean and Paul were immersed in each other. Les took pity on no more nestlings. Gregor found a local rugby club and was embroiled on most Saturdays with the healthy turbulence of the game that he had grown up playing. Dick became immersed in bachelorhood; there was a steady stream of different young women caught peering into the fridge for a bite to eat, wandering around barefooted and in various states of déshabillé.

As the school year came to a close, Gregor longed to breathe some good highland air, pined to have his spirits raised by the land of his birth, envisioned the train ride north to Inverness. He sought relief in his roots. So, he went through the motions of the last weeks of the school year. He was distracted and dreamy. Mentally he was reaching into the closet for his kilt for his summer holiday to come.

And the lessons learned from this first chapter in Gregor's working life were that mathematics teachers brew lousy beer, magnets that repel also attract, P.E. teachers should never be entrusted with baby sparrows, never, ever drink alcohol in the middle of the week and, most importantly, that there are fifty-year-old Londoners out there in different jobs and careers, with different interests and hobbies, bowled over by the delights and tragedies of ordinary life who remember that the speed of light is 186,000 miles per second.

"My hearts in the Highlands, my heart is not here."
- Robert Burns

CHAPTER 2

SCOTLAND

Gregor had come through his probationary year. It could hardly have been with flying colours, for Ms. Thomas had commented on his report that he wasn't "going to set the Thames alight." He had resisted the temptation to comment sardonically on whether he would have set the Taff alight but bit his lip and took it. There would be no Celtic aquiline nose, no lilting Welsh accent imposing itself upon him for the next six weeks.

"There's 'appy I am, bach," he mimicked as he drove home on the last day of the school year.

He knew that he would be back for the next year. His holiday beckoned. If he could not leave on the highest note then he could at least come back refreshed and ready to set alight any river at hand with a new-found panache and confidence. He had survived the experience of his first classroom. He had survived his flatmates. All had survived him. He was excited. The summer holidays stretched before him. Endless days of solitary contentment, no children to educate, no flatmates to placate, all that was before him.

As ever, it was the beacon of his childhood that called him. The smells of the glens, the heather and the gentle breezes of the highland air were a dreamy, lulling lilt in his mind's eye. The sights of loch and moor, mountain and tree, the vast acreage of unpeopled space were the call of the wild. Gregor could have driven his Morris 1300 north, could have had the independence of a car, could have had the motorized convenience of it; but he didn't. He also needed the memories of his youth. The present had been "too much with him late and soon," so why not a nostalgic, self-indulgent trip down memory lane? He had, therefore, bitten the bullet and booked an overnight sleeper from Euston to Inverness.

Euston Station in the early evening was bustling with excited people. Gregor found his compartment with the familiar bunks. Gregor wondered who his room-mates would be for the night. He had been used to having his two brothers and sister with him. It was part of his nature to like to meet and chat with new people. Strangers were inevitably interesting or inevitably not! Each had their own peccadilloes. Who knows, maybe there would be a party of twenty-something young women off to the Highlands for a camping and hiking trip. What an opportunity that would be. Gregor shrugged himself away from his fantasy and turned his eyes to the sliding door, which was slowly opening.

Gregor recognized the envelopes of three or four fly fishing rods before he saw their owner appearing in the doorway. Attached to the rods was a set of tweeds with a hat with flies pinned to its sides. A slightly overweight middle-aged man stumbled inside and flung himself onto the seat opposite Gregor. He was sweating and breathing heavily. Gregor stood up and offered to help him to deposit his luggage in the rack above. After much hustling and adjusting and tucking in of loose ends, they both flopped back to their seats. His companion extended his hand.

"Digby Blinding-Snotter. Thanks for your help."

At least that's what the name sounded like to Gregor. It could have been "Fortescue-Smythe" or "Tree-Fellers" for all that Gregor had heard. He had an inbuilt prejudice against plum sounding, posh-accented hyphens. Too many had strutted their stuff and tried to trample Gregor underfoot in his school days for him to have much truck with such people. He had gone from the dream of nubile nymphs to the nightmare of upper-class twitdom in a hyphenated moment. Life simply was not fair.

"Gregor MacCrimmon. Not a problem."

"Off fishing. Loch Maree. Staying at the Loch Maree Hotel, don't you know."

Gregor *did* know. He was in the presence of assumed greatness, generations of birthright and entitlement. All he had wanted was to talk and share with a pretty face, a single barrel of forthcoming femininity, anything but this. Such people had always been a class above therefore a class below as far as Gregor was concerned. Gregor had grown up and attended school with the trappings of the class system. He had his biases and prejudices. Generally, when he was confronted by such *his* own snobbery was equally evident but simply inverted. He felt like pretending the working-class hero, which he so obviously wasn't. Instead he was silent and smiling politely. But first he needed to transcend the grateness in Digby's greatness.

Digby reached into the interior of his roomy tweed jacket and brought out the largest hip flasks Gregor had ever seen. He unscrewed the top and offered it.

"Drink?"

There was a momentary hesitation from Gregor before he accepted. It was only a moment but Digby shrewdly caught the inference.

"I'm a victim too, you know. It is isolating to be me and to be everybody's image of what I should be. Have a drink with me and I will feel so much more confident."

How could Gregor resist? He reached and slugged. As he did so he was ashamed at his reaction. Obviously, he had somehow betrayed his attitude. He thought that he had given nothing away. But, maybe, not such an upper class twit? At any rate, it was not just the slug of alcohol which was red-rosing Gregor's cheeks.

"Slainte," he invoked the Gaelic toast, better late than never, as he shamelessly too a second swig.

"Slainte y Bha," he received in return.

It was the smoothest, most delicious whisky he had ever tasted. It slipped down all too fast. He instantly regretted **not** savouring, **not** rolling it around his cheeks, he felt ashamed of his Neanderthal swilling. His companion smiled his understanding.

"Don't worry, there is plenty more where that came from."

Gregor wondered whether anybody else would be joining them for the night and secretly hoped that he and Digby would not be disturbed. They shared another dram and soon their tongues were loosened. Digby had been in the army.

"Aaah, I see your assumptions written all over your face. Had it easy, officer class and such. Not true. Father insisted I enter as a squaddie. I was a private for three years before being commissioned. Imagine being a common soldier with my accent and upbringing, eh?"

"That would have been hard," Gregor admitted.

Digby nodded. "It was a great foundation, a great life lesson. I appreciate it to this day. Tell me about you."

So, the whisky and Digby's open-hearted friendliness launched Gregor into an unintended chapter and verse of his life story. Digby listened intently. Guiltily, Gregor concluded and apologized that he was talking too much.

"Hungry? Let's go and get something to eat."

So, the movement and the whisky lurched them three carriages forward until they found themselves in the buffet car. They were confronted by an extremely well-uniformed bar steward contrasting blatantly with shelves of plastic curled up sandwiches behind him.

"Yes gentlemen, behind me nestles the notorious British Rail Sandwich in all its glory."

"May we have two, my good man?" Digby reached in his pocket for change.

"What flavour, Sir?"

"Does it matter?"

The bar steward grinned and plopped two indiscriminate plastic containers on the counter.

"Gentlemen, these are my 'character-building specials.' They were delivered fresh from somewhere this morning, they looked like they were going nowhere this evening. You gentlemen **don't** look like you need your characters built so you will not be phased by their contents."

As they struggled back to their compartment, Gregor reflected on how much he was enjoying the company of his new-found friend and how pleasantly surprised he was to be doing so. He had come through college with people of his own age and most of his social life had been with people who were, by and large, his contemporaries. Digby had insisted and turned down Gregor's offer to pay for the sandwiches. So now he had encroached on Digby's hospitality for drink **and** food.

As they approached their compartment, Gregor felt the need to express his pleasure.

"It is really great to meet you, Digby. I am enjoying our conversation immensely. It is a shame that you won't let me buy you a drink and a real shame that your hip flask is empty, ha, ha!"

Digby said nothing but smiled impishly. On arriving back at the compartment, Digby pointed up to the luggage rack.

"Could you help me down with my case, laddie?"

Cushioned by the clothing within, Digby found what he was looking for. It was a full bottle of **Robert Burns**, the brand of whisky named for Scotland's bard.

"This is the nectar we were drinking before and, I must confess, I was saving this to share with a friend whom I am meeting in Inverness, but—" And he tilted his head to one side, smiling gently, "There are old friends and there are new friends and sometimes the old have to give way to the new. Let's continue where we left off. Ahh, I nearly forgot."

He reached his hand back into his case and produced some ivory drinking cups.

"The 'Rabbi' should not be toasted from the bottle."

Gregor appreciated the respect that Digby had for Scotland's and the world's poet and the affectionate way he had referred to Robbie Burns. Gregor had grown up with parents and grandparents who were steeped in quotations of the famed poet and was himself a fan of his genius.

The images of England's patchwork had long since faded from the landscape as the train rattled its way northward. The enveloping darkness and starlit night deepened as the conversation flitted back and forth from the serious to the humorous, the political and the religious. Such was the ease of this new-found camaraderie that no subject was taboo. The two of them had much in common. The whisky flowed easily. The train ground to a halt at a station. It was the town of Crewe in Cheshire. Digby expressed surprise and concern at the long delay at the station but Gregor remembered from his youth that it had always been a long stop. Gregor had never visited the town of Crewe but felt like he should have done. His family had spent many hours at Crewe Railway Station on their journeys northwards over the years. Recently he had found a riddle about Crewe Station, which he shared with Digby. The saying was:

"The place which is Crewe is not Crewe, and the place which is not Crewe is Crewe."

With the help of the whisky, the two of them had laughed and laughed at this. Gregor's attempt at the serious explanation, all to do with being part of the parish of Crewe and not part of the municipal boundary, did nothing to mitigate Digby's chuckling, which soon involved sides being split and tears being shed.

At a pause in their conversation, Gregor remembered the impatience he had felt all those years ago, the inertia, the stationary stationing at the Crewe Station that had caused the youngsters to ask the universal question of Dads, the "When are we going to get there?" which is still being asked by children to this day. Back then they had tossed and turned in their bunks. Now Gregor didn't care, he had the excellent conversation of Digby, the ear of Digby and the whisky of Digby. The night might not "drive on wi' songs and clatter" as the Bard would have it but "The ale was getting better."

There was no frustration at this hold up. Indeed, the delay prolonged the sociability of the night as Digby announced that there was no way he could sleep if they were not in motion. He was pulling the top off his bottle as he explained his predicament to Gregor. Digby explained that he preferred to be rocked asleep by the motion. So, he continued to tipple more whisky and they both pored and poured over more of life's exigencies. Finally, there was a nudge, a rattle and a slow movement and the train edged its way northwards with a staccato lurching. The two friends folded up the seats and took themselves contentedly to bed. It was not long before the gentle harmony of their snoring blended with the rhythmic motion of the train.

In the summertime, dawn comes early in the far north. Despite the alcohol and the late night, both Digby and Gregor were up with the lark. Up went the blinds and open went the small window. A cold rush of air greeted them both. They silently took in the aroma of moor and heather, sedge and bog, fair weather cumuli interrupted the azure sky. The early sun promised a glorious day. Newton More, Kingussie, Aviemore, Carrbridge. Little villages that had brushed Gregor's youth with such insouciant affection were passed as Inverness was getting ever closer.

The train slowed as it battled its way up to the Slochd Summit. Neither Digby nor Gregor minded the prolonging of the journey. The landscape took on a more windswept look, an almost treeless bleakness that in winter would have presented a white hostility to all but the most hardy. The tongues so loosened by alcohol the night before were now silent as they drank in the scene, savoured the endless changing panoramas. They knew that over the top was the steady run into the town of Inverness, the erstwhile capital of the Highlands, the hub which catered to the well-being of all who crofted in the far Islands, every little village school, every

Gaelic and English road sign, every health concern and every dot for every i and cross for every t in the beauteous land that surrounded the town.

The train slowly edged its way into the station. The bags were off the rack, the bunks were pushed back, Digby and Gregor continued to stare out of the window. It was Digby who finally broke the silence.

"Gregor, in my fifty or so years roaming the planet, your company last night has been a real highlight. We hit it off from the first, did we not? Two people of diverse backgrounds and different generations, buffeting their way north. True that we share a culture and common beliefs but bonhomie does not always break out well with new acquaintances. It certainly broke out with you and me and I am pretty sure that it was not just the alcohol. I suppose that the lesson for both of us is that scratching the surface of a first impression is what all people need to do, that human beings the world over can have common ground. Always remember, Gregor, 'Vive la difference, vive la meme chose.' Remember me when next you meet a complete stranger and please use that wonderful gift you have of putting people at their ease. Aaah we are at a stop. Goodbye my friend."

Digby shook Gregor's hand, grabbed his baggage and left the train. He found a baggage cart and with never a backward glance was lost in the crowd. Gregor was in less of a hurry and, truth be known, was a smidge hung-over. The train wasn't going anywhere. He donned his backpack and squeezed his way onto the platform. He was greeted by the smell of bacon butties and the distant skirl of the bagpipes. He ambled slowly towards the station exit.

Gregor knew what would greet him as he left the station and entered the town. He drooled as he passed the aromatic cafe, the morning after craving for grease was not new to him. But, for the moment, he curbed the urge. He had other priorities, he was determined not to give in to the temptation just yet. He had an uncontrollable desire to renew the acquaintance of an old friend. He entered the early weekday morning bustle of the centre of Inverness and there he was. The magnificent kilted figure with his busby on his head, standing as he had stood throughout the 20th century on his plinth of Portland stone, was suddenly before him. A solitary Queen's Own Cameron Highlander, placed there in 1893 to commemorate the centenary of the regiment. There were the names of Highlanders who were later to give their lives in the far-flung lands of Egypt and the Sudan. As he stood and stared he wondered at what it must have been like in those days before air flight, before television, before computers when roads were tracks and rail was the novelty. He wondered what it must have been like for the young crofter for whom Edinburgh was exotic to find himself in the desert staring up at pyramid or sphinx. Was it life's great adventure or was it needs must to absent oneself from a hardscrabble economy, a mouth less to feed in a land which yielded much that was beautiful but much, much less that one could eat? Were their travels away peopled by a desperate homesickness, many nights in the cold desert air with the plaintiff notes of *My Hearts in the Hielands*, a melancholic longing for "Hame and Hearth." Around the base of the cenotaph's base were 142 names of men who, as a result of disease or battle, did not make it home.

"Penny for your thoughts, old chap." There was Digby thrusting a black coffee and a bacon butty into his hands.

"Digby, you're a lifesaver." A broad smile beamed across Digby's face.

"Let's find a bench and scoff these."

They found a bench on the pavement and sat and ate and drank hungrily.

"Sooo, what were you thinking?" Digby enquired.

"Oh, I don't know, I suppose I was thinking of my grandfather who was 13 years old and growing up not far from here in Loch Flemington when this memorial was put up. I guess I was thinking that his life from 1880 until 1965 spanned a lot of technological development and many tragic wars. He was a doctor in WWI and in the Home Guard in WWII. He was 20 years old when the old Queen died and 85 when the young Queen was on the throne. It was sex, drugs and rock 'n roll by then, indeed the long-haired Beatles when he died. What must he have thought, Digby?"

"I don't know, Gregor, but from the day he was born until the day he died, it was **his** time. Look at you and me, a generation apart but your youth would never deny me my middle age. It is true that we live in a culture that has lost respect for their elders but that is a culture that will change. I know how lucky I am to have befriended a young chap like you and I think that you realize that you have had the same experience in reverse. And Gregor," he paused and focused his bright blue eyes intensely on Gregor's, "there has always been sex, drugs and rock 'n roll.

Let us not think of ourselves as superior to our forebears because of what we have developed scientifically and pragmatically over the years. There has been sex and drugs for thousands of years and popular festivals were not an invention of the 1960s. Our ancestors and your grandfather were part of the same, they were human, they felt as we feel, they loved as we love and they took their pleasures as we are taking ours. They knew their days."

"Are you my fairy godfather, Digby?" smiled Gregor.

"Not at all," laughed Digby cheerily, "But I pride myself on reading people and thus anticipating. I have shamefully exploited my talent and I hope that you are not offended. You're an honest man and, if I may say so, an extremely pheasant plucker. Of course, you needed to stop by something familiar when you disembarked the train. Look at this town, there is not much to recognize since your youth is there? This cenotaph, however, was there when you were a teenager in the 1960s. I knew you would be here. I'll say 'Farewell' again but remember if I have given to you then you have given to me."

They shook hands and Digby ambled over to the taxi ramp. This time, however, he did look back and with a wink and a grin, clambered into the back of a cab.

Gregor donned his backpack and decided to walk over the road bridge on the River Ness and find his way to Bught Park where he knew there was a campsite.

*   *   *

Gregor was often to think of his Digby encounter over the years. He would like to have acclaimed it as an enlightenment. He would like to have manufactured the belief that life was never the same for him again after that. The fact was that it was a chink of light that had somehow made its way through the clouds of his narrow view of life, its prejudices and stereotyping, his unremitting generalizations. The naiveté of judging the leopard by its spots was true of Gregor. He was supposed to be a child of the 1960s, enlightened by liberality but, in reality, when his peers had been manning the barricades, marching in the streets, he had slunk away fearfully and hid himself in the comforting corner of his past. He believed that that night on the train had taught him that a liberal view of life was not the exclusive purview of the young. So the "Digby" meeting *did* change Gregor, *did* encourage him to act in ways that he would not have acted before. He became the driver who picked up the homeless hitcher off the M4 some years later, rather than the two girls who were hitching alongside him. He thought that that would be far more interesting. It was the nuanced wisdom of the older van driver when he had worked as a van "boy" for the Nairnshire Laundry. It became the subtle, sometimes less than subtle, direction from a wiser head when he had failed to listen. Digby was not an epiphany for Gregor, but maybe he was the beginning of many wee nudges that sent him on a better, more accepting path.

CHAPTER 3

CAMPSITES

Making his way over the main road bridge and past the familiar sooty stone of the solid, no frills buildings, Gregor reflected that even though much of the centre of the town was now a cacophony of new stores and differently directed traffic, there was still a rhythm to the place, albeit an harmonious jazz-like cacophony, but a synchronicity nevertheless. Inverness had not seemed to have lost sight of its past.

Gregor's pack was light on his back, cheerily gossamer, weightless to match his light-hearted mood. Gregor had long ago mastered the art of looking around when he was hiking. His long-distance walks had never been head-down stare-at-ones-feet rapid yomps, struggles against the elements. They had always been stop and start, interesting ambles, meandering miasmas of myriad musings. So, it was some time before he found himself at the gates of the camping and caravan park. The sky was lightly overcast when he set his pack down on the green verdure beside the entranceway. He had introduced himself to the orotund, middle-aged camp owner, a retired policeman by the name of Macleod.

"Pitch where you want, laddie, nice wee bit of flat greenery right here near the office."

So, Gregor had looked skywards for rain, noted more blue than grey, observed the fair weather cumulus clouds and dumped his pack. He sat down, reached for his water bottle and lay back. Gregor enjoyed the pleasantness of nothingness. By rights he felt that he should have had a monstrous hangover due to Digby's generosity but either the early morning grease had headed it off at the pass or he had been waylaid by the humour and conversation into thinking that they had drunk more than they had. Either way he was now revelling in his own company and his renewed acquaintance with the town. He remembered that not far from where he lay was Highland Rugby Club, a club with which he had briefly played when living and working in Nairn. He smiled when he remembered Cliff Parr. There had been the trip down to Glasgow to play Strathclyde University and an overnight stay in the "dear green place" to go with it. Cliff had persuaded Gregor to go see a group called **Black Sabbath** on the Saturday night.

"Great place to pick up birds. Gregor, maybe they might fancy a bit of a Highland fling."

The pun was not lost on Gregor so he had laughed heartily, which had amused Cliff but he had no idea that he had punned at all. He was confused when Gregor had laughingly provided an explanation on puns and plays on words. Gregor chided himself inwardly for his teacher-ish explanation. It was a sleeping dog of condescension best left to lie.

Cliff had gone on to explain his literal meaning and the conversation had petered out, which was precisely what happened at the concert that night. The noise of the group in action precluded any chat lines; where all the "birds" could be seen but not heard, it was a pop concert that was all about the music. Nobody was to know at that point that Black Sabbath were to go on to be famous, indeed to be "Black Sabbath." The music was wonderful, but Cliff's hope was a flop.

Gregor stood up and began to unpack his pack. His one -man tent was debagged and ready for pitching. Gregor marvelled at how quick and easy it was in these days of superior "tentology." Soon it was up, his mat and sleeping bag were laid out inside. He decided on a stroll around the campsite which, in truth, was more of a caravan park. Children were out in force, riding their bikes, kicking balls, their cheery voices adding to the pleasant environs. Parents were lounging in deck chairs, drinking coffee and tea, and generally chewing the fat while keeping a watchful eye. Gregor found the launderette and decided on a wee keek inside. There was a typical batch of machines and a large sign by the drier, handwritten and with aggressive forcefulness.

"ABSOLUTELY _NO_ CARPETS IN THE DRIER ON PAIN
OF EXPULSION FROM THE CAMPSITE."

Gregor chuckled to himself speculating about what had happened to prompt the notice. Had somebody turned up out of the blue and proceeded to bundle their wall-to-wall into the drier without concern for its mass and weight? Had the overloaded machine spouted smoke and eventual flames so that the emergency services had to be contacted? Had an angry campsite owner been involved in a major confrontation over a carpet and a drier? Gregor wandered back to his tent and decided to go for a little dander down to the Ness Islands and maybe take in a look at the old rugby ground.

The River Ness is the heart of the city. In what towns throughout the world can a fisher cast his line from the bank in the very real hope of catching a salmon? Of course, when a fish was on the line, it was never long before a crowd of spectators gathered on the pavement to watch.

"A river runs through it," Gregor quoted silently.

Maybe the weather was cold but Gregor suspected that it really wasn't, it was just the contrast with balmy London. So, he grabbed water and waterproofs and strolled off through the campsite entrance. He meandered his dreamy way south, edging towards where he knew the river ran. Soon he was upon it, noting that it was still in a swollen state from previous rains. He knew that this would bring the fishers out, feeling that the salmon would be attracted up the river with the diminishing shallows. He noted people leaning over the pedestrian bridge attracted by a triumvirate of three kayakers paddling downstream. Suddenly one of them flipped himself over and performed a perfect Eskimo roll.

"Show off," Gregor muttered.

Soon Gregor found himself in sight of the islands and crossing the bridge. There is something about the flowing of water that is calming. Rivers can be in spate, burns can trickle, lochs can lap, seas can wave-crash but always Gregor felt calmed and reassured by their presence. It was primordial. Gregor had often pondered the "whys" of his feelings. He had decided that these were the same sounds that had been around for hundreds, maybe thousands, of years. Cities and traffic and the shouts of the people can change and vary, but the waters whether they be in Inverness or London remain. They are "The streams that stay yet still depart."

As he walked, Gregor wondered if it was the same for smell as it was for sound. He paused on a bench, closed his eyes, and listened and sniffed. He smelt the wood and the air and decided that if he transported himself back to his youth, then he could have sat on that bench and all would have been the same. He pondered on Inverness and thought that he had to get his bearings and spend the night and head off to the west coast and the islands. Sure and all he wanted to see his brother but he wanted to feel a highland under his feet also, sense the rough coarseness of the heather and eventually reach the coast and smell the 'tangle of the isles', the seaweed. He returned to the campsite.

The road to Ullapool was a thin, narrow strip. As he had walked out of Inverness, Gregor had kept his hitching thumb concealed from view. He would want a ride at some point but first of all he wanted was to breathe the air and take in all of the views. So, he headed to Beauly. After about an hour or so, he reached for his upright thumb and raised it in half-hearted hope. A car pulled over within minutes. A rumpled suit and tie wound down the window.

"Muir of Ord?"

Gregor accepted. It was only a short distance down the road but it was on the way.

Doddie was a sales rep. for a beer company. His stop in "The Muir" as he called it, was only a brief one, then he was headed back to Inverness. That was not what Gregor had intended. But when he explained about Ullapool and the ferry, Doddie opened up and said that he was headed home to Oban. He would enjoy the company and Ullapool was a mere pretension of a port compared to Oban, the one and true gateway to the Isles. Gregor was carried along with this little vignette of local jingoism. He had taken to Doddie's open, smiling energy from the beginning so changed his mind about Ullapool. After the call at the pub, they were barrelling back to Inverness and southwards to Oban.

Loyalty to a local town is an interesting concept. On the journey south, Doddie waxed long and lovingly about being born and growing up in Oban. Gregor reflected in the quiet moments on the journey, of which there were few, on instances of love of locale. There had been the native of Selkirk who had once proclaimed that "A day spent oot o' Selkirk is a day wasted." There was the 1912 headline in an Aberdeen newspaper: "Titanic sunk: Aberdeen man feared drowned." There had been the Scottish soldier who had been wounded during the Iraq War. When asked where he had been when he was hurt he answered, "A couple o' miles on the Rothiemurchus side o' Baghdad."

Gregor understood that being away from hearth and home, then the rose coloured spectacles could often come out. There would be an aching longing for the familiar and the friendly. But there are degrees of distance and Muir of Ord was hardly a pyramid away from Oban.

*"It is very unfair to judge anybody's conduct, without
an intimate knowledge of their situation."
- Jane Austen*

CHAPTER 4

THE HEBRIDES

There is and probably always will be a bleak beauty to the Outer Hebrides. They sit at the edge of the eastern Atlantic, rocky, windswept guardians of the mainland beyond. The beaches are blanched with sandy whiteness. They calmly bear the vigour of the sea with a silent insouciance, a philosophical acceptance of the constant pounding. Above the beaches there is often the machair, flatlands that suddenly give forth a blazing variety of colour when the wild flowers bloom. Beyond that, there are roads and crofts, the owners of which eke out a living through sheep and peat. Then there are peaks, sometimes steep, oftentimes rocky, easily accessed with a stout pair of boots and a walking stick. They are not high by mainland standards, certainly mere bumps when compared with the world's great mountain ranges, but their height is in stark contrast with the nearby sea level and their wildness gives forth mystery and awe.

Gregor had spent the night in the campsite at Oban and was excited to be heading for South Uist to stay with his brother. He had walked into Oban from the campsite on the point. The coastline of the island of Kerrera had accompanied him as he trudged. High, fluffy cirrus whispered their candyflossed ways in from the southwest, they varied the blue bright sky. A light breeze ruffled the calm sea. There was a spring in his step. Gregor was lightly perspiring when he reached the familiar ferry terminal next to the railway station. He bought his ticket and decided he had time to breakfast at the notorious Mactavish's Kitchen whose famed macaroni cheese had long tickled his senses. It was probably only Gregor who believed that the fragrance of the café wafted over the entire bay, but if the myth served the purpose then why debunk it? Macaroni cheese, Gregor decided, was like art. Everybody appreciated it in therr own unique way. He had once been told never to let the truth get in the way of a good story. The local macaroni cheese would always be part of the tale of Oban for Gregor. Thus, did he find himself with the full Scottish Breakfast: black pudding, mushrooms and fried bread, all that good stuff that made Scotland the coronary leader in the world. It was what visitors to the UK might call the "Full English" but with extra Scottish artery cloggers added rather like a North American side salad but with potentially more exciting consequences.

With a full stomach and fuller arteries, Gregor strolled aboard the ship and up to the viewing area. He ensconced himself comfortably and settled in to appreciate the spectacular panorama that he knew would be his reward when they started on their journey. Gradually, the seats around him filled up with young and old, families and lorry drivers. A large man plonked himself down beside him. He nodded a greeting but the man's demeanour forbade further communication so Gregor reached in his pack for his book.

The ferry began to shake, the safety announcement was made and slowly it eased away from the dock. Gregor closed his book and glanced about him. The bay was starting to recede behind them. The landscape on either side of them was beginning to share its magic. A deep sigh came from the man next to him.

"On holiday?"

"Yes, you?"

"Lorry driver."

Silence. The conversation was at an end it seemed. The man fidgeted his agitation. Gregor could see he was struggling with something.

"My lorry is stuck. Got onto the boat and the engine died. A've nae idea how I'm tae get it aff."

"Aah," replied Gregor with not much more to offer.

"'Ah think I'll awa up and speak tae the Captain," he muttered distractedly. He suddenly stood up and disappeared.

20 minutes later he was back and not looking happier or wiser.

"Did you speak to him?"

He nodded. "Ah got up tae the brig and there was naebody there,"

"Who's steering the boat?" Gregor asked.

"Ah dinnae ken, automatic pilot?"

There was no real answer to that so Gregor stood up and left.

The mainland, its peninsulas and inlets, its heathered hilltops and windswept, rocky outcrops were slipping away astern of the ship. The unusual calm of the Minch lay gently spread before them. Their destination was not yet in sight. Gregor settled himself, toyed with his book but was distracted by the comings and goings of the people. Islanders greeted each other with familiar nonchalance. Visitors craned their necks, strained their eyes for the first glimpse of their destination.

Gregor remembered his first visit to the islands. There had been something faintly exotic about that first trip over. Of course, he had read about the people and places. *The Tales of Para Handy* and *Whisky Galore* were tales of another time, a simpler period in history, but, for all the understatement, a harsher time when people were more attuned to the vagaries of their climate. It had been, he assumed, a more closeted world when the current ease of travel was less available. Gregor speculated that there must have been an inner warmth then, a closed intimacy, which helped the people meet triumph and disaster almost exclusively through the ties that bound.

The horizon began to take shape. There was a misty mysteriousness which soon formed a silhouette. The foreground of the machair was not as evident as the background of the hills. The Highlands had always held a brooding wisdom for Gregor. It was as if they knew things that humans did not. A nonchalant knowledge seemed to exude from every crag and every rock. It was the Scottish motto at its finest, "Nemo me impune lacessit" was surely written for every Munro and every Corbett.* They echoed their warning from every coire, from each waterfall, from every ancient rockfall, along every field of scree.

---

*   A Munro is a Scottish mountain with a height of 3,000 feet or more, a Corbett are those over 2,500 feet but under 3,000 feet.

"Wha daur meddle wi' me?"

The sun appeared through the light clouds to the west. It marked the boat's trail on the ready ripples on the water. The engine thrummed. The people gazed. Lochboisdale was less than an hour away.

Ben Kenneth, Beinn Ruigh Choinnich to give it its Gaelic name, Lochboisdale's little hill, its harbour sentinel, was soon over them as the ship nudged its way into the bay. The active sailors readied themselves. Car drivers were called to their cars. The opening and shutting of doors reverberated around the cavernous hold. Gregor saw the becalmed lorry, its driver in tune with his unresolved situation. The foot passengers were disgorged and Gregor found himself instantly in the heart of the village. The Lochboisdale Hotel lay on a rise slightly above the main street. The Macbrayne's offices were close at hand. Further up the street, Gregor spotted a Tourist Information Centre. He found a grassy verge, eased his pack off his back and sat down on it to await the arrival of his brother.

A battered old van was belching and farting its way towards him down the street and soon pulled up beside him. The friendly face of his brother, Brian, greeted him from the driver's side. Brian's passenger, his workmate, Chuggie, moved over so that Gregor could clamber into the back. The aroma that greeted him was a mixture of gasoline and fish. He made himself as comfortable as possible in his new surroundings.

The greeting had been polite but cursory, short but not unwelcoming.

"This is my brother, Gregor, from London. Gregor, this is Chuggie."

"Hmm, London!" Chuggie intoned enigmatically.

"We have to go to work, but we'll drop you at my caravan," Brian explained.

The roads were, of course, narrow. The passing places were frequent. Waved acknowledgements were exchanged with unseen strangers who were glimpsed only fleetingly from the back of the windowless van. Gregor craned to see out but was thwarted as he had to hold on to stop himself buffeting from side to side. No conversation passed between the three of them. As the stranger, Gregor searched for something to say, reached for some morsel of conversation with which to break the ice. The silence was awkward for him but obviously of no concern to the silent nodding shapes in front of him. No words sprung to mind that would not sound inane and nonsensical.

"The hills look lovely today" would have sounded so inappropriately effete for such strong silent types.

"There are a lot of sheep here," was just the bleeding obvious and would have elicited naught but knowing grins from the two "locals."

So, Gregor waited for some inspiration, some straw at which to grasp, some opportunity with which to break the ice. Soon, an example presented itself. Suddenly out of nowhere on the open moorland a concrete building appeared in front of them. It looked like some sort of factory, some place of small business. Its incongruous bulk rising up from the barren lands seemed completely out of place.

Gregor exclaimed, "What's that?!"

At that moment, he was flung forward as the vehicle screeched to a halt. He saw the two heads turn to each other with twinkling amusement.

"That's a sheep!" they exclaimed in unison.

A wool-weighted sheep lurched across the road in front of them and was gone. Gregor shook his head and turned his eyes to the heavens. He should have said, "I know that that's a sheep. I meant the building on the side of the road. I may be from London, a mere city slicker with little idea of how the countryside works, BUT I do know what a sheep is, you arrogant unsocial dolts."

But instead he kept his own counsel, slumped back into dispirited silence, his idea of a warm island welcome slipping into a doom-laden fiction.

In the evening of the first day, Gregor was introduced to Brian's caravan. It was a mobile home that had lost its ability to move. At least Brian hoped that it had but it was obvious that he was not confident of its stability. Ropes weighted by rocks were draped over the roof against the violent gales which occasionally swept the archipelago. They dropped Gregor and headed off to work.

Gregor then spent a happy day wandering down over the moor to the sea loch and pottering about on the littoral. He availed himself of Brian's fridge and made himself a fry up. He ate at the table by the window, ruminating on the fact that the low-hanging peaks over the heather-clad moor and the fjord-like inlet were picture postcard in outlook, a calendar picture if ever there was one. Gregor remembered his grandfather in Nairn saying to him once that "You can't live on a view," meaning, he supposed, that which was often said in the North of England,

"Where there's muck, there's money." Presumably where there was none, there was none! Well, looking out of that window, it would seem that one could have both.

During those years in the mid 1970s, South Uist burgeoned with youth and energy. There were ceilidhs and "Mairi" seemed to have a wedding every week. There was a pub life, a social whirl, a vibrancy. Gregor had visited several times. On one occasion, Brian picked up a young hitcher on the side of the road. He happened to be a young ornithologist from Norfolk, a hitcher twitcher, up to indulge his hobby by pursuing the amazing bird life of the islands. Brian was on his way to pick up his girlfriend from the ferry so he explained that there was not going to be room in the car afterwards. So, he agreed to drop him at the pub and pick him up later so that he could spend the night in the caravan. There was a certain naïvety about this twitcher, which appealed to both Brian and Gregor. Gregor had a feeling that there were other intentions behind Brian's altruism other than simply generosity of the spirit. Sure enough, after the pick up and drop-off of said girlfriend, Brian had dropped back to the pub. Gregor had waited in the car while Brian had popped in to retrieve the Englishman. It required three strongly built adult males to carry him to the vehicle where he was deposited—or rather poured—into the back seat. It was with difficulty that they had somehow manoeuvred the whisky-clad young man out of the pub and into the caravan. A sheepish "What happened to me?" look had surfaced in the caravan on the following morning. An apologetic desperation was uttered, a plea for forgiveness, which was accepted by Brian with cursory indifference. John, for such was his name, the introduction only having been made as he was attempting the welcome grease of the fry up that morning, remained blissfully unaware of the deliberate sabotage of the night before. It was hardly a Scottish Bannockburn of a victory but it was a chip away at English supremacy nevertheless. Best of all, the only thing hurt was a young Sassenach's liver which would soon recover with the enthusiasm at the sighting of the first rare bird.

These visits were in the halcyon days of the seventies when the communities on the islands were thriving entities. Now in the 21st century a picture of diminishment was presented. The population was not only evidently decreased with the depressing boarding-up of businesses along the main street of Lochboisdale. But the population was aging, the islands were being denuded of their young. It was the old, old story of how hard it was for the young to go back to the farm after they had seen "**Paree**."

"Every man's his own friend, my dear. He hasn't as good a one as himself anywhere."
- Fagan in **Oliver Twist** *by Charles Dickens*

CHAPTER 5

SKYE

Gregor reflected on the first time he had visited the island of Skye. It had been during the time that there had been no bridge but a ferry ride from Kyle of Lochalsh to Kyleakin. It had felt like going to an island then, nowadays it was just a continuation of the road. He hitched around the island and somehow found himself in Portree where he stocked up on fish and chips, bought groceries and hitched out again on the road to Sligachan. There, he pitched his tent opposite the famed Sligachan Hotel. The day after dawned sunny and bright so he hurriedly cooked a hasty breakfast, collapsed his tent, loaded his pack and started his walk along the pathway between the hills.

His day hike along Glen Sligachan was a festival of views of the Cuillins, craggy peaks whose magnetic content prohibited the effective use of a compass. No matter. The trail was clearly marked. Gregor knew that he would eventually find himself on the coast at Camus Sunary. Then it was a short hop up to the clear waters of the famed Loch Coruisk. Gregor enjoyed his hike but was tired and hungry as he found himself on the beach. The lovely sands were deserted as Gregor sought a sheltered area behind some dunes to pitch his tent. The breeze was sufficient to curtail any unpleasant midge activity. Gregor pitched his tent, found a comfortable niche in the sands and settled down with his cooker to make his supper. He paused to reflect on the potato and the can of beans that he was to eat. Why waste the gas?

Strewn across the beach were large clumps of driftwood, clusters of pale, weathered skeletons of long-dead trees. He decided to test his campcraft skills by having a real fire. He rummaged in his pack and found a bar of chocolate, sufficient unto his needs, he scoffed it down. The sugar energized him and so he began his forage.

He soon found that there was plenty of big wood but very little that was little. He would need to shave and cut to give himself an effective fire starter. His pile looked magnificent. It would burn until morning if he wanted it to, if he could at least get it started. Sitting by his tent with his impressive gathering of timber, Gregor looked about him. He noted the plethora of green, bushy growth but also noted that some of the reeds and ferns had been laid low by the weather. They were in a state of decay. There would be fire from these if he could create a spark. So, he found a sheltered spot far enough away from his tent to be safe. He recommenced the gathering process and soon had collected the small to match his pile of the big. He organized his pit, set up his scout-like pyramid of the dry, and the tinder. He crouched low, struck his first match, it was instantly blown out. Several others were tried but failed. Eventually he was lying prone, hands cupped against the breeze, sheltered behind a small clump of sand. This time, the flame caught on the leafless detritus. He shifted twigs and brown leaves onto the flame, praying that they would catch. Catch they did, and now Gregor was searching for something bigger, something longer lasting but something that would nurture his early flames. It wasn't long before he had a good blaze but he was still concerned for his fire's ultimate success. He knew that he needed hot embers embedded in the heart of the fire if he was to succeed. It was all too tempting to start ladling on the wood willy-nilly but Gregor knew that "hurry up and wait" was wiser than the fool rushing in. So, he nestled close to his creation, poked and fed, nurtured and blew. He experimented gently with the force of his blowing. Gentle, steady uninterrupted susurrations were better than forceful excessiveness, which risked blowing it out. Soon, he felt confident to load up the bigger stuff. Now he felt that it was ready for him to cook.

Gregor was never a well-prepared, carefully-planned camper, but today he had remembered to buy tinfoil. He preened himself as he pulled a strip from his roll and wrapped his potato in it. He found a hot spot, a nuanced nook, where he placed his potato. He reached for his tin of beans. They would not take as long to cook so he was in no hurry to heat them. It was then that he realized that his pride at his foresight with the tinfoil was premature. He had not brought a can opener.

Gregor flopped backwards on the sands and roundly cursed his foolishness. His pride at his success with the fire, his remembering of the tinfoil was now in ruins over the folly of the absent tin opener. He looked around him for something that might help him. He thought of a rock but knew that he would merely push the tin out of shape, that he would not be able to pierce the top unless he had something sharp. He did have his penknife.

"Penknife and rock?" he voiced aloud. "Rock and penknife, it's worth a try."

So, Gregor found a large, flat rock, stabilized his can in a bed of sand, opened his knife and tapped it gently with the rock on top of the can. Immediately, it slipped away beneath him, narrowly missing his thumb in the process. He realized that if he hit the knife too hard he was more likely to bend and damage the blade rather than penetrate the can. His eyes found their way to his tent and the tent pegs. He reached for the nearest peg and pulled it out.

"Pointed enough!" he exclaimed.

Gentle to hard bashing eventually produced a dent in the can, which encouraged Gregor to believe that he had made the start that would prevent the peg from slipping. Renewed vigour produced a hole through which the juice of the can began to appear. Gradually, he worked to enlarge it until at last the first sign of a baked bean began to appear. So, he prised and cajoled, holed and hacked until he was able to peel back a better expanse of lid. Not bothering with the pan, he stuck the can of beans next to his potato for cooking.

Gregor finished his repast. He could hardly have said that it had left him replete. Indeed, he felt that he could have eaten it again **and** he would have loved some meat. He had also finally settled back and noticed more fully his surroundings. He had heard the faint tinklings of a burn close at hand, following the sound to fill his water bottle and his kettle. He brewed his tea, reminding himself that he needed to drink a great deal. Gregor had had his bouts of headaches on many a path in the past when he had become so engrossed in his surroundings, wondering what was around that next bend, wandering around the side of the next buttress. Such had been his involvement in his enthrallment that he had forgotten to drink. The dehydration had taken hold, the head had started to bang. Gregor had been laid low and lower by the process.

He had become a curled, useless ball huddled tightly in his sleeping bag. So he drank more than he wanted and probably more than he needed.

The early breeze had dropped. The midges had started to leave the cover of the heather and were out to feed. Gregor supped his tea, hugging the fire closely more for the smoke's effect on the midges than for warmth. Still, the sun was red in the western sky. 8:00 p.m. and several more hours of daylight left. Gregor reflected that if he had been with a friend he might have suggested a dander up to Loch Coruisk that evening. But he was alone. He knew that he would want to linger by this most iconic of lochs, so he decided to leave his venture for the morning. The cooler evening air had sent the midges skulking for cover. He was now able, therefore, to lay outside his tent on his sleeping bag and reach for his book. D.K. Broster's *Flight of the Heron* soon had him transported back to 1746 and the flight of the Jacobite army through the heather after the defeat at Culloden.

Loch Coruisk is an enchanting place. Loch Maree has the magic of large sea trout in its waters, at least it did then. Lochindorb and Loch Ruthven were the fishing places of Gregor's youth so they would always be viewed with nostalgic insouciance by Gregor. Lochindorb was a short jog off the Nairn to Grantown-on-Spey road. It was treeless moor except for the shooting lodge that nestled in a wooded area at one side of the loch. On an island were the ruins of one of the Wolf of Badenoch's castles. The notorious Wolf had gained his notoriety by burning down a great deal of the town of Elgin, including its cathedral. His real name was Alexander Stewart, the Earl of Buchan, and the third son of King Robert II of Scotland. Gregor had always been haunted by childhood memories of fishing on Lochindorb. Its isolation on the moor, its enigmatic bleakness so near yet so far to the quaint little Highland town of Grantown-on-Spey. For several days over several summers, the loch had been peopled by him, his two brothers and his father, the only sound being the quiet toiling of the oars in the rowlocks as they pursued the elusive brown trout. But now he was after the different experience of Loch Coruisk. He had heard of it but never visited it.

He woke early. The waves of Loch Scavaig, the sea loch that served as a dropping-off place for boat trippers from Elgol, lapped the beach. A hasty breakfast of a bap and cheese, an even hastier retreat from his campsite, which had become a haven for the West Highland midgie, was required. Gregor reflected as he reached the littoral where sea met sand that if he lived long enough and travelled far in the world, the dangerous killing power of the mighty polar bear or the terrifying experience of a charging elephant would cause him little fear. He, Gregor the Brave, Gregor the Fearless, Gregor of the Thousand-yard Stare, had met and faced the West Highland midge. Nothing was more fearsome than these vicious little creatures.

As he walked west along the sands, he could see but not yet hear the waters of the River Scavaig, one of the shortest rivers in Scotland, trundling its short distance of metres rather than kilometres from the loch which, hidden from view, lay above it. As he came nearer, the gentle sounds of the sea diminished and those of the freshwater were heard. Gregor felt his heart quicken and his pace increase until finally he was at the mouth of the river and ready to climb up to the vista above him. Gregor had speculated about whether he would have to negotiate the famed "Bad Step." As ever, he had mistaken his route slightly. He need not have worried, quickly the calm blue of the loch appeared before him.

There was a rock and a green swarded bank off to his left. He lay himself down and drank in the scene. The clear azure sky allowed the early morning sun to show off the Cuillin at its dramatic best. There was a gentle breeze off the loch. The waters lapped gently, inches from his boots. The amphitheatre of the Black Cuillin, Gregor believed, would probably echo. But for the moment, Gregor was protective of his aloneness and did not want to disturb nature as it was intended with coarse human shouting. The midges were hiding from the breeze so Gregor was able to linger on his back for a wee bit longer and drink in the scene. He was shaken from his trance-like pleasure by the sound of voices coming up from below. Resolving to preserve his solitude for as long as possible, he stood up and began to stroll gently around the edge of the loch. He noted that it was not very wide but was indeed about three kilometres in length. The path was easy walking with little undulations and few steep pieces of terrain. He had had no intention of walking all of the way around the loch but he soon found himself at the far end. He had less intention of retracing his steps, so committed to complete the circuit. The people who had arrived 10 minutes after he had left were of similar intent. They, however, had tried the echo scenario to mixed effect. Of course, sound travels over water readily so Gregor was catching snatches of their conversation. Raptures at the scene, of course, laughter at the occasional trip and tumble, amusing references to common or uncommon experiences. Gregor almost felt a part of their group and, far from resenting their presence, he was taking a renewed appreciation of the scene and was uplifted by their pleasure.

All too soon, he saw and heard the waters of the River Scavaig and found himself descending to the bay below. He was on the strand and moving along the sands to his campsite. A tourist boat was appearing on the horizon, its motors pushing it along at a good clip. As it made its way into the bay, the engines and boat slowed to allow the punters to take in the scene. Gregor supposed that it might be possible for him to hail the craft and hitch a ride to Elgol, a lazy route out rather than the ten or so kilometres back through the glen. He shook the temptation and the idea from his head. It was a beautiful day. So many of his friends would be envious. How many such days did the vagaries of the Skye weather gift to the visitor. He had time, he was fit, he had food and drink. Slowly, he packed up his tent, arranged and balanced his pack, thrust some bread and cheese into his mouth, washed it down with large gulps of water, and turned into the glen. Gregor always felt a pang, a slight drooping in his mood, as if parting from an old friend for the last time. He shouldered his pack.

Was it deep-seated cowardice or simple lack of confidence? As Gregor wended his way towards the community at Sligachan, he found his eyes drawn ever upwards to the rocky crags. He had always a long felt want to climb each and every one of them but was so cautious that he resisted the urge as an exercise in dangerous futility, a venture of embarrassing negligence if rescue teams had to be called out because of an ankle twist or something worse. He had always liked his own company and had travelled frequently alone, but occasionally he wished he was there with a friend, a comrade with a common interest, a peak seeker who would not take Gregor's hesitation for an answer.

"Ho hum," he spoke aloud, "I wonder if I can buy fish 'n chips tonight."

The Sligachan Hotel was rapidly approaching. Gregor was tired and hungry. He pitched his tent and headed to the hotel bar. Pies, beans and chips fit the bill, washed down with a couple of pints of heavy. That was Sligachan then. Sligachan in 2015 was a different place.

In 2015, Gregor arrived at the campsite to find it crowded but not full. He was driving this time and planned to spend a couple of nights there. He assessed where to pitch. Places were peopled by young families, which Gregor had always found to be quiet to camp nearby. Sure, the children played late and noisily while parents lounged and socialized, but all was generally quieting down at about 10:00 p.m. Gregor could not decide so he parked and sat on a rock to watch and observe. A group of young guys were pitching their numerous tents. He watched with interest as one pitched his single man tent and placed his air bed inside and proceeded to blow it up. Laughter ensued from his mates as it became apparent that the air mattress was a double and was far too big for the tent. The faint amusement turned to side-splitting hilarity as the tent was completely engulfed from within. Gregor chuckled to himself. It would have been fun to camp next to these guys, but Gregor needed his sleep. He left the car and walked farther around the campsite. He found the perfect spot. It was a promontory with views up the glen on one side and a clear view down the sea loch in another direction. Gregor could not understand why nobody else had picked this wonderful location. So, there he pitched and there he camped.

The following day Gregor walked the Sligachan Glen again and again on a perfect day. On this occasion, he climbed and looked down on his old friend, Loch Coruisk, from above. He walked back to the campsite resolving to go for a drive on the following day and explore the area around Elgol.

The next day dawned with gloom and grey. Rain threatened. Gregor drove off, stopping to pick up a Dutch hitcher on the way. The rain spattered, the wind picked up. He dropped the young Dutchman at the ferry terminal at Armadale. The narrow road to Elgol was a soaking ribband across the moor, but Gregor parked up above the quayside. Gregor walked down to the little primary school in its idyllic setting above the sea. Typical playground equipment in the schoolyard but the children were of course on holiday. Gregor wondered what it would be like to be a pupil in such a quaint little outcrop. Even more he thought what it would be like to teach there. Of course, there would be the issues that every school faced, the stress that every teacher experienced. But there was always the view to fall back upon, always a dreamy escape from one's classroom window. Even on stormy days like this one, there came stress relief in the natural world. Gregor wandered down the hill to the quayside and looked towards where he knew Loch Scavaig and Camusunary lay. No view on this day, no sunlit upland, only wind, rain and black clouds over the Black Cuillins. Gregor turned to drive back to Sligachan.

The car rocked and the wind blew. Any resemblance of a midsummer day was gone. It was not the blackness of night, it was the blackness of a deep, dark abyssal hole. The gods were angry. He neared the Sligachan campsite with no great longing to be back, holed up in his tent where he knew that there would be the cacophony of noise, but he went anyway. He drove slowly into the campsite and edged closely to the promontory where his tent was pitched.

The scene that greeted him was not a pleasant one. The tent was flat, the poles were broken, the driving rain was forming puddles on the canvas. The situation could have been salvaged, perhaps, given a roll of duct tape, a knife and gentle sunny weather with which to right the situation at his leisure. Gregor was annoyed and his anger became his friend. With vigour, he picked up the mess and the detritus and flung it into the boot of the car without checking what was there and what was not. He rushed himself out of the rain, got behind the wheel and headed out, turning left on the way to Broadford. Gregor had no idea where to go but he had an idea of what to do. He would bite the bullet and give himself the luxury of a Bed & Breakfast. He could have stopped anywhere but he didn't. He crossed the bridge and departed from Skye. As the kilomteres drifted by, Gregor felt a smile creep onto his face. The smile became a chuckle. The chuckle became open laughter. He now knew why no logical camper had pitched his tent on that promontory. The possibility of bad weather from a variety of sides, the total exposure to all of the elements, even the most inexperienced of campers would have recognized the folly of making one's site there.

Gregor soon found himself at Loch Duich and Eilean Donan Castle. He thought that he might have better luck of accommodation some way off the beaten track. He came off the main road and found himself on the other side of the loch at the village of Letterfairn. It wasn't long before he found himself a comfortable looking B & B with a welcoming smile from a middle-aged lady who sounded like she was from Newcastle. He was given his room and pretty soon was luxuriating in a hot shower.

There is something about talking to a complete stranger, particularly one with whom one is never likely to meet again. After the German couple who were staying had left in the morning, Gregor, replete with the Full Scottish breakfast, including black pudding and fried bread, found himself alone with the landlady. He had given up speculating how people who pay for a B &

B can only eat the cereal. Still, Teutonic self-discipline is what contributed to several football World Cup Championships and the full British breakfast to no Scottish ones. Gregor paid his bill and lingered over his cup of coffee, passing the time of day comfortably with the lady of the house. She was an ex-nurse who had survived an abusive marriage back home in Newcastle. She had escaped, met a new man, married him and she had been very happy. They had gone for a boat trip and become the victims of a rogue wave, which had resulted in the drowning of her husband. After this tragedy, she had continued in her B & B business except that she had not. The sign outside that heralded "No Vacancies" was false. Her grief allowed for no customers, no company, her reclusiveness was her comfort. Coming out of her mourning, she met another man and yet again fell in love and married him. The Fates had not finished with her. Within a year, he had developed Alzheimers. She nursed him for five years until his death. So, now she was alone again and back in business and looking forward to a visit from her son from England, the only good thing to come out of her first marriage, she had stated with a wry smile. Before Gregor knew it, an hour had passed. He sensed that she was coming to the end of her story so moved to stand up and pay his bill. There was no tear in Gregor's eye, no lump in his throat at this tale of tragic sadness but there was a tremendous admiration for the courage and resilience of this remarkable woman. He reflected as he drove away how that hour of his holiday was the most, most worthwhile of his time in Scotland. The views and weather and walks and culture were as nothing to what he had just experienced. Certainly, he smiled ruefully, getting upset and feeling sorry for himself over a waterlogged tent was pretty pathetic in the light of what he had just heard. Every person has a tale to tell. Nobody is ever free from hardship and tragedy. All have a tent with a broken pole and a flattened windswept canvas to deal with at some points in their lives.

CHAPTER 6

AUSTRALIA

Every Briton born in the 1950s had heard about the "Ten pound Pom," the opportunity that the Australian government gave to the British to go and settle in the "Lucky Country." The pictures of sun and surf, bronzed bodies beneath endless azure skies, and the heat, sheep, corked hats and red centre were paramount. An escape from the wind and the rain, the moist hopelessness of a city council estate where the future was one of monotony in work and leisure; where the opportunity to better oneself was shrouded in the same gloom and drudge as the climate. The promised land of the antipodean continent had been an opportunity of a lifetime for so many.

So, after some four years teaching in London, Gregor applied for a "working holiday visa." Armed with his year-long work permit and a mate, Callum, whom he had happened to meet in a pub one night, Gregor flew out to Perth, Western Australia, in late November 1980.

The journey had an auspicious start. The plane left on time. The stop in Kuala Lumpur was somewhat eventful, however. Having heard tales of foreigners being thrown in jail and left to rot without trial for years, Callum and Gregor were nervous about such stopovers. The airline food and the alcohol had left the two friends desperate for a roomy toilet. They found one and settled down to inspirational relief. Gregor was just seated when there came a loud banging at his door.

"Gregor, Gregor, we have to get out of here fast and now!" a panicked Callum stammered. "Move, move, move!"

Such urgency had its effect and Gregor's bowels moved. There therefore came a delay, which prompted more increasingly strident pleadings from Callum. Eventually, Gregor rapidly adjusted his dress and rushed out into the concourse where he met a tremulous Callum, red in the face and sweating.

"Let's move away from here quickly"

So they moved to a café and ordered a coffee.

"Act normal. Read the menu. Let's order another coffee."

Was Callum a drug mule? Had he found a body in a cubicle? Had he been threatened? All these questions rushed in on Gregor with heart pumping, blind, unreasoned confusion. Finally he said, "What's happened Callum?"

"Lower your voice and listen carefully".

Callum looked around nervously, put his hand over his mouth and mumbled words that Gregor could not catch. Gregor leaned forward and gave Callum his ear.

"I, I flooded the toilet. I blocked it. Water and shit kept pouring out and I could not stop it. We're in deep trouble if they trace it to me. We could be flung in jail here. No trip to Australia. Not even a return home."

Callum could not settle until he was aboard the plane and into international airspace. Callum lightened up then and ordered a beer. The alcohol flowed, Callum smiled and laughed. His relief was palpable, his joy unbounded.

"Thought we were in the shit there," he grinned with relieved joviality.

"Well, you *were* in the shit. *I* wanted to be but was rushed out before I had finished!" Gregor observed with chagrin.

After a few days of exploration in the city of Perth they had settled on an apartment in the area of Subiaco-Floreat. Charlie, the caretaker, was from Nottingham and a pleasant old gentleman. He welcomed his two fellow Brits with open arms. Gregor and Callum's next mission was to try to find a job.

It was not a good time to arrive if one was seeking work. Australians were building up to their summer Christmas break and thinking more of their holidays than employing a couple of dubious looking, accented Poms. So they found a second-hand bookshop and bought what should have been labeled *The Complete Works of Robert Ludlum* but was just many dog-eared versions of his novels. They scanned the newspapers for "Situations Vacant." Nothing doing, so they went to the pub.

Australian beer is very cold after the lukewarm British version. Both of them felt the rush of blood to the head, the brain freeze that occurs from too quick consumption.

On the following day, Callum and Gregor were very hung-over. The seven dwarves were pick-axing their ways through their remaining brain cells. Their throats were like deserts in a sandstorm. Some sadistic joiner was banging nails into one of Gregor's frontal lobes. But it was rent day so they had to put one foot in front of the other and head down to Charlie's office and write out his cheques. Off they trudged silently with a patent air of self-pity. They knew enough about Charlie to know that he would be eager to reminisce about the "old country," that his garrulous greeting was likely to be a long-winded build up to the actual handing over of the money. They were offered chairs and slumped gratefully down in front of his desk. Gregor was aghast at the apparition before his eyes and caught a wide-eyed, startled Callum seated next to him. Gregor's thoughts raced ahead of him, a cacophony of chaotic consternation. He was never going to touch Australian beer again. This next year was going to be a sober one. No more alcohol. Charlie's chat of Tony Locke, the Nottinghamshire cricketer, who had migrated to Western Australia would normally have been of interest to the two cricket fans sitting before him but both were shuffling uneasily in their chairs. Gregor believed he was hallucinating and couldn't wait to leave.

"Make it stop!" he screamed inwardly.

Finally, the ordeal was over, the money was paid and they left the office. Silently they made their way back upstairs to their flat.

As they entered through the front door, Callum asked in a hoarse whisper, "Did you notice?"

Reaching for the life raft of reason, Gregor replied, "Do you mean did I notice that Charile's hair was a brilliant sky blue colour? Yes, I did."

"Phew, I thought that it was an alcohol induced mirage. If we both saw it then it must be real, must it not?"

They sat down at the kitchen table opposite each other and put their heads in their hands. Callum finally took a breath and managed to extrapolate.

"Charlie must have overdone the blue rinse!"

"Yes, yes, we are not hallucinating at all."

"The next time we go for a drink, let us sip rather than guzzle and let's not do it the night before the rent is due."

All that it really takes when our perceptions are askew is to have the confirmation from a friend, the reassurance of a like mind.

"Look back and smile on perils past."
- Sir Walter Scott

C H A P T E R   7

WANNEROO

The Perth suburb of Wanneroo was virtually all bush back in the New Year of 1981. Gregor had landed a job helping to lay pipes. He had to stand in the deep, sand-banked ditch to ensure that the mechanical digger above him did not dig too deep or too shallow. It was a job that he needed after the barren Christmas, so he was happy to collect his $200 per week for standing and doing very little. He was not happy at the idea that the rumblings of the digger would shake the ground so much that the wildlife in the bush (i.e., snakes) would be panicked and flee into Gregor's hole. It would be wrong to say that Gregor hated snakes, it would be right to say that he was terrified of them. Gregor spent his time in the hole ever alert to being surprised by the reptiles.

Gregor's wariness was not relieved by the upcoming entry of the last pipe into the approaching manhole. The manholes had been laid in place weeks before. To Gregor's active imagination that meant that they had become a nest of snakes. How was he going to pluck up the courage to enter and guide the last pipe into place? Tentatively he lifted the lid. No snakes. Sigh of relief. He lowered himself down as the last pipe was being lowered on the end of the digger awaiting his guiding hand. Slowly, he helped edge it into place. Quickly, he hoisted himself out and over the edge back into daylight. He went up to get a drink before commencing to pack the sand around the line of new pipes. He breathed a sigh and sat down. He looked up and Eric the digger driver was walking towards him shaking his head.

"How come you jumped into the manhole without checking," he demanded.

"I did check and it was clear. Not a snake in sight."

"Huh, whose talking about snakes? Did you not see the redbacks?"

"Redbacks, what are redbacks?"

"Spiders whose bite can make you sick."

"Nope, I didn't notice."

"Come with me."

Together they pulled back the manhole cover, and Eric flashed his torch into the darkness revealing a plethora of webs and several spiders lurking with intent.

"See?"

"I didn't notice them"

"Next time, check!"

It was strange to Gregor how much he feared snakes and how little he feared spiders. He had no understanding of how he feared the one and not the other. An innocent non-venomous corn snake would have him fleeing for his life, yet a spider with a nasty bite was of no consequence to him whatsoever. Gregor was always very careful to avoid the one, and careless about avoiding the other.

Gregor was enjoying his introduction to Australian life and culture. Callum was on the cusp of getting a job at a salt mine at a place called Useless Loop. He was fated to be going up north to a single man's camp, going "Troppo" as they called it when people moved north of the Tropic of Capricorn.

Every morning, Gregor was picked up by the boss in his "Beaut Ute," his utility vehicle. Gregor enjoyed the early morning conversations but was learning that Ockers were not fans of the local aboriginal people. Gregor listened with unease and growing anger about how they were lazy and a burden on the tax payer. He felt, however, that he had better keep his counsel because he was new to the country and wanted to keep his job. Gregor was very happy that the morning diatribe was a monologue, and he was never asked his opinion. It was his job just to be a wall. So he let sleeping dogs lie.

Early one Monday morning, Bruce, his boss, was 30 minutes late picking him up. Eventually the ute struggled around the corner. It was stuttering rather than moving along at its regular clip.

"Get in," stormed a grumpy boss with no apology for his tardiness. Silence ensued for five minutes and then he burst out with irritation. "Ran over a black boy on the weekend and I think there's a bit of if stuck in the radiator."

Gregor was aghast at the statement. Had Bruce just confessed to a hit-and-run murder? Had he just admitted, with more concern for his vehicle, that he had killed a lad? Gregor did not know what to say. He was questioning whether he should sneak off and phone the police when they arrived at work. Selfishly, he did not want to be guilty as an accessory. He did not know the laws in Australia, but he was sure that keeping quiet about the killing of a fellow human being may well be frowned upon. At the moment, however, he did not want to be in the same vehicle with this callous, indifferent man. Job or no job, he had to do something.

They reached the construction site. Bruce leapt out of his truck, flung open the bonnet and yelled, "OK, let's see if we can find the bastard."

Gregor's curiosity got the better of him. He half expected a mashed section of human limb to be extracted from the area around the radiator. He had noticed a mangled grill with a hole in it. He was drawn towards the ghastly sight.

"Got the bastard."

With that, a short branch still with some greenery on it, was flung decisively to the ground.

"What's that?" Gregor burst out, wide-eyed with consternation and alarm.

"I told you I ran over a black boy on the weekend and I was right. There it is."

"Oooooooooh, that's a black boy!" Gregor exclaimed with palpable relief.

"Yeah, what did *you* think it was. Oh no, you didn't," laughed Bruce as it dawned on him why Gregor was relieved. "I may not be a fan of our native people but I am not a murderer. A **'black boy'** is a short, stubby tree. Get down in your hole and start work you dopey Pommie bastard."

With that he turned his back and laughed all the way to the dunny for his morning constitutional.

Gregor had been exposed to the difference in the English of Australia before. He had been employed as a door-to-door peddler of encyclopedias. He had had the training. An erudite English woman had taken pity on him and persuaded him that he was just the man to convince young families that their children's future depended very much on the fact that they invested in the *World Book*. Margaret had shared the difficulty that her and her husband had had when they first had come to Australia. On one of her many interviews, she had been asked if her husband had actually got a job yet. She had induced smirks from the interview panel when she stated, "Not yet, but I am really rooting for him!" She was blissfully unaware that "rooting" was the Aussie word for the sexual act. It had further been explained to her that such was the unenlightenedness of the average Aussie male, that the lover was devoid of romance, that the typical Aussie lover was much like the dictionary definition of the wombat in that, "He eats, roots, shoots and leaves." There would be many more instances of the language barrier, the cultural separation between the old country and the new one as Gregor traipsed his wide-eyed naïvety around this "wide brown land" with the red centre.

For the moment, however, Gregor hoped to find a white Australian who would actually own up to the fact that the European settlers had treated the aboriginals appallingly. It would have been nice to have heard a bit of contrition but it was rare to find any. The Irish Potato Famine and the Highland Clearances had forced emigration, which in turn had hurt so many other indigenous peoples around the world. If all history is a history of colonization then the search for living space is rarely without conflict. These were thoughts that occurred to Gregor then and were to recur often, particularly when he eventually settled in Western Canada.

"Which of all my important nothings shall I tell you first?"
- Jane Austen

CHAPTER 8

BUNBURY, WESTERN AUSTRALIA

Bunbury in Western Australia is a city some 290 kilometres south of Perth. Gregor had found himself out of work, his ditch dwelling job having run out. So he decamped down to Bunbury, Callum having already headed up to Useless Loop. Gregor formed a quick, early opinion of Bunbury. It was a pleasant, sleepy port near the southwestern tip of W.A. On Sundays, the young guys would be out in their utes and cruising round the streets because there was little else to do. It seemed to Gregor, who had been teaching in London, that calling Bunbury a city was a triumph of belief over reality. It was a sleepy town at best, an elongated village at worst. But it had the Rose Hotel and it had a youth hostel. Gregor got off the bus, grabbed a local paper and walked the short distance up to the hostel, which was up a gentle slope just beneath the ridge of the hill over which was the beach and the Indian Ocean.

Searching the "Help Wanted" advertisements, Gregor came across a job called a "Grano worker." He had no idea what one of those was but gave the firm a call anyway. Thus did he find himself at very short notice, barrowing concrete from one side of a house pad to the other, for concrete was the "grano," and sweat and strength were the requirements. Gregor had an abundance of both to give.

Finding somewhere to live was the immediate problem because the hostel had its three nights rule. He approached Phil Collins, the owner, and asked for his advice. Phil beamed.

"You can stay here, mate. We have a room for the occasional permanent resident."

So, Gregor picked up his gear from the male dormitory and was shown his room at the side of the house. Later that evening he was introduced to Richard Sparrow, "Birdie," who was also living in the hostel. Gregor immediately took to this rugged looking Kiwi with a twinkle in his eye and a smile struggling to hide round the corners of his mouth. They decided to cement their early friendship with a companionable beer at the Rose Hotel. It was a midweek night so there were few customers leaning on the bar as Richard and Gregor entered. As they crossed to order their drinks, the locals were giving them the once over, again giving the lie that Bunbury was a "city." Nobody in Paris, New York or London would ever notice a stranger entering a bar. John, the barman, introduced himself and even shook them by the hand. After the beers had arrived, John asked Richard and Gregor about themselves. During the course of the conversation, it emerged that not only was John the barman but he was also the owner of the pub. He explained that Phil and Joan Collins who owned the youth hostel were new to the game of hostelling. Their real business was Collins Music, which was a large shop with a long frontage on the main street.

Richard and Gregor walked back to their beds and reflected that even though they had only been in Bunbury for a short time, they were now a part of the scenery. They would never be Bunburians or Bunburyites—or whatever the locals were called—but they felt that they might just fit in.

Gregor soon discovered that concrete work was physically hard but mentally unchallenging. He had hoped that this last would be mitigated by banter and beers with his workmates. He had hoped an easy camaraderie and the occasional jolly jape would light up the working day with laughter. He then discovered that Morgan and Sons was a concrete company that was mostly made up of Jehovah's Witnesses, a reflection of the boss's belief system. So much that passed for Gregor's character and his personality, which had been honed and styled by boarding school, college days and rugby clubs, simply didn't fit. But—he needed the work. His new friend, Birdie, was always an excellent presence at the end of the day so he vowed to stick it out until he had enough money to go and travel around the country.

After a fortnight or so, Richard decided that a weekend in the real city would be in order. So, excitedly, they purchased their tickets for Perth and mounted the bus on Saturday morning. After a couple of hours they were in Hay Street seeking food and entertainment. The food part was easy. Indeed, the drink part was easier. Neither of them admitted it to each other but the company of girls were what they were hoping for. That proved to be more difficult. There seems to be a cusp moment for young men seeking love and lust of an evening. That moment comes some time after the fifth or sixth beer when they realize that pursuit of the fairer sex is useless. At that point they give themselves up to more alcohol and the world becomes again an exclusively male domain with all the lack of planning and foresight that that involves. The hour came and the bar closed.

"Where are we spending the night?" Gregor slurred as they stumbled up the street.

"Good question, mate," Birdie replied with the goofiest of grins.

So on they walked, not knowing where they were going.

"Newspapers," nodded Birdie with emphasis and began to seek out any discarded papers he could find as they walked.

"A bridge," observed Gregor after they had walked on for another 30 minutes or so.

And so the two friends found themselves lying covered in the news media on a bank under a road bridge. Sleep was intermittent. It seemed that no sooner had they dropped off than they rolled over and felt bone chillingly cold. Daylight could not come soon enough. Eventually, rosy-fingered dawn, as the ancients would have it, made its appearance and Richard and Gregor could stand being still for no longer. Sandpapered throats, woodpeckers tap-tapping away at their sore heads, a rough taste in their mouths, their clothes covered in dust and dirt, they stumbled up the bank to the road.

"Th—th—that w—was an interesting evening," Birdie's teeth chattered.

"I thought that you had an address for the night," Gregor fumed aloud.

No answer was the loud reply. They found their bearings and headed back towards the city.

"We need a greasy breakfast, lashings of fried bacon, fried eggs, fried bread and anything else that is fried. Plus we need caffeine, lashings of coffee and water and water and water."

Birdie grinned lopsidedly. Gregor's diatribe continued.

"I'm from the far north of Europe, I grew up with wind and rain and snow and ice, I know what it is to be cold. I have skied and hiked and camped and sailed and played rugby on windswept, rain-drenched pitches, I know what bloody cold is. I tell you this, Richard Sparrow, I have never, ever been as cold as I was last night. Let's have our breakfast, get warm, get on that bus back to Bunbury, have a warm night and go to work in the morning."

So it was. The bus came and the two men slept all the way down to their home. As the bus pulled in to Bunbury, Birdie pushed Gregor awake. Bleary-eyed, they staggered out.

"Let's get a cleansing ale before we go back to the hostel," Gregor suggested.

Birdie nodded, so they stopped off at the Rose Hotel, which was quiet as befitted Sunday. John was behind the bar as usual.

"Good weekend, lads?" he asked in mid-pour not having asked them what they wanted to drink. He assumed rightly that the beer would be the same as they always drank. The ever generous Birdie reached into his pocket. John shook his head.

"These two are on the house, boys,"

"Thanks John." Gregor was surprised but reached for his beer, only to find that John was pulling it away from him.

"You can have *that* as soon as you've got rid of *that*," He nodded towards a heap of clothing on the floor in the corner.

Gregor and Birdie looked at each other quizzically. A messy pile of dirty looking clothing to be removed by them?

"Take a closer look." John tilted his head and sighed.

They wandered over and heard the snores from the floor. Warren, another resident of the hostel, was curled up asleep, the smile on his face showing a contented oblivion to his surroundings. Richard had been a mate of Warren's, indeed they worked on the same building project. So he did what all true mates do in such circumstances. He kicked him. Warren barely stirred. John handed Gregor a large jug of cold water.

"This should help."

It did. Warren spluttered and coughed and sat up. He gazed confused up at his two soakers. There was a slow, confused recognition dawning on his face. A silly grin broke out at his joy on seeing his two mates. They reached down, grabbed his elbows and pulled him to his feet.

It did not prove to be an easy task to get Warren up the hill to the hostel. Too often it was one step forward, two steps back. At one point, they all lost balance and toppled over onto a grassy bank. Gregor and Biridie were quickly back to their feet but Warren was lying with his eyes closed, asleep again.

"Get up you lousy drunken bastard!" Birdie had lost patience. "Get up and walk or so help me I'll grab your legs and drag you the rest of the way."

Yet again they got him on his feet and pushed and pulled him the last 100 yards to the hostel entrance. Phil was replacing a light bulb in the hallway as they entered.

"Hi lads, nice to see you." He spotted Warren. "I think?"

"Can you help us get him up to his room, Phil?"

More manhandling up the stairs, around the corner and eventually into his dormitory and onto the bed.

"I should have known this was likely to happen," Phil grinned as the three of them sat in the communal lounge recovering their breath. "He came up here earlier in the afternoon absolutely delighted that he had been able to buy a flagon of wine on sale for $5. He offered me a drink and, in the process, he tossed the screw top lid into the garbage, definitively stating that we would not need it again. 'As useful as tits on a bull,' were his very words, I believe, as the top sailed into the garbage. I only shared the one glass with him and then he grabbed his wine and disappeared into the park. Must have gone down to the Rose after the wine had run out."

"Oh well, thanks Phil, we're off back to the Rose for our free pint. Do you want to come?"

"Thanks boys but I'll stay here and keep an eye on things. And don't worry, Warren's a fine fellow I won't be asking him to leave. Ha, you see some wonderful sights in this job do you not?"

With a wide smile, Phil turned on his heels and went upstairs to check on his drunken lodger.

Bunbury was like that. You stayed there for a couple of weeks and it was as if you had become part of a family. Everybody seemed to know everybody else. There was a "Gudday" at the beginning, middle and end of the day. Some were remembered only as faces that one regularly saw, others were a name and a brief chat, still more were a shared blether in the public bar of the Rose Hotel.

Gregor and Birdie were there on the weekend when the New Zealand Navy came to visit. A large crew of Richard Sparrow's fellow countrymen were on shore leave and out for a good time. The two friends decided to join the horde and heaving mass of humanity in the public bar. Maori voices raised with gleeful good humour, accents which caused "Kevin" and "bed" to be "Kivin" and "bid." It was all an alcohol release from the confines of ship and rules and duties. Outside on the main street, the shore patrol paced and observed, ready to step in when behaviour got out of hand and the offenders had to be whisked back to their ship. It was good to see Richard interacting with his fellow countrymen.

A couple of days later, Richard revealed that his Canadian girlfriend, Wendy, was going to visit from Melbourne. On the day of her arrival, Richard had walked down to the bus stop to pick her up. Birdie had walked her back to the hostel and introduced her to their accommodation. Gregor was a bit surprised after he had been introduced that he was invited to join them for a drink. He had thought that they would want to be on their own. He protested this to Richard but he and Wendy were insistent. So, they had found themselves in the lounge bar with the ever present John pouring their drinks.

Sat around the table, Gregor had quizzed Wendy as to what Melbourne was like as a city. He had had a mind to visit it on his inevitable trip to the east. As she was explaining why she liked living there so much, she suddenly mentioned, "Of course, Richard has never been to Melbourne."

"Yes he has," Gregor intoned and received a violent kick on his shins for his trouble. "Ouch, what did you do that for?"

"Sorry, a sudden cramp. No, no I have never been to Melbourne," Birdie stated with hissing meaningfulness and an intense glare at Gregor.

It suddenly dawned on Gregor that he was not to reveal the Sparrow visit to Melbourne because it was too embarrassing to him.

The sorry tale of Richard Sparrow's sudden trip to Melbourne had been related to Gregor some weeks previously. The Birdie had been one of the groomsmen at a "weeding" ("weeding" being the Kiwi word for "wedding") in his hometown of Ashburton on the South Island of New Zealand. Drink had been consumed and as the evening had moved forward, his mates had come up with the plan to have a whip around and put the drunken Birdman on a flight to Australia. Richard had woken up in an airport lounge, assumed he was at Christchurch Airport, walked outside and hailed a taxi cab.

"Take me to Ashburton," he told the driver, who had never heard of Ashburton. After a lengthy explanation to the cabbie, Richard was questioned.

"Where do you think you are, mate? No, you're not in Christchurch, you're in Melbourne," and with emphasis, "in the beautiful state of Victoria, Australia."

Richard had been stuck with no money for three days over the Christmas holidays. Of course he did not want his new girlfriend to know about this escapade even though it had been in his distant past.

Gregor liked Richard Sparrow a great deal. He felt at ease in his company. If he had realized that when they had gone their inevitable separate ways that they were never to see or hear from each other again, he would have been terribly upset. But such is the self-centredness of youth, the vagabond nature of temporary jobs and accommodation that he cannot even remember saying "goodbye" to him. He knew that they never exchanged addresses. Email and mobile phones did not exist. The dog had barked and the caravan had passed. It was a shame.

"A continent cannot obviously be ruled by an island."
- Thomas Paine

CHAPTER 9

SYDNEY

Bunbury was a pleasant interlude. Gregor had enjoyed it. He had been enamoured of the intimacy of the place. He had liked working outside in the heat. He had enjoyed the temporary camaraderie of the hostellers who passed through the building on a daily basis. Some stayed only one night but all had a story to tell about their journey; an adventure to relate about their trip. Sometimes Gregor engaged in conversation with them as they cooked or as they ate. Most of the time he just listened, picking up tips here and there about what he wanted to see and how he wanted to experience this wonderful country. He heard how sleepy W.A. and Perth were compared to the "rat race" of the eastern states. He didn't really believe that at all. After all, he had worked in London. Although he had to admit there was a quick-wittedness in the cities that he missed. To him it had become a particular problem because his religious workmates were about as sharp-witted as a sloth using a plastic knife. Time for Gregor to head to Sydney.

Six p.m. in the Atlantic Hotel in Perth. Perth, the most isolated city in the world, sits on the edge of the Indian Ocean. Gregor had no idea how far the city was from the Atlantic Ocean. He did know, however, that as the crow flies, the crow wouldn't make it. The bus was due to leave for Sydney at any minute and Gregor was leaning on the bar resisting the urge to ask the barman how the hotel had got its name. Then came the announcement over the tannoy.

"The bus departing for Sydney calling at Kalgoorlie, Adelaide, Melbourne and many other points east has broken down."

That was it. No mention of when it would be fixed or whether it would be replaced or how long they would have to wait. Gregor asked for and bought another beer and settled in for a long wait. Maybe he would ask the barman about the origins of the Atlantic Hotel after all.

As he paid for his second beer he said, "So how did the Atlantic Hotel get its name, mate?"

"It's next to the ocean, mate. The city of Perth is on the ocean,"

This as if the answer to the question was so obvious that it was as if Gregor had asked which country in the world had the national anthem *Advance Australia Fair*. Could it be New Zealand? How about Denmark? Of course, Gregor should have known it was called the Atlantic Hotel because it was next to the Ocean!

How bleeding obvious was that?

"But, but Perth is next to the **Indian** Ocean."

"And your point is?"

Gregor took another slurp of his beer and looked away and glanced around the bar. In a corner there was a group of eight young men. Gregor couldn't quite believe it when he heard a Welsh voice raised with febrile exuberance. It was countered by the slow, lazy drawl of an Australian one. The animation of the discussion peaked his interest.

"They're more flexible, boyo, they don't crack with the pressure, they bend."

"Concrete props don't even notice the pressure."

One of the bystanders caught Gregor's eye.

"What are they discussing?" asked Gregor.

"They are talking about which type of pit prop is best, wooden ones or concrete ones. They are both miners in Kalgoorlie."

Gregor knew enough about his bus trip to know that Kalgoorlie was the first stop going east and it was a gold mining town.

"We apologise for the late departure of the 1800 bus to Sydney. It will now be leaving at 2200 hours."

An audlble groan went through the bar. Nothing for it but to order another beer. While his beer was being poured, Gregor reached in his pack for his book. *Catch 22* by Joseph Heller was almost a classic. It was well written. Gregor smiled as he remembered Heller being interviewed on TV, his arrogance to the fore.

"It has been said, Mr. Heller, that in all of the years since you wrote **Catch 22** you have never written anything to equal or better it."

"Who has?"

End of interview. Closing credits and music.

The Atlantic Hotel bar became a livelier place as the night wore on. Snatches of taped music tannoyed its way through the bar. Pieces of conversation occasionally penetrated Gregor's focus.

"You can reinforce concrete, you can't reinforce wood."

"Yes, you can. Wood always is good at supporting wood. You don't know what you are talking about. You've never even been down a Welsh coal mine have you?"

"OK, alright, how many miners have been killed in a gold mine compared to a coal mine. A lot more in a coal mine. Why? Because the pit props are not concrete. I rest my case."

Except that he didn't.

Finally the announcement they had waited hours to hear arrived.

"Would all passengers for the scheduled 1800 hours bus for Sydney please make their way to board at platform #12 please. We apologise for the late departure of this service."

Gregor finished the last little drop of his beer and dismounted his bar stool, returning *Catch 22* to his backpack. The barman approached him. For a moment, Gregor hoped he was going to explain the Indian versus Atlantic dilemma.

"You know, Young Pommie, there are no toilets on these busses."

"Thanks!"

This was a shock to the system and would be an even greater shock if they were a long way out from Kalgoorlie when he needed to go. So he rushed to the Gents toilet to find there was a bit of a queue. He did not want to risk missing the bus so he rushed out back onto the forecourt, hoping against hope that his young bladder was sufficient unto his needs. He found a window seat. Despite the fact that the bus was almost full, Gregor was grateful that nobody seemed to want to sit next to him.

The hours passed and Gregor tried to focus on his book. It was dark, so the scenery outside was black. He tried to doze but sleep wouldn't come. He was beginning to think that it would have been pleasant if he had had a companion next to him with whom to talk. He really, really needed to go and conversation would have helped to change his focus. There was no point in standing up and moving, for such action wouldn't diminish his need. He began to recite poems in his head. He tried not to look as the person on the seat opposite him opened his water bottle and began to drink. Kalgoorlie was getting slowly closer. He began to compose songs in his head. Johnny Cash came to mind.

"Kalgoorlie I love every inch of you…"

Then the Beatles: "Kalgoorlie, Kalgoorlie, nothing to do but say to you, how's your toilets?"

The Rolling Stones: "I can't get no Kalgoorlie. No, no, no."

All of a sudden, there was a road sign: "Welcome to Kalgoorlie." Gregor stood up but not before many others had done the same. He should have anticipated that so many needed to go. There was a mass urgency emergency and Gregor was at the back of the line. Gregor was all for selflessness but now it was every man for himself. The bus pulled to a halt, the doors opened. The exodus was quick.

The washrooms were large with plenty of urinals. Such was the relief as he stood that Gregor closed his ideas and his eyes to savour the moments of pent-up release. As he was in his entranced state of bliss, he heard a voice to his left.

"Besides, concrete pit props are good for the environment, they don't strip our forests."

Then immediately to his right.

"So here in Kalgoorlie I'm not going to see any wooden pit props?"

It was now about 2:00 a.m. and Gregor estimated that the pit prop discussion had been going on for about eight hours. As he completed his urination and was doing up his fly, he said loudly, "How about steel pit props?"

The Welshman and his Aussie mate looked at him as if it was none of his business and then as if he knew nothing about pit props anyway. Gregor returned to his seat on the bus. The two miners were disappearing into the darkness of the town. Before the bus had reached the edge of the town on its way eastwards, Gregor was contentedly asleep.

It was two and a half days later after the Nullarbor Plain and the Great Australian Bight had been left behind that Gregor was wide awake when the bus pulled into Sydney town.

"Men more frequently require to be reminded than informed."
- Samuel Johnson

CHAPTER 10

MALVERN'S MARAUDERS

Gregor had found the youth hostel and decided on the maximum stay of three nights to get his bearings and to find a way into the job market. It was true, as he knew it would be, that there was a faster pace of life here. The noise of the traffic, the vigour of the people when they walked, the sense of bustling business; an overriding feeling of confidence and a sense of confident, innovative self-belief. All this came across to Gregor as he walked the streets on that first day in the metropolis. He went to the Opera House, took the Manly Ferry and had a sandwich in the park. He was excited as he trekked back to the hostel with a supply of good food to cook for his evening meal.

Gregor was having a post-prandial nap in the large, communal lounge. People were chatting or playing cards, a small section were watching the news on the T.V. Suddenly, a tall, skinny, freckled red-headed young man stood up and climbed onto a table. In a loud voice he proclaimed to the people in the room, "I think the British should get out of Northern Ireland!" and then he sat down again and everybody else simply carried on. It occurred to Gregor that maybe this young guy did the same thing every day, shouted forth the same sentence at the same time every night. Then, honour and respect satisfied, he quietly sat down again and went about his business. He had done his bit for the cause, answered the call with his solution for the "troubles" across the religious divide in Northern Ireland.

Every visitor to Sydney at some point will find himself at Bondi Beach, the Opera House and Kings Cross. It was on his second day in the city that Gregor walked up the steps from Woolamaloo and found himself in Potts Point and eventually in Fitzroy Gardens at the heart of "The Cross." He rummaged and explored a bit longer and eventually found what he was looking for, a room to rent. He paid a month in advance, bought a newspaper and went about the business of finding himself a job.

"Hospital Porter" leapt off the page at him. A short hop on the train and Gregor was sitting outside Rob Malvern's office in the bowels of Princess Alexandra Hospital. Mr. Malvern asked him questions about the state of his visa, then sent him off to be fitted with the requisite green uniform and instructions that he would get paid $200 per week. He was to report in the morning for work. Gregor celebrated that night with a feast at the Rex Hotel, washed down with a few beers.

At work on the following day, Gregor learned that it was his job to move things and not people. If a television needed to be taken to a ward, then it was his job. If a patient needed to be returned to a ward, then it was the job of the white porters. The jobs were allocated on a strict rotation basis. The porters just had to be readily at hand in the office waiting for the call. Apart from that there was nothing to do but sup on endless cups of coffee, read books or write letters. So, he settled in to write to his friend, Callum, whom he knew was about to call it a day at his job in Useless Loop and begin to tour the country.

Gregor hadn't considered it much before but now that he had a regular job with regular hours and a Monday to Friday contract, he thought that he might like to play a little bit of rugby. So, he researched and found what he was looking for. Northern Suburbs RFC was just north of the Sydney Harbour Bridge. He found their training nights and took himself up there on a Thursday night. He received the welcome which only a rugby club can offer and was offered a game on the Saturday. He bought himself some boots and shorts and was ready for action, albeit with not much running stamina but with a healthy musculature due to his concrete work. Saturday's home game came and went. Gregor showered and ventured into the bar for a post-game beer. It was all good natured and friendly. The time came at about 7:30 p.m. when his new teammates were going on elsewhere to make a night of it. Not having been paid yet for his time at PAH and having spent money on his rent and his rugby gear, Gregor quietly declined the offer of going out. Eventually the wise old scrum half came up to him.

"No money, mate?"

"Not until I get paid next week."

He felt his hand being squeezed and when he opened it there was $20 there.

"Pay me back when you get paid."

"Thanks."

They all headed off to The Rocks area of Sydney, stood on the cobbles and bantered away the evening.

The following Saturday before the game, Gregor reached into his wallet, pulled out a $20 bill and gave it to Rob the scrum half. He refused it with a force that could not be countered.

"Just promise me that you'll pass it on."

There are so many different cultures in the world, each with their own set of rules and nuances. Gregor thought he knew all that he needed to know about mateship, about loyalty, about how to be a friend. He had been through boarding school where close proximity, intimacy, had been a fact of life. Yet that, surprisingly, had not bred the camaraderie that would have been expected in such an institution. He had heard all the trite sayings such as "To have a friend, you need to be a friend," and so on, but travelling in Australia brought home to him what it really was to be a mate. Maybe it was the convict history where life had been hard so that one helped one another out of jams and scrapes. Far from being altruistic, these were necessary deeds based on the belief that there but for the grace of god go I. That at some time in the future I am going to need them as they need me now. Gregor was to receive many acts of kindness throughout his time in Australia and he was going to try to give many in return. At any rate, it was *not* the small world of an English public school that gave him the deeper understanding of friendship. It had taken thousands of kilometres, a vast expanse of empty land, and a rigorous, sturdy culture to give him that understanding. There had been Digby in Scotland, there was a rugby club in Sydney. The passages of times and places were the givers of newer and broader perspectives.

"No one is useless in this world who lightens the burdens of it for anyone else."
- Charles Dickens

CHAPTER 11

A COMMUNITY OF EXILES

Among the portering community of Prince Alexandra Hospital were many people who were newly arrived in Australia. Of course, there was the usual batch of New Zealanders. Work was hard to come by in the land of the "long white cloud" in 1981 so Australia was also the "lucky country" for them. Life was also hard in Poland from whence Ralph had come. Ralph's English was weak, but it was coming along in leaps and bounds because he loved to speak and cared little if he murdered his new language in the process. "Solidarity," that organization spawned in Gdansk through the leadership of Lech Walesa, was coming to the fore but still Ralph had had to leave his fiancé back in his home and native land. The uncertainty and separation must have been hard for him but nobody would ever have known it. Ralph fizzed with joyous effervescence. He sang his way through the day, back slapped his way through each T.V. delivery, every bed that had to be moved. Really, he should have been a white porter because his joviality would have been a universal panacea for all ills. But he wasn't. He was confined to his green uniform and this most lively of men was confined to the movement of the lifeless.

Ralph drove a wreck of a car. Gregor was leaving work one day and was making his way to the train station for his commute home when a loud blast of the horn pulled him up short. The car window was down and the beaming smile and vigorous beckoning of the arm brooked no refusal. Gregor wandered over and got in.

"Gregor, Gregor, where you live? I take you home. Anywhere, anywhere, not a problem. I love you. You a funny guy."

He pulled away from the kerb without indicating, was blasted and sworn at by a bus driver, waved and smiled at him in return.

"How you Gregor? I love this country. You and I are a breath of fresh air, as you say, Australia needs us. We make country better. We teach them important things. They learn to love us, eh? We soon be dinkee di Aussies too. Fair dinkum."

There was no edgeways for Gregor to get in a word! The car was not a straight line machine. Ralph was starting to weave from side to side.

"So where you live?"

"Ah, Kings Cross. We get there soon. I know short cut."

A "No Entry" sign appeared on the left and Ralph swerved to enter. Quickly, they were on a one way street going against six lanes of traffic. Gregor slunk down in the passenger seat. Ralph had his window open, was gesturing, shouting in Polish, laughing and smiling in Universal. During intervals in this crisis, he turned to Gregor to reassure him.

"This does not matter, Gregor. My country has been invaded by the Germans, ruled by the Russians. Communism sucks, dinkum. Girlfriend is stuck in Poland. Miss her a lot." (Catch in the throat, dreamy look, one tear from his right eye, attention taken away from the situation!) "This, this does not matter. Strewth, Gregor." Suddenly he was back at one with the present.

All delivered with a waving of hands and a liveliness of verbiage. Gregor was very surprised when they made it home safely.

"Aaah, good company, Gregor, you are one nice fellow. I shall pick you up in the morning and we talk more?"

"No, no, it's OK, Ralph. I'll see you at work and we will have time to talk there. I have enjoyed our chat and thank you so much for not killing us both. I really appreciate it. I shall take the train in the morning. I *do* appreciate your kind offer but I have a peculiar desire to live so will not be a passenger with you again."

Far from taking offence at this brusque rebuff, Ralph grinned and pulled joyously back into traffic.

Working amongst the Kiwis was always pleasant. They had come over without the need of passport or identification. Those who didn't immediately sign on the dole, found work with ease. Legend had it that Fergus the porter from the South Island had gone home to the house that he was sharing with six of his compatriots. He had found them sunning themselves in the front garden.

"Found work yet, fellas?"

"Nope!" was chorused back at him.

"Wasn't there anything in the papers?"

"What papers?" Kevin asked.

Fergus reached for a beer from the chilly bin and sat down on the grass.

It wasn't long before Kevin found himself too at PAH but this time as a white porter. Kevin worked hard and worked well. He was liked by the patients who enjoyed his jokes. He exuded cheery bonhomie. Occasionally, he went too far. On one particular shift, he had become irritated by a patient whom he had to ferry back and forth for tests. Kevin could do no right for this middle-aged guy. During the last hour of his shift, he was called to pick up the same patient who had become an unwelcome bugbear to him. The patient was uncharacteristically nervous because he was going for a special treatment. His eyes were wide open with fear and he was talking nervously. Kevin had not much sympathy for him at this point. So when he was asked if he knew anything about the guy's upcoming treatment he had answered, "I don't know much about it, but I have heard that it is very, very painful."

The patient complained and Rob Malvern had hauled Kevin over the coals.

The other incident, which was much more serious, had produced no fraught interview with Rob for some reason. The hospital had decided to sweep it under the carpet. Kevin had pulled a night shift. There had been a road traffic accident with a fatality. Kevin was called to Casualty to pick up the body and deliver it to the morgue. The corpse was already shrouded and strapped to the gurney when he arrived there. It was a dark and very rainy night. The morgue was down a hill on a tarmaced pathway. Just before the foot of the hill there was a sharp bend on the other side of which was a steep, bushy bank. Not wanting to get wet, Kevin had set off with the gurney at a slow jog that gradually got faster as the rain fell more heavily. As he approached the corner he had tried to slow down but lost control, had stumbled and fallen. In the process the gurney was wrenched from his grasp. It disappeared over the bank and crashed its way through the bushes for 30 yards or so. Kevin was filled with concern and alarm, so he staggered down the bank to try to rescue the situation. He was pleased to see that the body was still secured to the gurney. He was less pleased to find that the gurney had lost a wheel and a leg and that the structure of the rest of it was buckled and bent. By now, Kevin was scratched and muddied and soaked to the skin. He debated whether he should go back and get a working gurney but thought that that would draw too much attention to the situation. He resolved to try to fix it himself. He managed to get the contraption disentangled and back onto the tarmac. Wheeling it, however, was now impossible. But he realized that he had come out near the laundry area and that there were several large laundry containers close at hand. He brought a half-full one back to the gurney, unstrapped the body and with some difficulty lifted it over the top of this container onto a pile of laundry that was waiting for cleaning.

Kevin took a deep breath. He decided to deliver the laundry to the morgue with aplomb. He would enter and deliver as if there was nothing unusual in the mode of transport. Of course, now his white uniform was not only sodden and soiled by the mud but was now bloodied as well from handling the body. Kevin pushed the laundry basket through the morgue doors to find that the two people on duty were sitting having their meal break and were in the midst of a game of dominoes.

"Corpse for delivery," he said.

The two technicians looked at each other and then at Kevin with undisguised disgust.

"Where is it?" said one.

"In the basket," said Kevin. "Busy shift so I have to get back. See you again." And he was gone.

Kevin had expected, and accepted, that he would need to have another fraught meeting with management over the incident. He had asked his friends, the green porters, to secretly pick up the wrecked gurney and deliver it to the Maintenance Department, which they had done. Surprisingly, he had heard nothing more except that he noticed builders about a month later engaged in putting up a protective barrier on the corner by the bank. He also noticed that he was never called to Casualty again to pick up a corpse.

That was Kevin the Kiwi, then there was Stewart, his compatriot and friend. Gregor liked Stewart a great deal. He was a trained teacher and a fellow green porter.

Stewart told Gregor one day, "You will be driving one of the hospital cars this afternoon, I know that you are dropping a doctor down to St. Martin's Square. Could you stop by the STD (Sexually Transmitted Diseases) clinic afterwards to pick me up? I'll be in there delivering some stuff. Just don't advertise it too much."

"No problem, Stewart."

The delivery of the doctor downtown was uneventful except that Gregor caused minor offence when he said that St. Martin's Square reminded him of George Square in Glasgow. How dare he liken the beautiful city of Sydney to the down at heel, uncultured, poverty-stricken vomit of humanity that was Glasgow was the arrogant—nay snobbish, self-righteous—retort. On his way back to the hospital, Gregor was blissfully happy that he had caused such offence. He blithely whistled a cheery tune. He pulled in at the STD (Sexually Transmitted Diseases) clinic, reached for the letter he was writing home and clicked on the radio whilst he waited for Stewart. After 20 minutes he thought that he had better pop into the clinic and let Stewart know that he was there. He locked the car and sauntered up to the door. The reception desk was manned by two middle-aged women.

"May I help you, sir?" One smiled politely.

"Yes, could you tell Stewart Strettle that I am here to pick him up?"

"I am sorry sir, but I am not at liberty to give out names."

Gregor frowned his confusion. Stewart was here on a job, delivering something. What was the problem with that?

"May I sit in here and wait?"

"Certainly, sir, if you wish."

Gregor thought that this was all strangely cloak and dagger but he wasn't going to argue. He sat down and pondered that he really should be getting back to his job. Still, a promise was a promise. He could always plead traffic for his delay. Ralph would understand if nobody else did! His thoughts wandered to his new friend, Stewart. He smiled to himself as he remembered the three or four times that he had been out in the evening with him. They had laughed and chuckled together but at some point during the evening, Stewart had become distracted by a pretty girl here or a wonderful young woman there. Gregor reflected on the fact that he had never completed the evening with Stewart. Such were his charms that he inevitably left with a member of the opposite sex on his arm. Gregor always seemed to stumble home on his own. Suddenly, a light bulb came on in Gregor's mind. Stewart *wasn't* here as a hospital porter, he was here as a Sexually Transmitted Disease patient. Gregor the Gullible had found his inner naïvety again. Gregor looked towards the reception desk again and noticed the paper thin walls of the cubicles behind. He guessed that they were the consulting rooms. He approached the desk again.

"I know that you can't tell me if **Stewart Strettle** is here, but if **Stewart Strettle** is here, would you be so good as to tell him that I have gone to wait in the car and have to leave in five minutes. That would be **Stewart Strettle** that I am talking about." All this was expressed loudly and slowly with special emphasis on the name of the person.

Gregor went out into the heat of the day to wait in the car. Stewart appeared soon after and returned Gregor's wave.

"What's the verdict?" Gregor asked nonchalantly.

"I have the clap."

"What's the solution?"

"Antibiotics, a chat with a social worker, and I have to let all the women that I have had sexual contact with over the last few months, know."

"Shouldn't be too hard, should it?"

"Hmmm, all is easy but the last requirement. I have absolutely no idea where to find some of these young women," This said with a worried look as he rubbed his furrowed brow.

They parked the car and were soon back in the porter's office.

"Where have you both been?" Rob asked from his office.

"Bad traffic, Boss," lied Gregor.

"On a job at the clinic so Gregor thought that he would save us both some time and dropped by to pick me up".

Rob frowned an irritated disbelief but said nothing.

The following day all of them were sitting around in the office with little to do. Some leant back reading the papers. A quiet game of dominoes took place in a corner of the room. Others were playing cards. Gregor was reading his book. He glanced up briefly to observe that Stewart was writing with febrile intent. Gregor was first on the list for a job so off he went to deliver dummies for a First Aid course. It proved to be an unusually long job so when he returned to the office all of his colleagues were out doing their rounds Five o'clock came and Gregor was getting ready to go home. Stewart approached him from the other end of the office.

"Would you mind posting these as there's a post box on the way to the station?" He handed him a dozen letters.

Gregor looked at him with raised eyebrows and gaping mouth.

"Are these what I think they are?"

"Eh, what? Oh no, no, these are to my extended family in New Zealand. Did you think they were letters about my unfortunate disease? How many women do you think that I slept with? Some fantastic Lothario me if I had slept with a dozen women over the last few months. Ha! Ha!!"

That night Gregor picked up his mail from the Poste Restante. He had a letter from Callum that said he had travelled around the country and seen what he wanted to see. He was due to arrive in a couple of days. Gregor was excited. He missed his old friend. He resolved to meet him off the bus on the Sunday.

Sunday came and Gregor was at the bus station early. The bus pulled in and, sure enough, there was Callum looking tanned and fit. They made their way to Kings Cross and dumped his stuff at Gregor's place. They went off for a pint and discussed what Callum was going to do. He still had two months before he was due to fly out. Gregor had extended his visa for six months but Callum was ready to go home.

"So, mate, what do you want to do for a couple of months, would you like to work?"

"Yes, that would be good."

On the following day, Gregor introduced Callum to Rob Malvern. After a five-minute chat, Gregor was walking him down to pick up his green uniform.

"That's amazing," said Callum as they walked back to the office with his new uniform neatly folded in front of him.

He started work as one of Malvern's Marauders the next day.

"All colours will agree in the dark."
- Francis Bacon.

C H A P T E R   1 2

R E M I T T A N C E   M E N

In the old days when the class system reigned supreme in Britain, there was a format for the male children of the aristocracy. One would join the church, one would go into the military and the least able would be sent to the colonies. He would receive a remittance from home as long as he promised to stay away. Of course not all "remittance men" were duds. For some, it was the making of them and, if they ever returned home, they did so with honour. Most, however, were not. One Australian wag on the sheep farm, commenting on his particular remittance man, said that "He got paid nothing and was worth it."

Gregor had found a particularly pleasant watering hole in the Cross called the Rex Hotel. It had three bars, a plushish restaurant-come-bar, a public bar at the front and at the back, a gay bar. Gregor had become friendly with one of the barmen. During a quiet period Wally was drying some glasses and passing the time of day.

"How would you like a part-time job here? We could do with a 'bar useful,' you know, somebody to pick up and clean the ashtrays and bring the glasses back to the bar. Also you're of a good size, a fit looking guy, I'm sure you wouldn't mind lending a hand if there was trouble."

"Thanks, Wally, but I'm already working."

"Please yourself. But adopt a false name, it's after hours. Will give you some extra travelling pocket money and, believe me, the taxman won't come chasing."

At work the following day, Gregor talked it over with Callum. Callum was enjoying his time at the hospital. He had found a place to live at what he called "Barney's Palace" and was really marking time until he went back to Perth to fly out.

"Take it mate, then you'll be able to make that Indian trip that you would like to do on your way home."

So "Peter Edgar" was born. He reported for work on the Saturday night and was given a roving assignment throughout the three bars. "Peter" did not like to be still and tried not to engage in too much conversation with the punters, particularly in the public bar where things inevitably became raucous on a weekend night. But inevitably he did speak and so his Britishness was revealed. So he became the "Pommie Bastard" that he had always been anyway. Gregor did not mind being a "bleeding one tubber," so called because Brits were reputed to bathe only once per week. He had some sympathy with the politics of republicanism, secretly agreeing that it was ridiculous that a far-flung country should still boast the Queen as the Head of State. So, he went along with the good-natured banter on his shifts, occasionally giving as good as he got. He never, however, referred to his customers as convicts.

Royal romance was in the air. It was announced that Prince Charles was to marry Diana Spencer. So, then Gregor was asked his opinion more frequently. This had started to irk him because he had a sublime indifference to the workings of the royal household. He had come to terms with the fact that the public bar was a bastion of deep-seated Australian republicanism, that the blue collar males who drank there were construction workers who loved the rough and tumble of Australian sport and, in particular, that most physical of games, Rugby League. So, on the day of the royal wedding, he expected that the T.V. in the public bar would be tuned to something like reruns of the Melbourne Cup, tackles of the week, player of the month, an Aussie winning Wimbledon, the final bowls of an Aussie cricketing victory. But no, it was tuned to live coverage of the wedding ceremony in London. There was no sign or sound of the raucous lack of respect that he had come to expect from his republican crowd. He could have expected hoots of disparagement and inappropriate cursings of the occasion. He anticipated that there would be a large faction that wanted the channel changed. If fruit and vegetables had been hurled at the screen he would not have been surprised.

Not a bit of it! Instead there were craning faces, rapt expressions and, but for the T.V. commentary, one could have heard a pin drop. Gregor continued his round of picking up glasses and emptying ashtrays but there were very few glasses to be picked up for the crowd of old who chugged their pints with "gabs that gaped" and refilled and chugged again, they were no more. Instead they were reduced to a rather effete sipping. Gregor reflected that but for their rough-hewn demeanours and casual dress, they would not have looked out of place sipping their beer from fine crafted china while inadvertently reaching for a cucumber sandwich. As he did his round past guys who usually gave him such a hard time, all he saw was rapt, entranced attention and total immersion in the scene in the cathedral. They were in the congregation hanging on every word.

Gregor took himself off into the other two bars to see the reactions there. All were glued to the scene. When he had finished his shift and "Peter" really became Gregor once again, it was too late at night for him to share his thoughts and amazement with Callum. But on the following day in the porter's office, he sat and listened as Mick Lynch, a probable ancestor of an Irish convict, a man with no respect for authority of any kind, an atavistic attitude of disdain for all who ruled or attempted to rule. Even Mick had watched and he was almost tearful as he expressed his enjoyment of the occasion. Gregor stole a "told-you-so" glance with Callum who was making himself a coffee at the other side of the room. Callum had paused in his stirring of the sugar as he listened, his face a picture of disbelief.

Many years before, Gregor had read *A Town Like Alice* by Neville Shute. He had wondered what it was that pulled so many Australians to talk about the "Mother Country." The young country had certainly not been found wanting in the First World War so much so that he had been surprised when they entered the fray again in 1939 when the novel began. To Gregor, the story was up there with one of the greatest love stories ever written, but he still didn't really understand the particular and peculiar relationship that Australia had with Britain. He had eventually rationalized it along the lines that it was more an Europhile attitude, a craving for old traditions, a deep desire to visit the Louvre, watch an Italian opera in Italy, ski in the Alps. The U.K. was the best place to start because they had a common language. They also had similar sports. They had friends who had lived in Earl's Court and worked in London. They had distant relatives there, distant in distance, distant in connection, but still desirous of the old link.

Gregor was still pondering this as Callum and he walked silently to the train station. Neither were at their best in the morning. Callum was sleepily glancing at the newspaper as he walked, Gregor was sipping from his water bottle. Suddenly, there was a loud crash on the pavement in front of them and the loud shouts of a dispute above. People stopped in their tracks. It only took a second for them to realize that the debris was the remnants of a small wardrobe that had been thrown from above. It took another nanosecond to realize that if they had been underneath at the time they would have been killed. Callum rustled his newspaper as Gregor and he skirted the wreckage. The silence between them continued but this time it was a different type of silence, no longer the gentle way to introduce the day, there was now a tenseness to it as they realized that sudden death could come at the least expected moment and from an unexpected direction.

"Live each day as if it is you last for one day you're bound to be right," Callum quoted as they walked up the hill from the train station to the hospital. "Gregor, I don't want to die in Australia." And with that they were ready for the day's work, two remittance men who would never be "ten pound Poms," always, always destined to return from whence they came.

"There is a wisdom of the head and a wisdom of the heart."
- Charles Dickens

C H A P T E R   1 3

GULLIBLE'S TRAVELS

It was with mixed emotions that Gregor said farewell to Sydney. He shook Rob Malvern's hand, bought Barney of "Barney's Palace" a case of beer, as Callum had done before he left. He caught the bus northwards to Toowoomba. There were many places that he wanted to see. Certainly he wanted to visit the Queensland coast but Surfer's Paradise and the Sunshine Coast held no appeal. Townsville and Rockhampton *did* appeal but he had no wish to take a boat trip out to the Great Barrier Reef. Gregor did not really understand why he had no real interest in one of the great wonders of the natural world. He was inexorably curious and did love to be out in nature. But he was also interested in literature and poetry and history so he guessed that his pressing interests were not those of the natural world but more how human beings related to it.

Gregor arrived at the Townsville Youth Hostel far too early to gain access. Nevertheless, he tried the door. He looked at his watch. It was an hour before it was due to open. He decided to go nowhere but simply sit around on the wooden deck and enjoy the weather.

He was settling to his task when he saw somebody entering the long driveway up to the hostel. There was an elongated, wiry thinness to this incomer. He was dressed rather like Gregor had pictured an Australian soldier. Bush hat, khaki shirt and shorts, knee-length green socks and brogues, incongruously made their way up the hill. He was marching towards Gregor like a time lord from the year 1945. Gregor thought that maybe he had come from work. Maybe he *was* a soldier. He was certainly a young, fit-looking individual.

"Good evening. Percival Fortescue-Smythe at your service. Hostel closed. Stinking hot day. Kettle on. Cup of tea?"

Gregor had met people before who were economical with subjects and verbs in their spoken language. Invariably they were from a tribe which had attended an English private school. Inexorably they had the air and confidence of the ruling classes. Gregor's Digby experience had taught him to take a step back from his instinct for stereotyping. Taking a step back was not difficult here.

Percival indicated Gregor to follow him around a corner where he did indeed have a kettle waiting to boil.

Percival, Gregor decided, was an anachronism, a throwback to a different time. He was a caricature of an upper-class Englishman. Gregor had come across his type before when had been flying back to the U.K. from Nassau after a wonderful wedding in the Bahamas. He was gathering his passport and ticket, ready to pass through the gates when a sixty-something mustachioed "Our Man in Havana" type had approached him and said, "Would you mind awfully old chap. Old girl's birthday in Sevenoaks in a couple of days. Been out in the islands. Clean forgot. Will pay for postage. Drop it in a letter box when you land. Ever so grateful. Wonderful old stick. Has me for a son. Ha! Thanks. Toodle Pip."

And he was gone.

Trouble was that Percival from Northampton was only 25 years old. He was the equivalent of the Bahamas version turning up in Dickensian fashion. So Gregor had one night with little England in the Townsville youth hostel. He had been interested to see how Percival related to the hoi polloi of society, the cool dudes from around the world, sporting their dreadlocks, their nose rings, their latter day hippiedom. The answer was that he went down very well. Percival had old world charm, an easy confidence, an easier conversation. Gregor prodded himself mentally. Of course, Percival fit in because nobody fit in. That was the point. He was not a solitary oak tree standing out in a field. He was just another tree in a very diverse forest. A little bit outré perhaps, noticeably his own person and definitely "uncool." But travelling is all about acceptance of new cultures and different people. If one wanted the daily mundane then one needed to stay at home. Percival and Gregor both fit in, different spokes of the same wheel.

Gregor went through the motions of looking at the Queensland coast. It wasn't as if he did not like the sea. Far from it, he loved it. He loved walking alone on a solitary beach far from the madding crowd, where no road brought the sounds of traffic. No flight path shattered his reverie. Ships and boats were beyond the horizon. He loved the fact that he was in exclusive possession of the same sights and sounds that were there and had been there for thousands of years. He could always feel the breeze on his cheeks, smell the salt and the tangle, hear the water lap and the waves crash. He could see the rollers coming in, some reaching up from close in, some building up from a distant swell. No, Gregor loved the sea. He guessed that he did not like it so much when there were other people oohing and aahing at colourful fish and languid leviathans. He was selfish in his passion. So he turned from the coast and caught a bus.

The drive took him west towards the town of Longreach, presumably so-called because it required a long reach to drive the cattle from the interior to the port at Rockhampton. He had been told that it had taken the jackaroos months to make the journey. Hard work no doubt, a hard drive ensuring water and feed for the beasts, billy canning their meals at night. But a sense of comradeship, a journey to show the true Aussie meaning of mateship. Certainly self-reliance, adaptability and independence but also the realization that at some time when things went awry, you needed your mates and they might need you. There was no phoning for an ambulance, no doctor or vet in these hot, dry lands in those days.

The bus stopped at a road house for 30 minutes. A one street town. Gregor took a few moments to wander up the street and explore a little bit behind the front of the stores and shops. He noticed a piece of rusty metal protruding from a bush. For some reason his interest was piqued. He moved forward for a glance. It was an old piece of farm equipment. He looked closely and noticed a metal plate. This machinery had been produced by Ruston Gas Turbines, Lincolnshire, England. Gregor should have not been surprised, but he was. It was such a world apart from Lincoln to rural Queensland. Gregor had visited Lincoln on many an occasion because he had old college friends there. He had seen the cathedral on the hill, the old Roman stone arch, the castle, the Strugglers Pub, so-named because it was on the site of where they used to hang the criminals. He knew the cobbled street up from the city below to the castle and cathedral, and the statue of Alfred Lord Tennyson. "Steep Hill" it was appropriately called. The distance from there to here was far in kilometres but even further in culture, history, geography and climate and yet, probably for the first time, Gregor saw the ties that bound. The links in the chain that led Australians to fight for King and Country, to die on far-flung Gallipolli, lay here rusting in the bushes and heat, a forgotten scrap of a history that was in danger of being mislaid.

The bus hooted its horn. Gregor turned and jogged back towards it. He nestled into his window seat, grateful that the coach was not too full, thankful that he was alone with his thoughts.

Soon they were pulling in to the small town of Longreach. Longreach was a pleasant little town with a magnificent swimming pool. Gregor was grateful for the dip and even more for the shower. He had found a bed for the night and, most importantly, an air conditioned room. Gregor had hesitated over the expense but common sense told him that there was no point in renting a room if he would be unable to sleep. So he cranked it up full bore and climbed beneath the sheets. He awoke an hour later shivering.

Gregor had decided that he would like to see the mining town of Mount Isa, so after a full breakfast he was at the bus station. Yet again the bus was relatively empty but he got talking to a young fellow on the other side of the aisle who was headed to the same place. All the usual questions that travellers asked travellers were exchanged. The two of them got along very well so Gregor suggested that they share accommodation for a night or two when they arrived.

As they entered the town it was so obviously a company town. No mine, no town. Everything resolved on the industry on the hill. Adam, his new-found friend, found a caravan for rent and accordingly they found themselves in a sort of trailer park. They sat outside in the sun and cracked open a beer. Adam was going to head from here to Darwin before heading south to Adelaide. Gregor, still rooted in *A Town Like Alice*, had decided on Alice Springs. On the following day, having returned from the tour of the mine and, it has to be said, been impressed by the company's propaganda, they discovered that the rains had washed out the road.

There was nothing for it; if they were to leave they would have to fly. Adam and Gregor soon were at the airport, the one going to Darwin and the other going to Alice Springs. Gregor had a moment's hesitation before he picked up his ticket, wondering if he shouldn't go up to Darwin and then come down by road. But he had also booked to fly out to Katmandu on a certain date and was limited in his time. He wanted to see the big rock in the red centre known then as Ayers Rock and time was short. He was committed to fly out from Perth on a certain date. He was to pick up an 11-week bus trip going from Katmandu to London. The road trip had seemed like a leisurely but exciting way to approach home. He wished his companion, Adam, the best and they went their separate ways.

A small plane ride to Alice Springs was a good plan albeit one that was forced upon him by the rainy season. Flying above the red, dusty sands of the red centre was a good way to view the country. Gregor, who had dwelled in three cities in his time in Australia, reflected that he had not met many real Australians. The aboriginal way of life remained a mystery to him. He had been sucked in by the British image of the country. He had read *For the Term of his Natural Life* by Clarke. He had loved the sporting rivalry. He had watched the movie *Breaker Morant*. He had taken to the poetry of Henry Lawson and "Banjo" Patterson but none of that was remotely linked to the people who had been there for 10,000 years and were in danger of becoming a footnote in their own land. Gregor thought about how he would have felt if Scotland had been overrun by a foreign power and the Celtic culture, the stories of the Clearances, Culloden and the Gaelic language, had ceased to exist. No, all Gregor had experienced of the aboriginal culture had been the prejudice of his boss while pipe-laying in Perth and the poor down-and-outs in Kings Cross and its surroundings. It was a sad commentary on the society he was visiting but it was more a very poor reflection of his own curiosity and his willingness to learn and understand. Gregor hoped that he could put this right on the next leg of his journey.

A strong blast of dry heat hit him as he left the plane. Gregor gasped and reached for his water bottle. He entered the small airport and sought out directions to the Youth Hostel. It was a "short hop" the lady at the information desk said. Gregor resisted the urge to say that he would flag down a kangaroo then.

Gregor had heard about Henley-on-Todd, the annual boat race that took place on the Todd River, which flowed through the town. It was the only boat race in the world where one did not need boating skills to participate. The competitors made boats from a variety of materials but they had no bottoms because there is very rarely any water in the Todd River. The boat race was a running race along the dry riverbed. Gregor was disappointed that he wouldn't be in town when it took place, but he shrugged it off and made the short walk up Anzac Hill. It was not particularly spectacular but gave him a good idea of the lay of the land and the town.

The hostel was friendly as they always are. Gregor ate his supper and took himself off to the pub. He had heard the tale of a friend of his who had worked in this hostelry in the 1970s. At that time there was limited T.V. coverage. She related the story of the bar being crowded on a Sunday night as that was the evening when *The Forsyte Saga* was to be shown on the T.V. At that time they also used to have the radio on for most of the day. His friend, Irene, had told him the story of the radio play, which included the crunch of snow underfoot, meaningful and poignant for somebody from a cold country. The sound of it had reduced a miner who had been in the town for 20 years or so to tears. He was an Icelander. Of course, a couple of pints would induce memories from the days of his youth and the realization that not only could he not reclaim his salad years but that he was also unlikely ever to feel or see or sense snow again. The world in the early 1980s was not the "bus" ride away that it is in 2019.

The following day, Gregor was back at the bus station and ready for the trip to Ayers Rock—or Uluru as it is now known. Part of the attraction was the much-lauded wonder of the Australian interior, the many pictures of the monolith that he had seen in tourist brochures, on calendars and in photograph galleries. But more than that, Gregor had read that it was a sacred place to the aboriginals. He hoped to escape the English farm equipment, the English Henley-on-Thames (Todd) and the British programmes on the T.V. Maybe at last he would experience at least a taster of aboriginal culture.

The bus journey was long and dusty. Like all such trips, Gregor was desperately keen to get off. So when it pulled into a lonely roadhouse, he was first to the door. He jogged over to the building, flung open the door and found himself at the end of a long bar. There were three men sat, nursing their cold beers, locals by the look of them, jackaroos by their clothing and their hats. Gregor noticed that the toilets were at the far end of the room so he had to walk the length to get to them. The three heads had turned as he had entered. He could feel the silent eyes on him, intrigued by the stranger, "watchful behind a fan" as he walked towards them. He felt that he had to offer some sort of greeting as he went past.

"Nice day isn't it?"

As he sauntered on through, he had no reply, just the traces of smiles on three sets of lips. He sat down in the cubicle and speculated why he had received the silent treatment, albeit also the impish grinning. After all, he had found Australians so pleasant throughout his trip that he had expected a greeting in this of all places where a bus coming through was an interesting event. Nothing daunted, he decided to persist and find an excuse to talk further. He came out and returned to the bar. He had every excuse to stand close to the three guys because the barman was already there talking happily to them.

"I'll have a Tooheys please."

"So, are you guys locals?"

"Yep."

"Do you work on a cattle ranch?'

"Yep."

"Are you all from these parts?"

"Yep."

"I'm from Britain."

"Rain there does it?"

The middle man spoke, while pulling on his left ear lobe with one hand and adjusting the tooth pick in his mouth with the other.

"Yes, we get a lot of rain When did it last rain here?"

"Bout three years ago."

"Aaaaah," with some hesitation, "Sooo I guess that today is not really a nice day. In fact, I'm guessing that today is pretty much like every other day over the last three years?"

"Yep," they all said in chorus.

Gullible tried not to have his tail between his legs as he left the bar and went back to the bus.

Monoliths have always had a fascination for humankind. Nothing seems to talk more about longevity. Isolated monoliths have an even more dramatic effect. Uluru rose from the red desert some way before the bus arrived. It waited and watched. It looked down on everything, an indifferent solitary guardian, a hardy sentinel who had seen it all. There had been controversy over its sacredness. The aborigines wanted to claim it back as their own and then forbid anybody climbing it. It was right that they should do so if for no other reason that they had been downtrodden for so long that almost anything that drew attention to their plight was worth it. As Gregor looked and gazed, entranced and amazed, he was with them in spirit. More power to them. This was an iconic picture that was seen the world over whether on calendar or tourist brochure. "Giving it back" to its people was a powerful gesture not only to Australians but to the rest of the world. Fair dinkum, too right, but he was still going to climb it!

Gregor had taken advice and had decided to time his climb up the rock for the early part of the day so as to avoid the heat. The following morning he had bread and cheese for breakfast at 5:00 a.m. and was at the foot of the rock soon thereafter. It was a steepish climb but not particularly arduous. He reached the top and had his picture taken by three guys from the southwest of England. The panoramic view, the surrounds of a vast throbbing wilderness, the joy of the moment, the sense of geography, of history, of story, of the dream time, crowded his thoughts. Now whenever Gregor reflects back on that time, nearly 40 years removed from the experience, he is drawn to the words of a recent Vancouver author, Michael Harris in *The End of Absence.* Mr. Harris had an epiphany when he stood atop the Eiffel Tower. He had decided to take a selfie of the sun coming up behind him. He was so moved to tears by the moment that he had to express his joy. So he posted his picture and expressed his feelings. Of course, he received posts back, "That's nice." "Wow" and "Awesome." He regretted that he had done so. Indeed, he even regretted taking the picture. It was **his** moment, not anybody else's. Like the old tale that one should never see the movie after you have read the book. Art is unique to every person. The personal image should never be spoilt by the palimpsest of other people. Gregor's moment on the rock was his and his alone.

On the following day, Gregor found himself on a crowded bus on the long route to Adelaide. He was sat next to a man who was on his way to Coober Pedy. This is a town that is roughly halfway between Alice Springs and Adelaide on the Stuart Highway. It is the opal mining capital of the world. It is famous for the fact that most of the residents live underground, which gives them a constant level of coolness and the ability to avoid the extreme desert temperatures. The two men chatted happily about this and that, about Europe and in particular the U.K. He had always wanted to travel but earning a living and saving money was not easy in Coober

Pedy. The stranger had expressed such an interest in Gregor and his experiences that there had not been much opportunity for Gregor to learn about the small town of Coober Pedy.

"So what's Coober Pedy like?"

"It's the arsehole of the world, mate."

He then went on to explain about the heat and the dust and the caves and the lack of female company and the hardscrabble existence. In Gregor's perverse way, he was tempted to interrupt his journey at the town so that he could see for himself. But his time was tight. He found himself craning to get a view of this particular "arsehole" as the bus entered the town, but it was too dark. The stranger shook his hand, grabbed his bag and got off the bus. Others embarked and soon Gregor was sat next to another different passenger. They mutually smiled a greeting as Gregor edged over in his seat to give him plenty of room. Pleasantries were passed.

"So where are you from?"

"Coober Pedy, mate."

Gregor's previous companion had **not** been from that town. He was one of many guest workers who populated the place from all over the world. Sitting next to somebody who was actually born and bred there, Gregor expected a level of a little local patriotism. His new companion would hardly be jingoistic enough to suggest that that small town was the best place in the world but Gregor did expect a soupcon of local loyalty, at least.

"So what's Coober Pedy like?"

No change of expression in his answer, no deep thought, no hesitation.

"It's the arsehole of the world, mate."

Gregor passed no comment but smiled to himself. That statement he thought should be on the sign at the entrance to the town.

"Welcome to Coober Pedy, the arsehole of the world."

And when leaving.

"Thank you for driving carefully through our town,
the arsehole of the world thanks you."

The conversation was over. Both men settled to sleep. Daylight came and they were still some way short of Adelaide but the red sandiness had given way to some semblances of green, which though not lushly verdant suggested that they had left much of the oppressive heat behind them. Adelaide had a reputation for being a centre of culture. It was an oasis. Gregor had some idea of what to expect but was looking forward to getting back to a city after his time on "walkabout."

Gregor determined to enjoy Adelaide. He went to a Sheffield Shield cricket game, walked by the river, perused the city centre. But really he was distracted. His thoughts were already in Katmandu and his bus trip home. He caught the bus out to Perth and was soon on his flight to Nepal.

Gregor said farewell to Australia with quiet appreciation but with little emotion. He knew that he had learned a great deal. He hoped that what he had learned would make him a better person. But he now had a greater awareness of self and, in particular, his own self. He was aware that any thoughts of a reflective nature were unlikely and, if they had been likely, would have been coloured by the immediate. Setting them on the back burner and taking the pot off the cooker after he had been home for a few months would give him a far better idea of what the country and the experience meant to him. For the present he was content to look forward to Katmandu and the beyond, which would be home.

"The cart is shaken all to pieces, and the rugged road is very near its end."
- Charles Dickens in **Bleak House**

G U L L I B L E   T R A V E L S   F A R T H E R

Gregor was excited but palpably nervous as his plane came in to land at Katmandu. He had seen the Himalayas from above. The sky was clear and he was sucking on the boiled sweet that he had been issued for the landing. With relative ease he found a room for the night. He was a few days away from his bus trip so he resolved to explore whether or not he could go on a short trek to get a feel of the country and the culture. Sure enough he found what he was looking for. Two guys, one a Sherpa and one a bearer, would lead him around the ridge of hills surrounding the city. It wasn't to Everest Base Camp but it was fine by him.

They set off on the following day. Gregor felt a bit of a fraud, somewhat guilt ridden. He had never before had somebody carry his pack for him on a camping trip, let alone cook for him. Still, he enjoyed the pleasure of walking without accoutrements and felt that he was contributing to the local economy, which assuaged some of his guilt. The scenery was spectacular and the weather was favourable. The people were open-hearted and friendly, greeting him with smiles wherever he went. He saw real poverty, which had Gregor producing his own law of social science. He came to believe that the bigger the smile, the poorer was the person. It wouldn't stand up to statistical analysis, but he was humbled as a human being who was and continued to be so privileged compared to the people who surrounded him. With most he could not make conversation, but he could signal his wishes and his pleasure with his body language. It was becoming sadly obvious to him that he was likely to learn more about the Nepalese and, eventually the Indians, in a few short weeks than he ever learnt about the Australian aboriginals in over a year. It was food for his thought that blind prejudice—and almost worse, bland indifference—were resulting in the sidelining of a race. Gregor had read *The Banality of Evil* by Hannah Arendt about the Nazi trials at Nuremberg. There, of course, had been a genocide, a state-sponsored plan to eliminate the Jewish people. There was one appalling scene in the book where a Nazi scientist is put on the stand and is questioned about his contribution to the killing design. He enthusiastically launched into a diatribe over the most effective means of killing. He was neither embarrassed nor ashamed about the part he had played. There was no humanity in his statement only "banality" as Arendt would have it. There **were** Australians of conscience. Nowadays, political power has been exerted to support the culture and well-being of the aboriginal peoples. But Gregor felt that he should have dug deeper during his time there.

Gregor was healthier in mind and body from his trek. A night in a bed in Katmandu and he was ready to report to the bus in the morning. The travel company had two double decker busses, one named **Gonnor** and the other called **Rhea.** Kiwi Stewart would have felt right at home, he reflected. The busses were designed so that the customers would sleep upstairs. They would cook and view downstairs. They were all westerners. Some were Brits going home. There was the occasional American and the odd Australian. Margaret was the "odd Australian." Margaret was a social worker from Sydney. She was the milk of human kindness. Gregor looked at Margaret and secretly hoped that she would outdo him in the gullibility stakes. Sure enough during the course of the trip she vied with him constantly to bring naïvety to another level.

The busses slowly edged their way over the border into India. Soon, they found themselves at the tourist campsite in Delhi. All sat around in the campsite having eaten their evening meal and consumed beer. In the background, Gregor, although never a pot smoker himself, smelt the unmistakable whiff of marijuana. They were looking forward to the next day when they were to visit the Taj Mahal in the city of Agra. Such was the mood of the crowd that they were already dreaming and speculating about what it would be like. They would see this magnificent white cupola at the end of a long, immaculate garden path. As they spoke their entrancement, they were all staring in the same direction, viewing the magnificence in their minds' eyes, there was a voice from the darkness.

"To me, it just looks like a wash hand basin?"

People looked confused, they peered at each other quizzically. Were they missing something? Was something lost in the translation? Gregor scratched his head.

"What do you mean, Margaret?"

"Well, it's not the Taj Mahal you are looking at is it, it's—it's just a sink."

Sure enough there was a sink on a wall clearly seen in the direction that they were all staring. Literallly, Margaret was correct, they were all staring at a sink. But, but, but!? Margaret was starting to take a starring role in the search for innocence.

The bus journeys had taken on a routine. Travel, stop and view. Travel, stop and eat lunch. It was a little disconcerting but every time that they stopped for lunch, locals came to watch them eat. Gregor had warmed to this zoo-like viewing with a need to monkey about. Accordingly, when three children couldn't keep their eyes off him, he resolved to make their acquaintance. He showed them a trick with three coins, which he had often done with young children in his classroom. Gregor enjoyed their smiling but really, really revelled in their engagement, their focus on the task. He felt confident that he could celebrate these new friendships by picking them up and giving them a swing. He hoped that it would not be too much of a cultural leap but took a risk and picked one up. He spun him around and was reassured by the laughter and the obvious pleasure. Soon, the other adults joined in and soon they were piggy-backing them around and trying to joust one on the other. It was fun and for Gregor it was a cultural breakthrough—something that he wished he had been able to do in Australia.

Lunch was over. They loaded up the busses and headed out of the village. They had driven about half a mile when somebody shouted, "Where's Margaret?"

She should have been on Gregor's bus, but she wasn't. The courier, Chris, asked the driver to signal the other bus to pull over. Quick check on both busses established that Margaret was not on either. So there was no alternative but to turn around and head back to the village.

After much manoeuvring on the narrow road, they were turned around and heading back from whence they came. They had not gone a hundred yards when they spotted a public bus heading towards them. It was the usual overcrowded Indian transport except that this one was unusual for it was all hands. That is that there were hundreds of hands from every window, including the driver's, waving the double deckers down. The busses stopped opposite each other like old western gunfighters about to draw. Gregor noted that with much hilarity and jovial hollering, a body was being ushered from the back of the bus to the front. And there was Margaret, standing on her own, paused, confused and slightly dishevelled standing between the three busses. She was Clint Eastwood, alone on the street as shutters on saloon and house were being closed and all waited for the shoot-out. The tourists were relieved that she was back, the local bus was relieved to give her back. There were bowed thanks from all of the tourists and generous beams of delight at a good deed well done from the deliverers.

Chris, the courier, asked her what had happened. Margaret revealed a manky, flea-bitten kitten from under her coat.

"I saw this cute little cat running from our lunch stop and figured that it was a stray so I picked up as I thought that we could do with a pet for the journey."

Chris said firmly and with a definitive lack of beating about the bush, "That's not coming on our busses."

Margaret looked crestfallen. Gregor stepped in.

"It's feral and disease-ridden, Margaret, and it would never get across the border, my friend. Leave it here. It's a survivor."

An arm around, Margaret. An escort of sympathetic fellow travellers back to the busses and they were back on their various ways.

The Taj Mahal was overwhelming. It is not true. Photographs *do* lie. No picture that Gregor had ever seen of its magnificence matched what it is like in real life. Some years after the visit, Gregor wished that he had looked more, had read more, had understood more before he had visited it. It certainly was a Michael Harris moment, a time that was his and was exclusive to the people he was with. He felt then that his companions felt the same and that any nightly conversation about the event would not be appropriate, it would somehow cheapen it.

They were back in Delhi at the same campsite that night and it was a subdued crowd. There was alcohol and possibly drugs, but it was so, so quiet.

On the following evening, somebody suggested that they take a night walk. Gregor was excited by the prospect of seeing the streets a little ways off the beaten track. Accordingly, they waited around the campsite until darkness came. They moved from the relative comfort of their place of rest out into the swim of humanity, which was so much the excitement of India.

As they moved into the throng, their western countenances forbade any anonymity. They were so obviously privileged Caucasians, that they were ready targets for street vendors. One voice suddenly was heard above the rest. They were being encouraged to come to see and bet on a spectacle. Ian, the big Scotsman from a farm outside Perth, was in the lead and his fellow tourists were following. There appeared a child, a Dickensian waif, tattered, toothless, scruffy, dirty and grinning. He was carrying a cage in which there was a mongoose. They were drawn towards him by the impish twinkle in his eye, the mischievous character in his personality. He lead them to his master who had a basket in which there was a cobra. The appearance of a dreaded snake was all that Gregor needed to make him give the scene a wide berth but somehow he was fascinated from a distance. It soon became obvious that this was a roving betting shop. That the bet was between the mongoose and the cobra; that they would both be released after bets had been taken. It was to be a fight to the death between the mongoose and the snake.

This was not something that Gregor wanted to witness, yet he remained entranced by the scene, drawn in by the child's demeanour and his master's patter. They were very, very good. Soon, along with his mates, he was reaching in his pocket, drawing out his cash and betting on the cobra. After all, every creature in the world was frightened of snakes, were they not?

All bets taken, the moment of release was upon them. With much drama, many tenterhooks drawn out for the big moment, the lids of the baskets were opened and the two creatures were off and running. Gregor did not know what to expect from the experience. He had thought that there would have been a long gladiatorial battle, many moments of bluff charging with each protagonist feeling each other out before engagement. He had expected loud cheering, cajoling from the sidelines, moments of tension as they circled each other, thrusting and parrying.

Seconds after release, the cobra was dead. It took the mongoose a mere scurry, a lightening thrust, an expert drive and he had killed his foe.

The crowd of westerners was silent, shocked by what they had just witnessed. Through the silence came the eager, enthusiastic voice of the ringmaster.

"Look, look, mongoose is winning, mongoose is winning."

At Gregor's side came the muttered anger, which was rarely heard, the shocked horror of a Scotsman who has just been fleeced and conned.

"Mongoose is winning?! My arse. Mongoose has fuckin' won."

And with that, a disgusted and embittered Ian turned on his heel and headed back to the camp compound.

"We forge the chains we wear in life."
- Charles Dickens

CHAPTER 15

JAIPUR, SRINIGAR AND HOME

The colours of Rajastan were something that Gregor had heard about. He was nevertheless astounded at the bright variety of colours as they entered the city of Jaipur. He loved the idea of the city and its history. The group were taken to a palace forecourt and introduced to their guide, a very well-dressed, elegant, middle-aged gentleman. They were standing around the old stone courtyard waiting for instructions. The guide spoke about safety instructions, where the facilities were and the timing of the tour for lunch and coffee breaks.

"And one more thing. Should you hear a siren go off that means that there are incoming Pakistani war planes on a bombing run. Immediately you should lay flat on the ground near the walls and put your hands over your heads. Can't guarantee your safety but it is safer than doing nothing."

Gregor gulped and saw the colour drain from many of his friend's faces. None of them thought that they were going to be in a war zone. At that moment the siren went off.

They all rushed to the wall and lay prone as instructed. Gregor's life passed before him, his mind filling with all the things that he had wanted to do with his life. Now it was going to be sadly curtailed by a war that was not his. All he wanted was home and to be away from this place. Suddenly, the draw of this exotic land was as nothing to the green-fielded warmth of home. But, of course, all of his friends had the same thoughts but knew that flight was pointless. It was a terrible moment in his life. But, as he lay there contemplating the booted feet of the American guy in front of him, he caught sight of their guide still standing in the middle of the courtyard. He looked relaxed and had just lit up a cigarette. He nonchalantly looked up and suddenly the siren stopped. He said that it was safe and that they could all stand up. Sheepishly they got to their feet and brushed the dust off their bodies. Their guide, Paveen, spoke to them.

"In England I believe you have something called April Fool's Day. That siren was the signal for the end of the shift at a local factory."

April 1, 1982 was the day when an Indian guide called Paveen was nearly lynched by an angry mob of westerners.

Gregor recovered himself and decided that he couldn't come to India without going for a ride on an elephant. He had read somewhere that Indian elephants were completely different from their African cousins in that the latter were untrainable; that the Indian subcontinent had the advantage of this magnificent creature to do their heavy lifting for them. No such advantage on the African continent.

Gregor's elephant was a lovely elephant, a friendly elephant, a powerful elephant, a headless elephant? A little bit of direction from the mahout and Gregor was finally facing the right way. It was a rolling ship, a ponderous side-to-side movement, it was very relaxing. Somehow, however, Gregor managed to get a piece of painful grit in his eye, which he tried not to rub. He hoped his gentle tears would wash his eyeball clean. Instead it seemed to get worse. He could no longer focus on the pleasure of the ride and was happy when it ended.

Getting back to the busses, Gregor went upstairs to lie down. His eye was now very sore. Covering his face with a scarf was a relief but laying down was the only real relief.

On the following day, the busses were heading to Srinigar in Kashmir. It was a journey that Gregor would love to view but now one which he would gladly have foregone. He was coming to the conclusion that he was going to have to visit a doctor and particularly an eye doctor. He explained this to Chris, who agreed to help him out. Chris was Australian but was a veteran of these trips. He had been in India for years. Chris found Gregor an eye specialist to be visited on the following day. In the meantime, a round of golf had been arranged. Gregor was not a golfer, but he decided that it would be a distraction from his ailment.

The golf course was brown with bits of green vegetation. The greens were not the manicured magnificence of what Gregor imagined would be the "Old Course" at St. Andrews. They were each given a set of clubs and a caddy to carry them. It was at the ninth hole that events took an amusing turn. There being no map of the course, it was impossible to tell whether the green was to the right or to the left of the long fairway. Ian from Perth was in Gregor's foursome. He took the game seriously and was a competitor. Gregor at this point was playing with one eye, having bought a patch for his injured one. There was much addressing of the ball by Ian at the ninth tee. He was wiggling his stance, practicing his swing. Eventually he was ready to take his shot. The other three players were already following the presumed flight of his ball. Finally he stepped back and spoke to his caddy. With hand gestures and slow, simple English he asked which side he should aim for to put him nearest to the hole. In the near distance there was a manky, hairy, scruffy looking mongrel dog lying asleep close to the right hand side of the fairway. The caddy pointed towards the dog and said, "Dog, dog," by which Ian was able to guess that if he aimed at the dog, his ball would be headed in the right direction for the hole. Yet again a few practice swings, a wiggling of his posterior and Ian addressed the ball. It was the perfect shot. It came off the club with the sweetest of sounds and soared powerfully into the air and dropped majestically to Earth. It landed firmly on the stretched prone body of the dog, which yelped, stood up and ran off into the bushes. At this point, caddies and golfers alike collapsed in giggles and belly-rumbling laughter. Ian turned to his audience with a sheepish grin. Gregor forgot his painful eye. It was a storied moment on a memorable day.

On the following morning, Gregor got himself a cab, an auto rickshaw. Gregor muffled himself in his scarf and nurtured his misery in the back of the cab.

Suddenly, there was a crash and a jolt and, amid shouting and recrimination, Gregor should have been outside taking an interest but instead he sunk lower into his seat. The cab driver was now in the midst of a heated argument with the driver of a large bus. Suddenly, his door was opened and a very excited man appeared. He noticed that Gregor was European and launched into English.

"This can happen in any country, this can happen in any country, you wanna come and see my carpets?"

Something about Gregor's unusually unsocial demeanour caused the man to desist and he was rapidly gone. Remarkably, there was little damage to the cab and an apologetic driver soon had them underway again. Gregor paid him off after he had indicated a long line that he said led to the eye doctor's office. By this time Gregor had become accustomed to long queues so settled himself at the back and pulled out his novel. Better to try to read a book than to look into the painfully bright sunshine.

Gregor had been there for about five minutes when the woman in front of him turned around and noticed him for the first time. She immediately politely pushed him in front of her, Gregor shook his head and went back behind her. She spoke to the men and women immediately in front of her and soon Gregor was being pushed and ushered against his will to the front of the line. Finally, he had found culture shock in operation. Gregor was at the front of the line, sweating and embarrassed but the smiling faces behind him refused to let him retreat to his original position. He did not understand how these poor people, because they were very poor by western standards, who were giving up their day to sort out their own far greater problems, could behave like that to a stranger. He consulted with the specialist. He had no grit in his eye. He had a herpes infection—in effect, a cold sore—in his eyeball. He was given ointment. He paid his money and, walking past the waiting line, caught a cab back to the busses.

Gregor talked to the courier and his friend the bus driver and decided sorrowfully that he was going to have to leave the trip. It was an emotional moment, indeed the cause of cold sores often lies in one's mental state, tired and stressed. Gregor had not felt that way before the illness but he certainly did after he had contracted it. He was not an emotional man but he certainly was when he left his friends at the Pakistan border and caught a public bus back to Delhi. A quickly-acquired ticket and he was on his way to London.

There was an extremely interesting gentleman sat next to him on the way home. He was an English guy who had been an officer in the Ghurkas during the Second World War. He was just returning from Nepal where he had handed over a cheque to help fund the schooling of Gurka children. Gregor was interested in his war story. His name was Reggie.

"You know, war does funny things to human relationships. You are going through the most intense and frightening experiences in battle, you build a comradeship that becomes your family. That juxtaposition you would think would mean the closest relationships in your life. These men were your brothers in arms. Yet you try not to get too close because you know they may be killed."

He went on to relate how a fellow officer was shot in an action with the Japanese. Reggie saw him go down and knew that there was nothing he could do for him. Reggie had lost his glasses a couple of days previously and he really needed them. He reached down and removed his friend's spectacles intending them for his own use because he knew that his comrade was dead or dying.

"And you know, Gregor," he said with a smile, "He still reminds me of that brazen thievery to this day."

Back home in the bosom of his family with his herpetic eye better, albeit with a permanent scar across its surface, Gregor received a package in the mail. It was a beige coloured t-shirt covered with sayings. Gregor wondered where it had come from. The comments on it meant very little to him on first perusal.

"Amazing"

"Aim for the dog!"

"The mongoose is winning"

Gregor appreciated that it was XXL so that it would fit but there was no covering script so he had no idea from whom or from whence it had come. He studied the verbiage again and came across a statement that he had missed. It simply read: "Margaret is missing."

PART II

HOME AGAIN

"Good judgment comes from experience which comes from bad judgment."
- Anon

CHAPTER 16

LINCOLNSHIRE

Immediately after getting back from his trip, Gregor realized that he had to get back into the "real" world. Gregor had always hated that phrase. Surely the ***real world*** was always where one was at the time whether that was down a mine in Australia or gazing at one of the wonders of the world in India. Surely those sites and sights were equally real at the time. Better to say that it was simply time for Gregor to resume teaching and further his career. He had old college friends in Lincolnshire and was able to drum up a reference letter from them, so he soon found his way to an old English Manor House in Lincolnshire that had become a boarding school for 40 or so "***maladjusted boys***." Nowadays, the politically correct terminology is "***emotionally and behaviourly disturbed***." Whatever the label, Gregor knew it was going to be hard work. Somehow he managed to get the job. He was to start work at Brampton School in the village of Spital-by-Brampton on Monday morning.

Gregor was living in the village of Saxilby with his Canadian girlfriend, Mae. They had met in Australia. Early on the Monday, Gregor set off for his new job. He had travelled but three kilometres when his car stuttered to a halt. Gregor got out and flung open the bonnet. This was a futile gesture because he knew little about cars. But he checked the connections, rattled a few wires and got back into it. All of the time he was muttering curses at the terrible timing of the incident. A new job, a new beginning, the first day, a bad impression, all came to mind when he slammed down the hood with much more emphasis than was necessary. Miraculously the car started, but he was late. He was trying to control his fluster as he pulled into the driveway of his new school. He opened the front door and headed straight for the headmaster's office to find him on the telephone to Mae. He apologized profusely. The Head was happy and took him forth to introduce him to boys, teachers and houseparents.

Gregor was nervous as he stood before the children who were lined up in their five classes at the end of their break in the courtyard. He showed them his "Black book" in which he would list miscreants, he said. He was told later that they were impressed by that. The other teachers filed off with their classes and he was left to lead off his. It was a lovely day so he would have liked to have gone around this beautiful quaint village and got to know his young charges that way. But he thought better of it. They might have run off, he speculated and *that* would not have been an auspicious start to his time at the school.

He trekked them off back to their usual classroom and his new one. He formed them up in a circle and asked them to introduce themselves and state where they were from. They varied from Newcastle-upon-Tyne, Birmingham, a few from Nottingham, and a couple of boys from London. He was surprised that he had no children from Lincolnshire itself. He told them a bit about himself but only a small bit. He was cautious of being too familiar. He then decided to read them a story. They were 12 years old so he had to think carefully what it was that he read. He settled on *Kes*, which had proved a good standby for him in the past. Also he knew there was an excellent film about the book, which maybe he could show to them at a later date. The bell went and it was time for lunch. Gregor asked Steve, the Head, if it was OK if he took his class for an afternoon walk after the lunch break.

"Good idea, there is a path between the fields that goes for a few of kilometres parallel with the main road. Ask a houseparent to go with you."

He approached Julia, whom he had met earlier and asked her.

"Certainly, I would love to."

Nick, the senior teacher, invited Gregor to walk around the grounds with him during break time. They were out beyond the courtyard where there were some grassy nooks and some gnarled looking apple trees. The maintenance crew had designed and made some playground equipment. There was a wonderful cable runway with a handle from which the children could hang and career downhill for well over an hundred yards. It was known as the "Death Slide."

As they were walking and Nick was talking, a boy was running past them. Nick automatically stuck out his foot. So fast was the boy going that he sailed into the air and landed heavily in a clump of nettles.

"That's Dwayne Dorrien. Nice kid. He's in my class," said Nick without changing pace.

Gregor looked back to see Dwayne pulling himself out of the stingers, ouching and grimacing his way from the bushes.

Gregor and his class enjoyed their walk through the fields. The kids were allowed to run ahead. They did so and if they found a tree or bush to hide behind then they took a natural joy in climbing and hiding in it. It was the teacher's job to pretend not to see them and to do a convincing imitation of somebody who is shocked and surprised when the hider is found. So far Gregor was enjoying his time at his new place of work. He drove home and slept well after his first day.

On the following day, Gregor was given his first break duty. It was dry so the children could use the grassy playground and the Death Slide. Wanting to do his duty properly, Gregor paced back and forth watching closely as each child seemed to be playing happily. He was watching a game of hide-and-go-seek when there was a cry of pain from behind him. He turned to find the bulky form of 15-year-old Stephen from Blackpool rolling about in pain and holding his wrist. Gregor hurried over, knelt down and tried to keep him still.

"Where does it hurt, Stephen?"

"It's my wrist, my wrist!"

Gregor turned to Paddy and said, "Go and get help."

It wasn't long before help arrived, followed quickly by an ambulance. Time revealed that Stephen had indeed broken his wrist.

"Get one of the houseparents to show you how to fill out an accident form," the headmaster said to Gregor.

"Will do, Boss."

"And don't call me 'Boss.'"

"Sorry, boss."

Gregor closeted himself in the houseparents' office and spent a great deal of time and thought filling out his form. With satisfaction he read it through for the final time. He was proud of his creation. He made copies, left one for the chief houseparent and dropped one in the Head's letter box. He then went home, having been told that Stephen was being kept in hospital overnight.

On the following day, Gregor was called to the Head's office to be confronted not only by Steve but also by Dave, the high heedjun of the houseparents. It all looked a bit ominous. Yesterday's incident passed before his eyes. He didn't think he had behaved wrongly. He had been moving around the various activities. He had never sat down. He had never stood still. What was the problem? His first week at the school and he was going to be sacked! The two were sat behind the desk and had obviously been putting their heads together.

"B, B, Boss?" Gregor stammered nervously.

Eyes to the Heavens. "Don't call me Boss."

"Sorry, sorry Steve. Errrrr, hi Dave." He raised his hand in an effete acknowledgement of Dave's presence. "W—wh—what's the problem?"

Dave spoke. "We've been reading your accident report. It's very well written, by the way. But we cannot submit it as is."

"Why not?"

Dave showed Gregor the report.

"You use the term 'Death Slide.' Would you mind changing it to 'aerial runway,' as 'Death Slide' suggests, umm, well, death and danger and the possibility of well, ah, a broken wrist, if you get my drift."

"Of course, of course, I'll change it," Gregor blurted with relief. He reached for the report. "I'll change it right away. I thought that I was going to be sacked. Phew. What a relief. Thanks, thanks for your time." He reached for the door. "See you at lunch, Boss."

"Don't call—" but by the end of the sentence, Gregor had closed the door.

T H E I R   D I G N I T I E S
A N D   A L L   T H A T

Case conferences were a frequent part of the school's life. Each teacher and houseparent was given four or five pupils who they were required to read about and report on to their social workers. Eric, the jovial Londoner who was a housefather, always took his job seriously. Although he presented a devil-may-care attitude to all and sundry, he cared deeply about his charges. Every child wanted to be in Eric's group because they knew he would do the best for them and that it would be fun. It was case conference time for one of Eric's teenagers so all of them were gathered in the headmaster's office, sampling tea and biscuits, as they awaited the arrival of Social Services. The head, the chief houseparent, Eric, and Gregor (as the young man's teacher) were all there.

Steve said, "While we wait, Eric, could you open up Maybury's file and tell us a bit more about him?"

Eric wafted the crumbs off the top of his file folder, opened it, perused it quietly for a few moments, then spoke, "Well, umm, Maybury has a brother called Desmond."

There was silence which was eventually broken by Steve, "Hmmm, does Desmond have a barrow?"

Gregor interrupted Eric before he could answer. "And, err … is that barrow in the marketplace?"

Dave dove in. "Ob la di, ob la da," spoken in a dull monotone.

Steve took charge. "So don't let me get this wrong. You are saying that Desmond has a barrow in the marketplace, ob la di, ob la da. I say to you, 'Life goes on.'"

With that he was up out of his seat and soon all of them had joined him and were dancing around the office, singing lustily the Beatles song with all of their might and main.

"In a couple of years—"

And at that moment the secretary came through the door. They quickly dashed to their seats and adopted a serious, professional mode before the visitors entered the room.

Such spontaneous interludes of silliness and humour were frequently necessary in an environment that was often stressful and fraught.

As the years went by, Gregor became more confident in his role at the school so was able to reduce his personal stress and sleep better at night. The headmaster changed and a new man came in who did not have Steve's relaxed bonhomie. Gregor tried calling Harry "Boss" on the latter's first day and noted that he did not object. Gregor felt that this said something about the fact that Harry wanted to be above them; he wanted to have a sense of his own power and security; he wanted more of a hierarchy and less of a network.

So, when some distinguished guests were due to visit the school, Dennis the gardener was asked to produce plants in pots to spruce-up the outside. There was a touching up of scarred paintwork. Children were given lectures about their behaviour and bribed with extravagant promises if things went well. The "Boss" was a flurry of nervous energy, flitting into a classroom here, inspecting a dormitory there. He was even seen dashing into one of the toilets with a spray can of disinfectant and a few wipes. The cooks were instructed to pull out all the stops for a special luncheon for the boys and all. The staff were to be dressed in their best. It was all a bit much for Gregor who had experienced a year or so of Aussie honesty, mateship and their healthy lack of respect for authority. It was, however, what it was and Gregor would go along with it. Gregor always went along with it. If there was a fence to sit on as far as making a decision was concerned then Gregor was a gold medalist in that particular sport.

Gregor was on duty in the courtyard that day. He was now an old hand at playground duties, so was happy to take such things in his stride. Broken-wristed Stephen had long since recovered from his injury. His enforced idleness, however, had meant that he had not been getting the exercise he needed. Always a big boy, he had now ballooned to well over 300 pounds. He had left the 20 stone mark trailing in his bulky wake some months ago.

Stephen was at the far end of the playground playing Frisbee with one of his mates. It all looked innocent enough. Suddenly, Gregor heard an angry shout. He looked across and Stephen had Nathan by the throat and was forcing him onto the ground.

"You !@#%%$@ cheating bastard. I'll ^^&%%$& kill you!" screamed Stephen.

Nathan was helpless against the weight, the strength and the adrenalin of his opponent. Gregor ran as fast as he could to interrupt this contretemps and possibly save Nathan's life. He arrived at the scene just as Stephen had taken Nathan by the collar and was about to headbutt him. Gregor was a prop forward for his rugby club at this point in his life, so he was fit and strong. With some effort he managed to get Stephen's hands away from Nathan and behind his back. This was normally "game over" and the culprit's hands would be immobilized. But such was Stephen's rage and resulting strength that Gregor failed in this effort. Instead, Gregor was behind him and clinging onto his wrists for dear life. He had little or no control over where the raging bull was going. Stephen somehow got to his feet and moved forward. To his credit, Gregor had not let go of his arms. He found himself as a dryland water skier with no control over the powerboat ahead of him. Out of the courtyard they went, round the corner where cars were parked. Soon, they were past the main building, all the time the country air was filled with expletive-loaded anger.

They were heading past the windows of the head's office. Gregor glimpsed three figures as they stormed past. Indeed, for a fleeting moment Gregor thought about taking his right hand away to give them a friendly wave but realized that he risked a different hell breaking loose. He was starting to wonder whether anybody was going to come along and offer him some help, but nobody materialized. Finally, they were at the back door of the main building, which Stephen proceeded to kick open. As he entered, Stephen tripped on the lip and went down. Gregor wasted no time in getting his knee to Stephen's back to restrict his movements.

Stephen's expletives were now peopled with bouts of muffled carpet. Gregor realized that Stephen could not keep this up for much longer before exhaustion would set in and it would all be over. Indeed, the situation was already easing as the anger was subsiding into tears. Round the corner of the hallway came Eddie the housefather, an ex-army PTI, an athletic guy who had been responsible for making squaddies fit to fight. He helped in the restraint but also spoke soothingly to Stephen, which calmed him down.

The punishments at Brampton School were always carefully thought out. There had to be consequences because they were trying to train children for the real world. If the behaviour was unacceptable to the world beyond the school then it was the duty of the institution to make the boys aware that bad behaviour was unacceptable also within the confines of the institution, albeit with kind counselling and advice in the process. Stephen lost his outside break time for a week and had to sit alone in an office with an adult.

What of the "Boss" and his visitors? The visitors needed to see a special school in action, so they were pleased to be a witness to the Stephen incident rather than simply saying admiring things about the planters and the lunch. Gregor was called into the head's office, and expected some form of recrimination. He was surprised to be praised at how well he had dealt with the situation.

"Phew, thanks Boss," Gregor sighed as he left.

"You can call me Harry, don't call me 'Boss,'" the head said as Gregor closed the door behind him.

It was a sunny Sunday so Gregor and Frank were on duty. Gregor had been kindly exempted from Saturday duties as he was playing rugby every weekend. The school was always half empty on the weekend as so many of the boys went off home, so Gregor liked to get the lads on a bus and out for the day. On this beautiful Sunday morning, Gregor and Frank had ordered a picnic lunch. Gregor was going to drive half the group to the bird sanctuary at Gibraltar Point on the northern side of The Wash. Frank was to drive his group to Mablethorpe, have some fun there, then walk them south along the beach until their paths crossed. They would then swap bus keys and carry-on their various ways. Nothing could go wrong.

There is something very quaint about driving through Lincolnshire. It is a large county but not densely populated. It is a flat county, which makes it ideal for Royal Air Force bases. It is a fertile county, which makes it magnificent farmland. On days like this, Gregor always reflected on his reasoning for coming to the flatlands when he was really a lover of hill and glen. But the county grew on one. He liked its distinctive seasons. He loved the fact that occasionally in the winter that chilly east wind blew in from the Urals, froze the ground and gave them all that occasional cold snap of snow and ice. So, here he was driving on country roads to areas of natural beauty and wild bleakness.

The two busses had set off together but long since gone their separate ways. At approximately 10:30 a.m., Gregor pulled into the car park at Gibraltar Point. He gave the boys the obligatory tour of the Visitor Centre, and they set off north along the beach. They had footballs to kick, Frisbees to throw and dunes to run up. Also, the strand (the shoreline to the road) was not that far, so there was no chance of them missing the other group coming towards them.

They had gone over halfway when Gregor had a feeling of unease. He became extra vigilant. The two groups should have crossed paths by now. Having accomplished three-quarters of the route with still no sighting, Gregor was now worried, for it was too late to turn back. These were the days before cell phones, so there was no way of contacting Frank. His equanimity got no better when he saw Frank's bus parked on a promontory on the outside of the town. The group arrived with the wrong set of keys and no way of communication. The boys were too tired to walk back, and they were going to get hungry sooner than later. Of course, these were sharp-witted characters whose understanding of the situation was very good. Gregor told the children to go and play, as he had to sit on a rock and think things through. It was certain now that the busses were not going to be back at school to pick the boys up from the railway station, which always happened on a Sunday night. So that was a problem. True, it was not going to get dark soon. Also on the plus side was the fact that they were in a town, and Gregor could buy them fish and chips if he had to. Gregor's head was not in his hands yet, but it was obvious to the boys that he was disconcerted. Gregor did, however, run his hand anxiously through his hair as he glanced around and saw big Tyler lumbering towards him.

"What's happened now?" he muttered to himself.

"Mr. MacCrimmon, can I say something?"

"What is it, Tyler?"

"This has been the funnest day ever," he beamed.

Almost as he spoke, a taxi came around the corner. Two teenage boys got out, rushed up to Gregor and gave him the keys to Frank's mini-bus.

Frank did give his version of what had happened. Gregor had nodded wisely but did not understand. Gregor had given his version of what had happened. Frank had nodded wisely but did not understand. As it turned out, they were not that late on their return to school, and the bus trips to the railway station went off as planned.

Freddie Godwin was a nice fellow. He was 15 years old, and he was from Yorkshire. His dad and the Social Services had come from Wakefield for Freddie's case conference. Freddie met them in the hallway. It seemed to Gregor that the likes of Freddie should have been allowed to attend their own conference, but this was the 1980s and that was not the way things were done back then. So Freddie greeted his dad, his Social Worker and an education officer in the head's hallway and then went back to class. Gregor was not the teacher involved with Freddie, so he viewed all this from a distance. He did, however, happen to be in the lounge when Freddie came in with his dad.

"Now Dad, you don't have to worry about getting to the station at Newark because the school will get you there. Give me your wallet. Now I am putting your ticket in it. You will need to cross the tracks to Platform Two; do you want me to write that down for you? No? OK."

This was a teenager talking to his 40-year-old father as if he was a child in primary school. It was an example of the child raising the parent. Gregor was desperately saddened by the exchange that he had just witnessed.

A few weeks later, it was the Friday of the end of term. Gregor was on duty. It meant checking off the children as they were picked up by a bus or bussed to the station. A phone call came through. Freddie's people from Wakefield were going to be late arriving. He was the only student left in the school.

"Would you like to go for a walk around the village, Freddie? Something to pass the time?"

"Yes ah would, Mr. Macrimmon."

So off they went. They walked through the churchyard and into a lane that ran parallel to the main street. They paused outside the magnificent Elizabethan house that had a lychgate and a very old hedge. They sauntered up the road to the village green and the pond. They had seen nobody. People were either at work in Lincoln or Newark. The village was deserted. There were clouds gathering overhead, but rain looked unlikely in the immediate future. They came to a path through a wooded area at the end of the village, and they decided to walk down it. The beech trees leaned over them protectively as they walked down the hill back towards the school. There was a carpet of wildflowers—snowdrops, daffodils and bluebells—on either side of them. Freddie was very quiet. Gregor was content with the silence. Indeed, he sensed that Freddie was wrapped and rapt in a world that was new to him. Eventually, they arrived at the main street, the length of which they would have to walk to get back to the school. There was the pub, the butcher's shop, the local garage. There were now just a few people going about their business and none of it seemed urgent. As they neared the school, Freddie looked at Gregor and said in his broadest, deepest Yorkshire, "Ah liked that. 'Twere relaxing t't brain."

After Freddie had left and Gregor was free, he reflected on that statement. Freddie was going home on "holiday" except that he was not. He was going to a place where he had to be the adult, had to show responsibility. He was going to a place that was messy, downtrodden and which contained no structure. He was going from order to chaos. He was taking the bus from childhood to adulthood in two short hours. Tyler and Freddie both had the wisdom to pick their moments and pick their words. These two boys both saved and enhanced situations. They became memorable boys because of their memorable timing.

"Be who you are and you'll become who you want to be."
- Peter Davidson

A L   F R E S C O

Gregor had always realized that time spent outside for him was a re-creation in the purest sense of the word. Because he was a notoriously slow learner it had taken him some time to realize that it might be the same for other people as well. And, well, children were people the last time he had looked. Now during his time at Brampton School he had come more and more to realize this. He had met the roughest, toughest, most disturbed teenager and seen him on the Gower Coast in South Wales when a housemother had looked and said out of the blue, "I think I'm going to buy Peter a bucket and spade."

So she did. Then this boy who could not focus on sweeping the floor, writing a sentence or playing a team sport, this poor, poor lad sat on the beach and played with his new bucket and spade for hours. It was the childhood that every child should have but that he had never had. At the time when those who were there witnessed it, this simple example of a child at play was the greatest happiness and yet the greatest tragedy.

Back in Lincolnshire, Jim had run a weekend fishing trip to a local river. Peter had been given a rod and line and settled on a riverbank. For hours he changed bait, moved the angle of his cast and sat and looked at the river. As far as anybody knew, no fish came to his line; no perch, chub or carp broke the surface. There could have been no fish in that stream. It had not mattered. There was a contented, tranquil solitariness that was such a sharp contrast to the inner city turmoil that had almost stolen his childhood. There was hope for Peter Lynch.

So, because of incidents like these and Gregor's many weekend excursions, he really wanted to better his outdoor experience. He applied to do a three month outdoor leadership course at Plas y Brenin in North Wales. This was difficult to manage because he was now married to the wonderful Mae and had two young children at home. But she agreed. He bought himself a beat-up old mini car and, after a fond farewell, was off to Plas Y Brenin for six weeks followed by a further six weeks at Plas Menai on the waters of the Menai Strait.

There were six male teachers on this course. They ranged in age from the early twenties to the mid-thirties, Gregor falling into the latter category. It said much for the type of people that they were that half of them had arrived in V.W. camper vans.

The course was full of "tasters," which included rock climbing, kayaking, orienteering and mountain leadership. All had an educational bent as to how they could be applied in the teaching of children. The course at Plas Menai involved sea kayaking, sailing, Canadian canoeing, and sail boarding. Gregor was average at all of them but took such pleasure in the company of all the other guys and the leaders.

"Today we are studying the lower limbs, and they are both called legs," said one of the Kiwi instructors at the beginning of an afternoon First Aid course. This man had stood atop Everest.

"Can you here the footfall of the old tin miners?" intoned Derek as they walked across the debris of an old tin mine.

"With his appetite I am surprised he couldn't manage the whole roll!" was said after Dean had bragged about doing half an Eskimo roll in a kayak in the swimming pool.

There had been many funny occasions. The sailing course was going to take them in two large sailing ships to visit the Isle of Man. Sadly, the weather was so bad that they spent their time at sea in the topsy-turvy turbulence but, in the evening, in some sheltered bay that happened to have a pub.

Then there had been the film crew who visited. They were creating a video to sell the course to interested punters. What a memorable occasion of frolic and folly that had turned out to be. The plan had been for the six novices to position themselves in the Menai Strait behind one of the ancient, solid, wide portals of the Menai Bridge. In pairs, they were to appear from behind the portal in their canoes, surfing down the tide race. The film crew were a pragmatic and phlegmatic looking bunch. Gregor felt that they had probably filmed riots, wars, elections and, most terrifying of all, a royal wedding or a session in parliament. Their leader, however, was a different kettle of fish.

"Gentlemen, for you the camera is not there. When you appear around the corner, focus on where you're going, your next dip of the paddle, focus on the focus. Got it?"

Gregor was in the last pair so as Dean and Phillip disappeared around the corner of the upright, it was the privilege of the remaining four to be stood watching from behind the cameras.

"So don't talk because the microphone will pick up everything."

One of the offsiders appeared around the edge of the portal and put his thumbs up meaning to start the cameras rolling. They all waited with bated breath. Considering they weren't very far upstream, they were a long time coming. Eventually, a single paddle came around the corner bobbing up and down. Seconds later a second one appeared, followed closely by the capsized canoe and the two bobbing heads of Dean and Phillip as, buoyed up by their life vests, they floated past at a creditable rate of knots.

"Cut!" A flustered squawk from the director.

The four students rushed down the bank to rescue Phillip and Dean who were stumbling and spluttering out in the shallows. Gregor managed to grab the canoe, which had briefly become snagged on a rock, but the two paddles evaded them all.

"OK, OK, let's try again," "Alfred Hitchcock" tried a smile that didn't quite appear genuine.

The second pair disappeared behind the portal. Again there was a delay. Everybody strained their eyes to see the appearance. First around the corner this time was the floating head of Big John, then came paddles, overturned canoe and, finally, Wee Alan who was actually hamming it up for the cameras. By this time the spectators could control themselves no longer. Tears of laughter were flooding down their cheeks.

"Cut, cut, cut!"

It was Wee John and Gregor's turn. They walked up behind the portal. To John it didn't seem to be a problem. There was a calm shallows before they reached the vigorous flow of the current.

"Up to us, Gregor, we'll show them." He punched the air with confidence.

Gregor imitated the punch half-heartedly. He *so* wanted to believe, but he knew full well that the four who had gone before were far better athletes than he and Wee John. If the previous four couldn't manage it then how the hell were he and John going to? Wee John held the canoe as Gregor embarked. Then lightsomely and with a single flowing movement he was in the stern and they were making their way into the current. Their paddles were poised, ready for the onslaughtt. There was grim determination and intense focus on both faces. They hit the flow and immediately were over. Like a bull rider at a rodeo, they had mounted at one side and immediately fallen off on the other. Gregor gulped in water. Just before they floated under the bridge, Gregor felt his hand gripped by Wee John so they appeared together with both hands in the air in front of the film crew.

By the time the intrepid students had rescued all of the remaining equipment as well as their two last voyageurs, the angry and frustrated director had stomped up the bank, loaded up the trucks and screeched off into the distance never to be seen again. Drew, their instructor, smiled widely.

"Serves him right. I told him that you were beginners and wouldn't be able to manage vicious water like this. Let's find some calm and paddle gently back to Plas Menai. Everybody warm enough? Are you all OK?"

They were all fine. Their journey back was a slow and steady progress. No dramatic events. Just a slow, steady, gentle, germane chance to practice the jay stroke, and an opportunity to take in the views.

The "solo experience" was something that Gregor enjoyed the most of all of the activities they completed in their three months. They all had to pick a local spot on the map and spend 24 hours there on their own. One of their number, for example, had chosen a deserted car park. Gregor had a spot marked for him high up on the backside of Carnedd LLewelyn and Carnedd Daffydd, a little hollow removed from the beaten track. He could have picked something less arduous perhaps, but he liked the hills and the only way up a hill was to climb it. So, he set off up Pen yr Oleu Wenn early in the morning and by late afternoon had found a quaint little flat green spot next to a gurgling brook. He had an afternoon nap then cooked up his evening meal. Satisfied, he wrote in his journal and settled in to read his book. He slept well that night. In the morning, he woke to find a mist shrouding the ridge over which he had to climb. It took him most of the day to find his way back down to the road. He was tired and hungry by the time he had driven back down Llanberis Pass to Plas Menai. After supper, the six of them had gathered in the conference room for a debrief with their leaders. The room was hot. Gregor noted that all his comrades were rested and lively, ready to participate. Gregor was not sure how long he lasted but he was asleep in minutes.

Weeks later when the course had come to an end, they were gathered together for a full course debrief. Among the many questions they were asked, was one about which aspect of the course they had found most psychologically challenging. For Gregor, it was an easy answer. Rock climbing. Despite the fact that he knew that he was roped in and secure, the perceived danger was real to him. His legs shook uncontrollably. He found grips for his hands and feet but lacked the conviction to trust himself to them. He had been cajoled and babied up the rock faces of North Wales. He had expected others of the group to have had similar fears of the water, the weather, the river and so on. He was surprised indeed when three out of the six stated that they found the solo experience the most hard. He had never realized before how aloneness could be traumatic to some. Gregor was gregarious but had always been content with his own company. He was glad that he had picked an arduous solo for, despite the exhaustion and the rigour, it had given him such a wonderful memory. It had also given him further insight into the human condition. Despite close proximity to five other people over a prolonged period of time, the end of course debrief proved again to Gregor that he did not really understand people on a certain level at all. It was another lesson on his path through life.

"He had a genius for backing into the limelight."
- Said of T.E. Lawrence.

CHAPTER 19

RUGBY

As Gregor played his last game of rugby at the age of 42, he reflected on the 30 or so years that he had played the game. He knew with a certainty unusual in one who was not always very sure of himself that the game had given him far more than he had given it. Growing up, Gregor had not been very athletic, but there had been a turning point when he suddenly found himself not only in sport but also enjoying being in sport.

At the age of 10 in an all-boys school, the boys had been given a choice. Giving boys and girls choices was innovative, creative thinking in the early 1960s. It was during those days when children should be seen but not heard at the dinner table. It was also the era of corporal punishment. Gregor remembered the hackneyed phrase of one of his teachers: "A boy has ears in his backside. Beat him and he understands."

He remembers the phrase not because he was scarred for life by the thought of it but because it was frequently used by a teacher who was kind and gentle. As far as anybody knew, Mr. Crumbly-Eaton had never raised a finger or cane to a boy in his life. Better than that, he always gave full noisy warning well before he arrived in the classroom by quoting Shakespeare loudly: "Something is rotten in the state of Denmark!" could be heard as he approached, which allowed the watcher at the classroom door to shout "Cave" (Latin for "Beware"). This permitted the miscreants to leave off squeezing Nobby Clarke's spots or lighting Nigel Ball's farts. So when

Crumbly-Eaton turned the corner into the classroom, they were all sat at their desks, staring innocently to the front, eager to learn the follies and tragedies of *Macbeth* or *Julius Caesar*.

Gregor had thought, along with most of his peers, that Mr. Crumbly-Eaton was a silly old duffer who, had he arrived quietly and out of the blue, could have had a field day of punishing many misdemeanours. But, of course, they were all so wrong. The warning signal of pending arrival was the whole point. Mr. C-E was a wise man. He knew exactly what everybody was doing and was determined that he should not have the hassle of dealing out punishments. To him all boys were sinners, it was their natural state. It wasn't until after his death that Gregor discovered that John Crumbly-Eaton had been parachuted into Holland to hasten the end of the Second World War by trying to take the bridges at Nijmegen and Arnhem. To pull the wool over the eyes of a brave, aware hero like that would not have been within the skill set of ten year old boys. John Crumbly-Eaton was never going to be flustered by a set of school boys. After all, he had met his bridge too far many, many years ago in the heart of war-torn Europe.

The turning point had come when John Crumbly-Eaton had announced at Assembly one day that there was to be a choice. On Friday afternoons, the boys in the two classes in Gregor's grade could either go for a cross-country run on the lower cliff path or go to choir with Mrs. Lees. Gregor and his peers had experienced Mrs. Lees before. She was a well-endowed middle-aged lady who played the piano with panache and style whilst cajoling the boys to shrug off their reticence and give full voice to their music. Most of the boys were far more interested in speculating as to how she could see to play the correct notes, given her buxom obstruction. Much though Gregor had the stirrings of an interest that he didn't really understand, the only real choice for him was the cross-country run.

About 20 pupils lined up for Gordon Frame, the P.E. teacher, to set them off at the school gates. There was a fair bit of pavement to run before they actually reached the ups and downs of the dirt path. The "Lower Cliff Path" hugged the shore of the Bristol Channel littoral. It was a beautiful part of the town's rural backdrop. It undulated over slight gradients, always about twenty feet or so above the craggy shoreline. The banks were surrounded by gorse and broom, nettles and bramble. Gregor learned to settle in behind his friend, Guy, who always took the lead and set off at a goodly pace. It was never possible on the narrow path for Gregor to contemplate overtaking him, but as they hit the pavement again on the way back, Gregor was always at his heels and he could still have had enough fleetness in his foot to finish first. He never did. Somehow it became a routine. Guy would always finish first and Gregor a near second. The front runners would then have to hang around and cheer the stragglers in. After they had greeted the huffers and puffers, the front runners and the rest would have to wait and greet Nobby Clarke. Sometimes it was getting dark when Nobby finally made an appearance. There was an unspoken wish that Nobby would have a change of heart and resort to Mrs. Lees, her breasts and her choir, rather than put himself through this obvious agony week after week. But that was never going to happen, especially when, incredibly to Guy and Gregor, Nobby was singled-out for his guts, determination and stamina at Assembly by Mr. Frame. Despite their consistent success, Guy and Gregor never got a mention. There was a bit of chagrin about this in later life. When Gregor and Guy met many years afterwards they came to the conclusion that this bit of weekly exercise was it for Nobby whereas Mr. Frame knew that Guy and Gregor were always going to persist with sport. That was an interesting theory and certainly, Gregor thought, Guy putting an interesting spin on something that probably wasn't the case.

The next step for Gregor was the rugby field. He wasn't very good. He didn't know how to tackle because he was too frightened. He didn't like to run with the ball because he was too frightened to be tackled. At the age of 13, Gregor left the school and headed off to boarding school in rural Somerset.

In his first week in the school, Gregor had to practice with his age appropriate rugby team. He was terrified because that was how he had always been when he took to the rugby field. But Mr. Arwel Thomas, his Welsh speaking rugby coach, took him to one side and taught him how to tackle properly. There were also a great number of one-on-one physical drills, which Gregor coped with. Gregor discovered that they didn't hurt as much as he thought they might. After two weeks or so, he found himself selected for the Junior XV as a prop forward. There were a few butterflies prior to the first game, but Gregor acquitted himself well and they won.

Gregor was not a social animal during the five years of his boarding school life. He was bullied a bit and that tended to push him inwards. He became a solitary character around the school. It worked for him. He did not press his company on anybody else and they were happy to ignore him. It was June of his penultimate year, just before the summer holidays, when Gregor received a letter in his pigeon hole. It was a moment to cherish for him. He had been chosen as one of 20 or so rugby players to come back to school early to prepare for the upcoming rugby season. It was a huge honour. Gregor lost all interest in his traditional fishing holiday with the family at his grandparents' house in the town of Nairn on the Moray Firth. For the first and only time in his school career he could not wait to get back to school.

The time came. Gregor had played a great deal of football with his brothers during the summer so it had not been a time of indolent insouciance. His dad dropped him off at the school and he was greeted by the three senior rugby coaches, teachers whom he had admired from afar for years and with whom he was now sitting around the dinner table. Breaking bread with legends and seeing their humanity for the first time was an enormous boost for Gregor who had spent four years flying under the radar—"watchful behind a fan," it is true—but for whom saying boo to a goose was *his* bridge too far. Gregor was in awe. He determined that week to not put a foot wrong.

The real term started. Gregor daydreamed his way through class, was distracted when he should have been doing his homework. His whole focus was on his rugby practice and whether or not he would be selected for the first XV on the Saturday for that first game. The team was to be announced after Thursday's practice. As usual Gregor gave his all. They were all called together at the end and the team was announced. Gregor beamed when his name was called. The remainder of his week was an unaccustomed bounce in his step, a smile that could not be wiped, a head held unusually high.

On Friday, school seemed very long. Gregor was all of a fidget in class on Saturday morning. In those days it was mandated that the whole school turn out to watch the first XV play. Gregor boarded the bus that took the team to the grounds. He saw the other busses with boys and girls he knew getting on board. Gregor was terrified yet he wanted so much to take that field. He wanted the game yet he wanted the game to be over. He wanted to shrink away into his shell and disappear into the crowd. He wanted to run out onto that field and become immersed in the game. He wanted to play well and not let his teammates down.

The first XV ran out of the changing room through the crowd and onto the field. Gregor's nerves were no more. He jumped up and down in his warm-up. He felt as fit as a butcher's dog. He lined up for the kick-off, supported the catcher of the ball and played the game. It seemed all a blur to Gregor. No sooner had it begun than the final whistle blew. They won, shook hands with the opposition and were soon back in the changing room. He was told that he had played well enough to keep his place but that he needed to become more of a competitor. It was one thing to be honoured to play for a team but it was another thing altogether to give one's all to win for that team. Gregor did not yet have that overwhelming desire to win, which makes a good player better.

Gregor never forgot the first Monday after the game. He had caught the bus into the school along with the 79 other boys from his boarding house. He got off the bus and was walking to class. As he walked he was greeted by smiles and "Good game" from people he did not know. Teachers and students who had never acknowledged him before were doing so now. He went to his first class, which happened to be Latin. Mr. Black was a scholarly man who had always tried, in a kindly manner, to bring Gregor's language skills up to a level where he might actually pass an "A" level. Gregor knew that Mr. Black attended all of the rugby games because, although he had not seen him there on Saturday, he had seen him there many times before. Gregor was not as distracted as he had been the previous week, but he must have appeared confused and uncertain because Mr. Black called him to one side after the class. He beckoned him to sit down next to the desk

"Gregor, Gregor, you don't understand do you?" He smiled benignly.

"Understand, Sir?"

"Gregor, your life changed at 3:00 p.m. on Saturday afternoon. It will never be the same. How you use it will be up to you."

"Sir?" Gregor scratched his bowed head.

"You think nobody has noticed all these years. You have avoided the limelight because all too often the limelight has been nothing but bullying and teasing and cruelty. So, you hid in a crowd, cowered away from the attention because the attention was so soul-destroying. Now, because you played for that team on that Saturday you have become recognized in a good way.

Your peers are never going to bully you again, Gregor, because they saw character in you on Saturday, and they respected what you did. Get out there young man, hold your head up high and make some friends. It's about time. Now hurry away to your next class, you're late. And, Gregor, work hard in class and you'll enjoy your rugby more."

The greatest lessons Gregor ever learnt at his school were from his rugby coaches but they were not about rugby. The greatest lesson that Gregor was ever taught at that school was from his Latin teacher but it was not about Latin.

"What we hope ever to do with ease, we must learn first to do with diligence."
- Samuel Johnson

CHAPTER 20

RUGBY CLUBS

Gregor left school but did not leave rugby. Indeed, Gregor thought that he could never fully leave the game. It had consumed him latterly at school and continued to consume long after he finished playing it. He thought again about his Australian rugby experience, and to him it became a metaphor for the cosmopolitan nature of the game.

Immediately after he had left school, now a reasonably confident 18-year-old, Gregor's new-found confidence attained through his school experience of the game served him well. He was confident when he went into his first game as an adult for his local club in Somerset. Wiveliscombe, a quaint village in rural Somerset, were the adversaries. Gregor had played against some really good players whilst at school, indeed some who had gone on to play for their countries at junior level. It is a fine line for a young man to develop confidence but also to know how to avoid arrogance. Gregor had taken to the field with what he thought was the former and discovered in the first scrum that it was the latter. He left the pitch defeated, dispirited and dismayed. His opposite number had toyed with him, had twisted him, had buried him, had lifted him, had dominated him through strength, experience and merciless cunning. Gregor thought that he would never be able to play the game again. He sat in the changing room unable to muster the strength to pull his shirt off, let alone able to make the short walk into the showers. The chastening of Gregor's hubris was complete. Andy, his loosehead prop, saw his head down and came over to commiserate. Andy was one of those elder statesmen who had played men's rugby for over 20 years and knew the game inside and out.

"Man strength, Gregor, man strength. That's all it is. You've not got yours yet but it will come. Get changed. A pint will be waiting for you on the bar. Let's have a night."

And they had a night, the season went on, and Gregor learned something new every game. He never forgot, however, that if one thinks that one is the fastest gun in the west, then eventually one is going to find one faster. He learned never to assume, both in and out of the classroom, but also on a rugby field.

Gregor met many characters in and around rugby clubs. He had played with an Irish guy called Eddie. Eddie had truly kissed the Blarney Stone. His gifts with language on the field of play were not appreciated by the referees or his opponents. Indeed, Eddie was the scrum half and occasionally he was not appreciated by his own forwards. Giving him bad ball at a lineout meant him giving the ball away when he threw it back at his forwards in vituperative anger. A forward pass in rugby ends up being the opposition ball either from scrum or advantage. But Eddie, short of stature, was a little dynamo who bullied his big, ugly forwards. He'd snipe away at them, cajole them, call them by name, praise them, drive them. All the forwards loved Eddie even when they didn't love Eddie.

The bar was always knee-deep in bodies after a game. Gregor, after one particularly hot game, was gasping for a pint. Just when he thought he had the barman's attention, he hadn't. He had shuffled his way to the front to find the barmaid had moved away to the other end of the bar. He had moved his position again. Eddie arrived, having just held forth in the changing room, standing stark naked before his forward pack, giving them his Irish brogue that brooked no interruption. Eddy was always the last out of the changing room.

"What's up Gregor?"

Gregor rubbed his forehead in exasperation. "Eddie, get me a pint."

In thirty seconds Eddie was back with two foaming pints of bitter.

"Thanks Eddie. How did you do that?"

"I'm Irish. Off to speak to the opposition. See you later."

Colin and Daffydd were Welsh speaking, both centres and both played for the same team. One of the most useful aspects of their game was that they could talk openly about what they were going to do with the ball next and nobody on the opposition could understand them. One of the least useful aspects of their game was that nobody on their own team could understand them either. They were a little bit of Wales in the heart of England. They were characters. Sadly, Colin took a job in a different town, so life in the first XV clubhouses and on away trips was very different.

Daffydd came to practice one Monday with a blank schedule. In the bar afterwards he explained that Colin was coming for a visit on Saturday and this was the shift schedule for the night's activities. Gregor was given a thirty-minute shift rather than an hour. He was married with children at this stage so was forgiven the hour that the single lads were given.

Come the night, and the prodigal son was in fine form. Gregor was coming to the end of his shift and was grateful for an anticipated early evening Chinese take away and time with the family. He left the pub as Colin was standing on a fragile-looking circular table. Gregor witnessed the precarious balancing act. He heard Colin's statement of intent.

"Boys, I am standing on a table, balancing on one leg with a pint in one hand and a pickled egg in the other. I am about to eat the pickled egg and then down the pint."

Loud cheers from the gathered throng. Gregor left before fun became a mess.

In Somerset, Bootsie packed down in the front row with Gregor and Andy. At scrummaging practice on the Thursday night, he was talking up a storm as befits somebody who worked in the T.V. industry.

"Boys, I have a plan. We're playing Blagdon on Saturday. There is not much to do in that little village of a weekend except play rugby, drink and go pigeon shooting. There will be an occasion when we should try to steal one of their balls at scrummage time. The best way to do this, I feel, is to give them that split second of distraction so that I can get my foot to the ball."

Andy and Gregor nodded. To Andy, distraction in the front row meant a headbutt to the bridge of his opposite number's nose. To Gregor, distraction meant getting his shoulders and neck under his opposition's ribs so that the only way he could go was feet off the ground (i.e., upwards).

"Here's what we do," Bootsie was enthused now. "Just before the scrum half puts the ball in, we coo like pigeons. Let's practice it. All together now: 'coo, coo, coo.' Drag it out a bit, make it slower and at a high pitch."

"What's the point of this?" Andy was not convinced. Gregor was looking doubtful.

"The point is, fellas, that they will hear the 'pigeons' and look up and try to pinpoint them by which point I will have struck, and we will have the ball. Verstehen sie?"

"Versteh," said Gregor teutonically.

Cometh the Saturday, cometh the crisis. There was a Blagdon scrum that was two yards short of the opposition line. Bootsie announced gleefully. Gregor and Andy were so focused on their, by now, operatic 'Coo' that they forgot that the basis of good scrummaging is a good body position and a determination to push. Up went the 'Coo,' in came the ball, forwards went Blagdon, try scored, Blagdon win. Andy was not happy after the game.

"Listen you two," finger waving at Bootsie and Gregor, "I do one thing on a Saturday afternoon and I do one thing well and that is push and dominate the scrum. None of your clever, fancy damn ideas ever again, Bootsie, or YOU are dead to me. Get it?"

Bootsie got it. Gregor retreated mumbling something about it not being his idea and he hadn't wanted to do it in the first place.

In London, there was Peter Carroll, the full back and captain of the second XV. He was the most unlikely of Australians because he was cultured, articulate and urbane. He even spoke like an Englishman, referring to "Cavalier rugby, chaps," which meant that every ball that was kicked at him or the backs was run back at the opposition. No awareness of the fact that his forwards would have liked him to kick into touch so that they could have a break and catch a breath. It was the spirit of his age, the flamboyance of his nature; it was fun-filled and exciting. If one was a forward it was trekking back to cover for mistakes in the backs, it was catch-up support play for the next breakdown, it was the faint hope of a scoring pass from a generous back. The forwards were always the grunts, the more arrogant of the backs regarded them as a sort of "forlorn hope," a group of "berserkers" who were sent in to soften up the opposition so that the elite could have an easier time and more room to show their class. Gregor, Paul and Dick were the front row on the day they played Blackheath. They were endearingly known as "The Good, the Bad and the Ugly." None of them had ever asked who was supposed to be whom.

There was far too much Carrollian cavaliering that day. Blackheath liked to kick away their possession. Peter liked to field their "Garry Owens" and run them straight back at them.

Gregor and co were up against a Blackheath front row who had all been dropped from the first XV from the previous weekend. They were not a happy band of brothers. Early in the second half they were lined up opposite each other for a scrum. They had just covered ground after a rather ridiculous excursion, which Peter had masterminded from his own try line. Both Gregor and his opposite number were hands-on-knees out of breath. The Blackheath loosehead and Gregor looked at each other. They bound up for the scrum. Before the referee let them connect, Gregor's opponent spoke across the divide.

"See that captain of yours, either you guys smack him, or I will. ***Get him off the field***."

After the game, all six of the front rowers took over a corner of the bar and commiserated as all true "roundheads" do about the extrovert flamboyance of "cavalier rugby."

In his days playing rugby in Lincolnshire, the goal had always been to reach and play in a 3 Counties Final. The cup winners of Lincolnshire, Derbyshire and Nottinghamshire would play one semi-final to play a final. Why the powers that were could not have found a fourth county so that they could have two semi-finals was a mystery to Gregor. It was what it was. As Lincolnshire County Champions one year, the club found themselves in the 3 Counties Cup Final at the home of Paviors RFC, Burnt Stump Lane. The day of the game was a glorious spring sunny spread of open English hedgerows, wooded deciduousness all panoramic from the Paviors' rugby field, which sat atop a hill. The grounds were packed with people, most of them home supporters who expected that a feast of carnage would be delivered on the lesser abilities of their Lincolnshire neighbours. But, the away team had their best kept secret in their left winger.

Marcus was very, very fast. When he had joined the club, Gregor had spoken to one of his mates who had known him from his college days. Gregor had asked if he was as fleet as foot as his reputation suggested. His old pal, Barry, had replied, "Fast, Gregor, you bet he's fast. He's shit slipping off a very, very shiny shovel."

Gregor had chuckled at the description and had, years later, thought about how a BBC athletics pundit might have described a young Usain Bolt. No list of races won, no expert talk of his powerful stride, his running style, his diet, his training regime. Just, "Usain Bolt, fast? He's shit slipping off a very, very shiny shovel!"

As the club was to discover, it was one thing to be fast to be able to catch, tackle, time a pass to perfection and score frequent tries. All those skills Marcus had. The only trouble was that Marcus was described by Dick Hawforth, the second row and local farmer as being "mazed."

"What do you mean mazed?" Gregor had asked naïvely.

"I mean mazed, Gregor. You know, all dreamy like. One moment you'll be talking to him and the next he'll suddenly be staring into space, away with the fairies like. You ask him what he's thinking and he'll quote you a bit of poetry and explain how you made him think of it. He's mazed, mate, mazed I tell you."

Marcus was picked on the left wing for that cup final. There had been a ruckus in the changing room before the game when the captain had slapped him a couple of times on the chops.

"No dreamy bloody poetry for thee this day, laddie. Thou 'ad better keep thy mind on't job."

Marcus had smiled wistfully at the taps to his cheeks. The captain would have preferred that he had growled with determined anger so shook his head with woeful disgust as he left him to tie up his boots.

The final had started unexpectedly well for the Lincolnshire team. They had pressed on the Paviors' try line and won a couple of scrums and a lineout. Suddenly, they had found themselves 10 metres short with a ruck won and Marcus on the left wing, unopposed with just the final pass needed and he would have been over for a try. Eddie slipped the ball to him as he was tackled, the Irishman's beautifully timed pass could not have been better. Inexplicably, Marcus had his back turned towards Eddie. The ball hit him in the square of the back. Marcus was in a trance-like state, almost catatonic. Wherever he was, was not on a rugby field let alone in a cup final. He was looking out over the folding English fields beneath. The ball was dropped. The opportunity was missed. A grateful Paviors cleared their lines and the chance of an early lead and a possible victory was gone. As expected, it ended up as a very heavy defeat for the away team.

In the bar afterwards, Del the loose head prop, confronted Marcus about his lack of awareness. Del was a man who dug ditches for a living and whose only poetry was scatological limericks peopled with huge chunks of less than subtle sexual innuendo. He was not, therefore, impressed when Marcus conjured up pictures from the Lake Poets and John Clare's rural idylls. Del retreated to the other corner of the bar where Dick Haworth was shaking his head and muttering, "Mazed, f!@#$%& mazed," into the froth of his pint.

There had been the Yoshi experience. He had come to Lincoln from Japan to learn English. He had been fixed up with an exchange job at Ruston Gas Turbines (RGT). In those days, the workforce at RGT was very much a man's world with all the rough and readiness of a factory shop floor. But Yoshi was a winger. He *did* slip off a shovel very quickly. Yoshi's English was very basic, yet he had an advanced degree in open-hearted friendliness. He slotted into the club as if to the manner born. Everybody liked Yoshi and Yoshi liked everybody. He would be found in the bar after a game surrounded by a group of players, most of whom seemed to have been from the opposition from that afternoon. Many of the club's opponents hailed from the neighbouring county of Yorkshire, so Yoshi's English was becoming tinged with a Yorkshire accent while being immersed during the working week in a Lincolnshire one. It came the time for Yoshi to head back to Japan, so the players of the club decided to throw him a bit of a party. Eddie wanted it to be a lively and bantering affair so brought along his own props, which consisted of a hammer, a spanner and a screwdriver. The beer-sodden crowd was quickly hushed as Eddie stood on a chair with one hand resting on the beaming Yoshi's shoulder.

"Now then, Yoshi, we surely have had a good time getting to know you. We know that when you go home and you're back on the floor of your factory in Tokyo all of your mates are going to gather around during your lunch break and they are going to want you to try out your English on them. I am here to help you today. So I am going to hand you some of the tools you have been using at RGT and give you their full definition. Take this one, for example. (He hands Yoshi an implement.) That which you are now holding is a "fookin' 'ammer." (He takes it away and hands him another.) That's a "bloody spanner." (Takes it away, hands over another.) And that's a "bastard screwdriver." As the night proceeds we will help you to remember these useful English tools. Now which one of you bastards is going to get this poor bugger a fucking pint?"

So that was Yushi's last night. Nobody would have been surprised if they had run into one of Yoshi's mates some months later wandering up the aisles of the local hardwear shop looking for the ***"Bastard Tool Section."***

Gregor had experienced so much that was wonderful in the sport of rugby over the years. He had discovered that he could be impoverished and a bit homesick, and he could turn up as a complete stranger at a rugby club anywhere in the world and he would be at home. He saw and heard of tragedy and saw and been a part of the network of practical and down-to-earth support that the bereaved received. Most of the time it was not a gung-holier than thou exuberant act of agitated altruism but simply the quiet slipping of money into a hand here or the arrival at a house with a hot meal and a beer there. It had become worth so much more because it was so undemonstrative. Gregor loved rugby clubs.

PART III

CANADA

"A fish only recognizes water when it discovers air."
- Anon

CHAPTER 21

CANADA

Gregor's wife, Mae, was Canadian. They had met in Australia, a chance meeting at the youth hostel in Bunbury, an even chancier meeting several thousand kilometres away and some months later at a train station in Sydney. Fate flung them together. Mae followed Gregor to England and stuck with him through two children and nine years in Lincolnshire before she suggested a return to Canada for her and a new beginning in her birthplace of Vancouver, B.C. for her husband and their children. So it was after some bureaucracy, the administration of selling a house, and the necessity of a change of bank account and other administrivia, that the MacCrimmon family found themselves in a motel in the West End of the city of Vancouver for a week, the city in which they intended to settle. No job, some savings, nowhere to live, two young children, but an exciting beginning in a new land for Gregor and a ready-made guide in Mae. Gregor had not realized that he had married such a risk-taker in Mae but was very grateful that he had. He was excited by the mountains, the prospect of wilderness and wide open spaces in the distance. He was even more excited by the wind and the very, very white teeth.

Firstly, he was surprised that there was little or none of the former as he ventured out onto the Stanley Park seawall on a beautiful spring day a week after they had landed. He also had never seen so many good-looking women and wondered why. Were they an illusion? Was it the simple fact that he was hypersensitive with the adventure that they were all embarked upon. He pondered the issue and decided that it was nothing more than a superior dental system compared to that of the National Health in the U.K. He was probably still jet-lagged but there definitely was no wind. The teeth on the women were very, very white. He supposed that the teeth on the men were white as well but, for some reason, he hadn't noticed them.

They found a place to rent in the Marpole district of the city. They really **did** have to rent it even though they may have seemed to have been hesitating at the time because their three-year-old boy pulled his pants down and had a pee while they were being shown the bathroom. He was the little coyote marking his territory. That simple act decided them. So they took it.

Mae found a job working on the 1991 census. Gregor found a job for Burns Security. The boss had found him a job one day, which gave him a regular shift.

"Hey, Gregor, you're a teacher," he had said with impish intent. "I have you a job in a school. Just what you want."

So Gregor found himself at Langara College doing the graveyard shift from 11:00 p.m. until 7:00 a.m. Every so often he walked around the building checking doors and signing clipboards as proof of his checking. Then suddenly he was removed from there and given the check-in for the cruise ships at Canada Harbour Place. That gave him people contact, well, **American** people contact. He had heard that they were different from Canadians but was not really sure whether this was true or not. Then he stumbled on a G.K. Chesterton quotation:

"The real American is all right; it is the ideal American who is all wrong."

He decided to put this to the test at work and discovered that, lo and behold, they were open-hearted and friendly, just as the English had been when he first met them at the age of 8. They were like the Indians, the Australians, the Kiwis and Ralph the Pole. Well, actually, nobody was like Ralph the Pole but that had little to do with his nationality. What he did find about the incoming Americans, who were all picking up a cruise from Vancouver to Alaska, was that they expected Canada to be like America. They made assumptions that guns in their baggage were acceptable. Gregor came across one when he was scanning a suitcase. The gentleman concerned was adamant that he had broken no law. That was serious. Less serious was the woman who had converted her American dollars to pounds sterling because she was coming to *"British"* Columbia. All in all, Gregor got along well with the customers as they walked, deer caught in the headlights, towards security. Gregor was open-hearted and smiling which, apparently, Americans were unused to from authority in uniform. Indeed, some of his colleagues liked the feeling of power that the uniform and the status of security gave them. They were not marines, not special forces, they were mostly immigrants who had just got off a plane and were making their first incursion into the work force in their new country. Gregor was enjoying his summer of security work but he knew that if he was to become the breadwinner then he had to resume his teaching career somewhere.

Eventually, three interviews came his way and he found himself being offered a job at Eldertree Independent School in West Vancouver.

"The future is purchased by the present."
- Samuel Johnson

CHAPTER 22

DIFFERENT CULTURE, SAME GIG

There were times during that first year teaching in his new school, in his new city, in his new country that Gregor was absolutely terrified. He had a wide spectrum of ages to teach and manage. He was, on top of that, suddenly landed with coaching the senior rugby team in October because a colleague had been selected to represent Canada in the Rugby World Cup. Gregor had played rugby for a long time but had never, ever coached it. But, off he went on Saturday morning in his blazer and tie with boys in their #1 uniforms to catch a ferry and play a game against a Vancouver Island school and catch a ferry back again. A three- to four-hour journey it was and very pleasant, too. Gregor stumbled and fumbled his way through coaching, much as he was muddling his way through every day in the classroom. There was a cusp for Gregor in that first year when he decided that if the boss wanted him to coach tiddlywinks to Kindergarten or clean the toilets with a toothbrush at the end of every day then he was going to do so. He liked the school, the students and his colleagues so much that he vowed that he would eat the humblest of pies just to stay. Then there was another cusp when he realized it wasn't about the dire necessity of having a job anymore but more about the sheer pleasure he was getting out of going to work every day. He still had doubts about his ability. He was still intimidated by the wealth. The parents often put pressure on teachers. But his doubts were becoming less prevalent. Particularly reassuring was the day that a senior maths teacher came charging into the staffroom declaring in vituperative frustration, "These children are a management problem."

Well, they weren't. How could they be compared to EBD Brampton School? Gregor felt for the first time that even though he had nothing like the paper qualifications of his colleagues, that he might have something to offer. He didn't know what it was but it was there and he started to relax, to become less defensive.

CHAPTER 23

FLOWER RIDGE

One of the minor frustrations in Gregor's new life was that he saw all of this beautiful scenery but wasn't really able to get out into it as much as he would have liked. He knew that, unlike crowded Europe, there was unlikely to be a main road or a pub over the next ridge. That it was likely that there was more of the same. That was the beauty and the danger and the thrill. But Gregor appreciated what Mae had done for him. She had two young children and given up house, secure job and stability in the U.K. so that the whole family could have an adventure. Mae was always going to be staying at home with the children to begin with, so it was integral that Gregor not only work hard but also try to make himself indispensable. So it was with great appreciation that Gregor was given an opportunity at the end of his school year at Eldertree.

Colin Dalhousie, the head of the school's Outdoor Education Programme, approached him in June. He explained that he was in charge of the Duke of Edinburgh Awards Scheme and was going to run an expedition in the summertime to an area called Flower Ridge in Strathcona Park on Vancouver Island. Would Gregor like to come? He was honoured to be asked but would have to check in with Mae.

So it was that in July of 1992, Gregor found himself in a mini-bus being driven off the ferry at Nanaimo and northwards up the Island Highway. The trip was to have a four-day wilderness component, a practice expedition for those students who were setting out to complete their Gold Awards. Eighty kilometres were to be hiked in the four days with all the wild camping and campcraft that it included. The fifteen or so students were given groups and had been responsible for their own menus. The school provided tents and cookers. Their clothing and sleeping bags were their own.

It was Gregor's first real time out of Vancouver apart from his rugby trips to the Island, so he was agog at the coast, the peaks, the trees, craning to see what was around the next corner. He was not a participant in the bantering back and forth between the students behind him because his mind and eyes were too enraptured with the panoramas before him. Finally, they turned left and were leaving the coastline behind them. The scenery edged ever wilder, the peaks became higher, the ridges and coires became more defined and more rugged. Finally, they were at a campsite just outside of Strathcona Park. The students pitched their tents and began to cook as if to the manner born. It was so, so different to the many outdoor trips he had made with children in Britain. There were no arguments or discussions over how to put up the tent. No debate about who was going to fetch the water. No confusion over how to cook the dehydrated food. It was all quiet efficiency. Gregor was impressed with the young men and women. At the same time, he was watching closely the man who had so impressively trained them.

Colin Dalhousie was a Scot with a degree in psychology from Glasgow University. He was lean and wiry and a very, very fit man in his mid-forties. Gregor observed a different style of leadership from what he had been used to. Colin quietly pitched his own tent and cooked a meal for himself and Gregor. There was no advice given to the students, no forceful directions. It was simply, "Here's the campsite; do what needs to be done." Gregor had not experienced the like before. He was either in the presence of gross incompetence or sublime, cerebral, subtle control. By the way the pupils were performing it was likely to be the latter.

On the following morning, Gregor was having to rush to keep up. The smell of cooking and the quiet murmurings and movements of the students had stirred him from his sleep. By the time he had performed his morning ablutions, tents were down and breakfasts were being eaten. Gregor was inwardly flustered. He was about to set up his cooker so that his breakfast porridge could throb away gently while he took down his tent when a bowl of steaming porridge appeared in front of him.

"Get this down you."

This was Colin's welcome to the morning.

"Thanks."

"Hope you slept well."

And he was gone back to complete his own tasks.

Gregor alternated spoonfuls with the taking down of his tent. He was soon almost ready to leave and was edging ahead of the students at this point. He only had himself to care for, after all. Eventually his pack was ready. He saw Colin travelling around each of the students, lifting up their packs, checking their weights and balance. He also noted that he was asking them how they had slept, how they felt, had they drunk and eaten enough. Pretty soon, Colin was ready to go. He was standing with his pack on, his bush hat pulled down over his brows and leaning on his formidable hiking stick. He was surveying the students who were loading up themselves but also making sure that there was no detritus left, no evidence of them having camped there. He suddenly lifted his chin off his stick and pointed to something in the bushes. He bounced over and reached in, pulling out a drinks container. He didn't say anything but held it up before him for all to see and shook his head with a wry smile.

"Ready to go then? I'll lead. Mr. MacCrimmon, are you OK at the back?"

Gregor nodded.

They set off along the road to the trailhead. It was only a short distance. Salal bushes abounded, the last sorry blooms of wild flowers drooped their heads, deciduous trees with leafy shades and protective canopy were giving way to the more stolid looking conifers. Colin stopped the group and turned to speak to them.

"Last night and this morning were very impressive. A few things to remember today. As you know, we only travel as fast as the slowest person. When I stop we all drink. If you see something that you want to observe or take a picture of, then we all stop. We snack, we drink, we dress for the temperature. Most importantly, this is bear country so we make noise. All OK? Mr. MacCrimmon, have you anything to add?"

"Not at this point."

So, up they climbed through the trees, which soon gave way to low shrubs. The path was easy underfoot but contained steep intermittent rock and bouncy peat. Red osier dogwood, sheep's sorrel and the ever-present salal accompanied them on their ascent. As they gained height, the bushes became less dense. Mountain sorrel began to appear, its erect purple stems shown off best by the garland of neatly presented leaves underneath. They boasted their presence with blooming bravado. Gregor was grateful for the weather, which was warm and still with the promise of more heat as the day advanced. The group came to a halt. As ever, Colin reached for his water bottle, so Gregor did the same. They both noted which of the students followed suit, but Colin said nothing. The only problem with the cessation of movement was that the stillness in the summer air alerted the flies whenever there was a warm stationary body. Cousins of the West Highland midge must have migrated with Gregor! Colin seemed immune to it all.

All was forgotten as they walked along the ridge. The peaks of the Golden Hinde and other lesser hills in the distance glistened in the sunlight. Not a cloud in the sky, a natural blue, far from any city pollution; it was a feast for the eyes. Gregor reflected that people would pay a great deal of money to fly to the west coast and seek out sights like this. Yet here he was, a lad from urban U.K., experiencing this virtually in his own backyard. He was almost overwhelmed. They reached a point on the rich, verdant trail that seemed convenient for a lunch break. Before he ate, Colin circled the group and spoke quietly to individuals. Gregor picked up snatches of the conversations, "Not drinking enough," "Put your hat on," "Did you apply sunscreen?" "You're too hot, take a layer off," and so on. These were all delivered sotto voce with a smile and a generous compliment to go with them.

Flies again were abundant.

"Mr. Dalhousie, what are we going to do about the flies when we camp tonight?" John said, swatting with mounting frustration.

"No flies in the campsite," was the short reply.

Gregor was intrigued. He saw looks of disbelief from the students as they contended with the onslaught. He wondered if some of them would make it through the four days if they had to contend with this every time they stopped. A bit of rain or a gentle breeze would have been very welcome at this point, but no such relief was at hand.

Eventually, they reached a path that descended off the saddle. Almost immediately below them was a small lake with a mini glacier above it on the sheltered south side of the opposite peak. Slowly, they picked their way down the saddle. It was early evening and they were all tired from the heat, the walk, the flies. Colin introduced them to a green patch akin the lake, which he suggested would be a good place to camp. The group set down their packs and sighed their relief. There was a constant breeze steadily coming off the lake so, as Colin had promised, there were no flies. He said nothing but smiled at the group. He could not resist stretching his arms wide and saying, "See. Like I said. No flies."

"No explanation either," reflected Gregor ruefully to himself.

Colin had guaranteed a fly free zone and they had one. How? What? Gregor was learning something very quickly about this new colleague of his, and the more he learned, the more he felt that he was in the presence of someone amazing.

As on the previous night, the tents sprung up, and cooking smells permeated the campsite. The sun was still high, but the breeze ameliorated the heat and gave respite to tired bodies.

"Eat your food. Tidy up. We'll sit down for a bit of a chat. A debrief if you want to be technical," Colin announced to the throng.

Colin gathered them all in after all the chores were completed.

"So, what have you learned from today?"

Gregor was to become aware over this trip and other subsequent trips that Colin never asked the students how they felt. It wasn't that he did not care, it was just that he would learn how they felt by asking them what they had learnt. Gregor had ruminated on this modus operandi and related it to some of the "touchy-feely" professional developments he had been involved in over the years. It made sense to him. Asking somebody how they felt might produce everything from an ingrown toenail to a death wish. Colin, Gregor surmised, would get a better feel for these issues by asking everybody what they had learned. He would learn who was stoic about the annoying bugs, who was limping along on blistered feet, who wanted to be in the wilderness and who wished to be back in their own beds. These answers would come when he asked everybody what they had ***learnt.***

"I learned that stopping too long to eat was a mistake," Doug grinned, creating amusement by swatting at imaginary bugs.

"I learned that getting to the ridge and experiencing that view was worth the effort."

This came from slightly-built Penny who carried a pack that was probably too heavy for her. Very obviously Penny was a wiry, tough, self-sufficient character who could move and outdo the strongest, if outdoing was required.

There were many such contributions. There were two, however, who did not contribute. Frank had his head down and was drawing doodles in the soil with a stick for the whole meeting. Christopher looked distracted, stared away from the group and twitched nervously when he felt awkward. Then there was Alison.

"I think I know why there is a wind here," she said.

"Why is there a wind here?" asked Jon.

"I think that it is because of the glacier," she said.

All eyes moved to Colin. He said nothing, merely indicated with open palms that they should discuss it further amongst themselves. The discussion centred around cold going low and heat rising. Eventually, they turned to Colin for an answer.

He explained that the wind rushing down from the glacier was a katabatic wind from the Greek word "katabasis" meaning "descending." The heat of the day on the plateau had caused rising air, and the wind at the campsite was merely the cold air descending to replace it.

"What have you noticed about where we have camped apart from the obvious lake and glacier?"

"I've noticed a trail leading up the hillside on the left of the lake," Doug offered.

Colin stood up. "Who wants to explore the path?"

Most of the students and Gregor got to their feet.

"Mr. MacCrimmon, do you want to do the honours?"

Gregor led off up the hill. Gregor noted that Frank and Christopher did not move nor make any attempt to join them. Halfway up the 400-metre path, Gregor noted that Colin was also not with them. He looked back down the hill and saw him crouched down and talking to the two young men.

They came to the end of the path. It was a dead end with a large rock blocking any further progress. They all looked around the rock and found no evidence of a continued path on the other side. Puzzled, they walked back down to the campsite to find Frank and Christopher brewing hot chocolate for everybody. When they had all been served up a cup, they asked Colin what the significance of the path was. He did not answer them directly but instead asked them what they thought was unusual about the rock. Nothing unusual, they decided, just a different colour than the rest of them.

"There is your *eureka* moment," said Colin with enthusiasm. "That rock is the destination of most large animals in the area. It is their mineral lick. Also up at the top of the glacier is a bergschrund, which is a crevice between the top of the glacier and the rock face. It's a German word."

Christopher asked what it meant in English upon which Colin repeated his phrase of a definition. Christopher persisted.

"But what's one word for it in English?"

"There isn't one because glaciers did not exist in England at the time the language had evolved. Long day tomorrow. We need a good night's sleep."

The group moved off and started to get ready for bed.

On the fourth day of the hike, Jon was ecstatic. He was dreaming of Dairy Queen on the way home and his own bed that night. He knew that the route out was flat. No climbs, no descents and a short distance to go. The weather was as good as it had been all week. Jon was packed and ready before anyone else. He sat on his pack, bantering with the group, his leg twitching, his impatience to get going showing all too easily. The group was ready. They began. As usual, Colin was in the front and Gregor was at the back. Gregor had noticed that a long sheath had appeared on Colin's hip with a large looking machete included within. At least it looked like a machete.

The campsite was checked. All was clear. Colin glittered his impish eyes around the site, saw no debris and nodded his approval. The beginning of the lowland trail was easy enough, but ahead of them Gregor noticed that the trail seemed to come to an abrupt end as vegetation appeared to block their way. Alder trees flattened by the snow were slowly bouncing their way back to a semblance of perpendicular as winter had given way to spring. The trees were about

20 feet tall, but the snow had almost flattened and intertwined them so that they seemed impenetrable. Colin stopped, paused as if about to throw down the gauntlet, reached for his "sword" and moved forward with blade flashing.

As the group moved forward, all that Gregor could see was the sunlight glittering off Colin's lively machete. Purposeful hacking and slow, steady progress emanated from every stroke. Heavy packs, balancing on and stepping over awkward branches, no smooth, flowing strides, staccato steps, sweaty shirts, and tired limbs. Gregor suddenly found Jon next to him. Jon had started near the front, eager to complete the hike and look back on the ordeal. Now he presented a disillusioned, disheartened, distraught figure. Eventually, Jon stopped and sat on a branch that bore the scars of the Colin cuts. The volcano erupted.

"I can't f*&&^%$$% believe this. There's no bloody trail. We are lost. We have no idea where we are going. We are not going to get out of here."

He clenched his fists and pounded on the trees in front of him. All the time he spat and foamed, swore and cursed. Tears rolled down his cheeks and he brought his open hands to his face and sobbed.

"Give me your pack."

Gregor did not know what else to say. He was already reaching forward and slipping a pack strap from his shoulder.

"What?"

"Give me your pack."

Meekly, Jon obeyed. Gregor rigged it up on his front so he was carrying his own on his back and Jon's on his front.

"Let's go!"

Jon arose and began to walk. Now he was light and maneuverable. Gregor dropped back, slowed to a crawl. He saw Jon start to move forward easily. Gregor saw the lightness return to Jon's step. The flash of the blade was no longer in sight, but the evidence of the destruction left them an easy route to follow. It seemed like hours to Gregor, but eventually the alder began to thin. He saw Jon moving back towards him. They stopped as they met. Gregor took off Jon's pack and handed it to him.

"Nearly finished now, Jon."

Jon took his pack guiltily and they walked out onto the open trail together.

Colin was standing at the trailhead with the rest of the group to greet the two stragglers. He was dripping with sweat. He had sheathed his machete. The group looked tired and distracted. They hauled themselves along the short stretch of road and pitched their tents in the campsite.

On the following day, they drove back down the island and took a ferry over the seas to Horseshoe Bay. Gregor thought that he would never see Jon on an expedition again. He was wrong. Jon was one who persisted and eventually completed his Duke of Edinburgh Gold Award. Gregor took a leaf out of Colin's book. He never mentioned the breakdown at the rear of the group to anybody. Partly that was due to a lack of confidence on his part, but mostly it was out of respect for the student. There could have been a debrief, a breakdown of the breakdown, an analysis of his attitude at the time, some advice on how he could better have coped with his crisis. There was no need. Gregor sensed that he was embarrassed about it. He knew that Jon was intelligent and was likely to learn from the experience. If he had gone to Colin or Gregor for advice, then no doubt it would have been given. But Gregor was learning from Colin about empowering students to find their own way. Jon certainly did find his own way.

"Language is the dress of thought; every time you talk your mind is on parade."
- Samuel Johnson

CHAPTER 24

RAMPAGING THROUGH THE ROCKIES

G regor was still a neophyte to Canada as a country and still a naïve to Canada as a countryside. He really had no idea whether he had acquitted himself well or badly on Flower Ridge. Colin had not volunteered anything, and Gregor had not dared to ask. But the school came up with an outdoor format for Grades 8 and 9 whereby the homeroom teacher would be asked to go on any expeditions that were going out during the term. Not every teacher was a hiker and some saw it as an unreasonable request of their time. So, Gregor volunteered and found himself on several trips, particularly up to Elfin Lakes above Squamish. He thought that he had made himself useful but was never sure. Come the following June, however, Colin approached asked him if he would like to make a 10-day trip to the Rockies as a final assessment for the Duke of Edinburgh Gold Award. What an opportunity! He talked to his family. Mae kindly agreed.

The plan was to take two or three Eldertree students, pile them and gear into a mini-bus, and drive the twelve or so hours to Banff where they would meet a group of 20 to 25 students from the U.K. who had already been on a residential at Olds Agricultural College in Alberta for 10 days. They would move their base to Banff Youth Hostel, where they would prepare for their expedition; groups, menus, packs, mapping skills, bear proofing, all would come together and they would be dispatched on their three-night, eighty-kilometre excursion with leaders walking behind or ahead but always camping beside them at night.

They set off one sunny day in West Vancouver in August. Colin drove. Every rest stop required a Dairy Queen. Kamloops, Salmon Arm, Revelstoke all provided the necessary breaks for hungry teenagers and flagging drivers. Eventually they were in Banff. Hail fellows, well met exchanges were made with Colin and the English leaders, whom he knew well. All the students were settled into the hostel and the planning began.

Gregor enjoyed the chance to stroll around the town. He noted the high prevalence of Japanese tourists. The Bow River was a magnificent green and the stroll up Tunnel Mountain was a warm-up.

The students were a mixed bag of those who really wanted to get out into the countryside and those who simply wanted to put the award on their resumé. But they were mostly in their early twenties, were working or at university. They had been determined enough to save funds. So, there was obviously a bit of character and grit about them.

The first day of the hike was to take one group and Gregor and his fellow leader, John, up to Mystic Pass by way of the Inkpots. John was from Plymouth in Devon. Like all of his fellow British leaders he was a volunteer. His real job was working with ships in Devonport Services.

John and Gregor watched as the group they were to be responsible for set off up the trail ahead of them. Gregor was a bit concerned when a young fellow from Birmingham immediately plugged his earphones in. Surrounded by the sights and sounds of some of the most spectacular scenery in the world, it seemed sacrilegious to interfere with the experience by wiring oneself up for sound. Still, as per Colin's example, Gregor was not a naysayer but rather a nothing sayer.

John and Gregor hung back to allow the group to get a good head start. To be apart, yet still a part, was the philosophy for the leaders. The trail up towards the Inkpots was more of a paved pathway than a mountain trail. It was a tourist route. So, there was a thick throng of visitors, day-trippers making their way up to the honey pot that was the Ink Pots. John overheard a couple on their way down laughing at what they considered to be the ridiculous idea of taking such large packs on a short trip up to see a well-visited tourist attraction. The assumption must have been that the group of students ahead were only out for the day. John and Gregor caught up to the group while they were paused by the Inkpots having a break and a snack. The two leaders asked how they were but did not stop and wait. They took the opportunity to get ahead of them by tackling the steep trail that led up to Mystic Pass.

As they rounded the corner at the end of their climb and were entering the pass, Gregor understood why it had been given the moniker "mystic." It was a truly enchanting place. Too much of a mountain environment for much of tree growth but with still little clusters of Indian Paint Brush, the last of the alpine flowers stoically sharing their glories here in August. Steep scree slopes creeping up the sides of the hills guarded a clearly marked ribbon of a trail set before them. After initial expressions of joy as they entered this wonderful place, John and Gregor lapsed into companionable silence, the best to be aware of where they were and what they were seeing. Even the faint sound of footfall as they strode onwards seemed to be out of place, a slight insult to the awe of such beauty. They were both glad that they were ahead of the students so their progress slowed to a more leisurely pace. They stopped every 100 yards or so to drink in this view and breathe in their appreciaton. They were about thirty minutes into their valley crossing when they heard the voices in the distance coming up behind.

The trees gradually appeared again, the shrubbery came across as more green. Soon, they saw the sign that showed the campsite. They decided to pitch their tents and take a leisurely walk up to the lake.

After they had pitched their tents and hoisted the food up the bear poles, they trekked off up to Mystic Lake. John was a man of a few words. Gregor was more of a social animal. They came around a corner and were suddenly in a natural amphitheatre the like of which they had only ever seen in photographs. A craggy ridge about 1000 feet above them was already encroaching on the early evening sunlight. Small patches of snow still clung desperately in pockets in the hollows on the mountainside. There was little vegetation sprouting from the talus on the slopes. Had they a mind to do so, the incline in places could probably be scrambled up. The lake lapped gently by their feet. There was a wee rivulet trickling close to where they were standing and some short scrubby marshland close by. There were a couple of rocks, conveniently flat and large. Gregor and John sat down and silently immersed themselves in the view, grateful that they had arrived before the students. They were not able to sit for long because the inevitable bugs suddenly rose up from the sedge and sphagnum moss, dispelling any romantic images of an earthly paradise. They took a last lingering look, turned on their heels and headed back to the campsite.

When they arrived, the group had turned up, making a great deal of noise and matching progress. Gregor began to boil water for his tea and his food. He was crouched over his cooker when he sensed a presence leaning over him. Wendy, a 19-year-old from Devon, was embracing him with her shadow.

"Good evening, Wendy."

"Good evening, Gregor."

"What can I do for you, Wendy?"

"May I have some of your water for my food please?"

Gregor was nonplussed. These students were being examined. They were, in effect, sitting their *final* exam. This was based on excellent campcraft and individual, independent integrity. Gregor considered Colin's response. He decided that Colin would say nothing and would give over the water with good grace, but he would not forget.

"Sure you can, Wendy, help yourself."

She took it all.

"Thanks, Gregor."

"No uh problem, ummm, I think."

He headed off to refill his pan from the creek. Gregor had watched Colin in action frequently. He had wanted to refuse Wendy the water and give her the reasons why. He had wanted to stand frowningly on his high horse and give her an old style dressing down, preaching her the sermon of self-reliance and independence and restating the purpose of the award. But he didn't. He let it go. He did what Colin would have done but, like Colin, the information was filed for future use, if necessary.

On the following morning, John was up early and watching the students lowering their foodstuffs from the bear poles. Gregor had lingered longer abed but stuck his head out to watch the shenanigans. Needs must and Gregor noted that the outhouse was free. He quickly grabbed his headlight and some reading material and headed off to do his business before anybody else. Gregor had frequently sought inspiration in the toilet. Indeed, while laying concrete in Australia, the "dunny" had been a place in which to have a rest and recoup. He also enjoyed it as a place of solitude, a haven of aloneness, of which there was not too much in his chosen profession. So he settled down, clicked on his flashlight and opened his book. Two minutes later he heard a voice.

"Gregor? Gregor, are you in there?"

There was a moment of panic as Gregor flashed his light around the confined space because the voice was either one from god or there was somebody else in there with him. He reasserted himself and answered Wendy, albeit disconcerted by this unusual connection in such a sacred place.

"Y-Yes, Wendy, I'm here. W—w—what do you want?" This delivered in a tone suggesting that this was inappropriate and not the time.

"It's a lovely day, isn't it?"

"Yes, yes, Wendy, but what do you want?"

"I was just thinking hmmm, I was just thinking aaaah…"

"Get on with it, Wendy." Now real irritation in his voice but obliviousness from the other side of the door.

"Well, I was just thinking that I should never have asked you for water last night. Then, of course, without thinking I took it all and you had to start afresh, filling up again and boiling it all over. Mmm!"

A welcome silence.

"Gregor, are you still there?"

"Where else would I be!!??"

"That was very kind of you last night."

"Wendy." Real annoyance now.

"Yes, yes of course. I just thought that I would return the favour. May I get you some water and boil it up for you?"

"Please, please, please. Go ahead and do it. Please do it *now*."

Silence and she was gone. Gregor's time in the outhouse was coming to an end. It had not been the moment of peace that he had craved. Indeed, he reflected that it had not been like any other toilet experience he had ever had. He thought that he might confront Wendy with the inappropriateness of the place and timing of the conversation, but then she would be mortified and embarrassed. Maybe he would take a moment to make light of it to her when the trip was over. The plus side was that she had realized that she was offside on the previous evening. She wanted to make recompense on her own. She was, most of the time, an outstanding candidate. She was physically very strong, organizationally excellent and she worked well with her peers. She was everything one expected in an outstanding Gold Award recipient. But speaking to one's leader when he is on the toilet is not likely to get you brownie points.

"Brownie points," Gregor muttered as he mulled the incident over with an impish grin. "That's what *I* was there for!!"

"Kindness is in our power, even when fondness is not."
- Samuel Johnson

CHAPTER 25

A MINNEWANKA MEMORY

It was Gregor's third year on the annual summer Rockies expedition. He had never yet been permitted to hike with Colin on these trips. The logic of the English trip leaders was always to split the two of them. So on this occasion, Gregor found himself with a husband and wife team, Bill and Millie. They were from Devon in England and were avid bird watchers. They were also enthused by everything else. Their joy and excitement at each twist in the trail was something that Gregor liked immensely. He had hiked with the morose and the mundane before. By the end of four days in that type of company, Gregor's natural giant ebullience had been suborned to a mouse-like depression. No, Gregor much preferred jovial, skipping jollity to the reverse. People who burst into rapturous glee when they found a bag of prunes in their pack were Gregor's type. So Bill and Millie were proving to be good company as they set out on the round of Lake Minnewanka.

It was an overcast day. The group that they were assessing were a keen, fit-looking bunch of characters. They set out on that morning, the third day of the expedition, with German accents. They had agreed to be German for the day. So, Gregor had been amused when he witnessed the fry up at breakfast. William had been the designated chef for the meal. Penny had approached him with her very excellent accent and asked him, "Soooo, Wilhelm, venn am I becoming a sausage?"

"Venn ihre sausage is becoming fried, Fraulein Pennstein," was the reply.

Gregor had found this very creative and amusing. He would have liked to have been close enough to have heard more of this banter during the day but that went against protocol, so he would seek his amusement with Bill and Millie. The group cleared their campsite with Teutonic efficiency and were ready to head out a long time before Gregor, Bill and Millie.

Rosie had announced, "Ach so, vee go now, nichts zu langsam, nichts zu schnell," and "zay" had gone.

The lead group had progressed only a short distance from the tourist spot when Bill and Millie wanted a stop to study the map. They had cut their outdoor teeth on *Dartmoor*, the best maps in the world. The Ordnance Survey maps of Great Britain had long been renowned for their accuracy. It was an exactitude that even showed large, errant boulders appearing among the contour lines. Rocky Mountain maps are very rudimentary by comparison. Gregor had explained gently to them that they should not be too map reliant as they would become very frustrated very quickly when they discovered that they hadn't covered the distance they thought they had covered. Still, Bill and Millie loved maps and every stop for snack or lunch was also a map stop.

The map was folded away and they were on their way again. They had gone but half a mile when Millie signalled a stop. A loon was bobbing up and down on the lake's surface below them.

"Look, Bill, a Great Northern Diver!"

For such are loons called in the U.K. When Gregor had arrived in Canada, he had known little about the animal life. He knew there were bears, polar bears, cougars, moose, skunks and raccoons but the only birds he had known of were the Canada geese because they were found in other countries, too, and eagles, of course, because they were iconic. He had certainly never heard of loons. But on car camping trips into the interior of British Columbia, he had come to understand why this bird found its way onto the dollar coin, which was thus nicknamed a "Loonie." It is a solitary, dignified bird that could be forgiven for being labeled a "duck" except anybody who has ever camped near a Canadian lake would not make that mistake. There was that old saying: if it walks like a duck, looks like a duck and quacks like a duck, then it must be a duck. Well a loon did **not** quack like a duck. It's call is so distinctive, so recognizable, so eerie and so wonderful. Gregor had a friend who said that it was like that of a hyena. Gregor disagreed. It was just unique, maybe eccentric, and iconically and absurdly Canadian.

"Let's stop for a moment so that we can hear its call. What do you think, Gregor?"

Gregor had noted the ominous storm clouds appearing overhead, knew that they had something over 24 kilometres to go before the waded crossing at the narrows at the head of the lake. IF the rains came, then the crossing would become too deep, too quickly, and they would have to make the extra couple of kilometres to the head of the lake before they could camp at the foot of Carrot Canyon.

"I think that I live here and I can hear the cry of the loon at any time but you don't so we should wait and give it a chance to speak. But, it will likely get dark early tonight here in the valley. The cloudiness may be a factor as well. We still have a long way to go. So we need to be aware. That's all."

So they paused in their tracks. None of them took off their packs. Gregor expected the loon to show off its cry any second. That had been his previous experience. But either this character had a bout of laryngitis, had been struck dumb at birth or realized it was being watched and was not going to cooperate. No sound came. No haunting call echoing around the valley. Not a murmur, not a whisper, not even a squawk. They waited and waited. Mr. Loon sat there as "idle as a painted ship upon a painted ocean." Finally, Gregor had to be the spoiler.

"If we start moving, we can still hear it for some way along the trail."

Bill and Millie shouldered their disappointment as an added burden to their packs. Sure enough, the bird let out its signature cry as they moved away. The noise carried easily across the waters of the lake and gave a generous reverberation off the echoing rocks. It was an ornithological moment they wouldn't forget. Gregor was happy for them but gently trying to up the pace slightly. Still, however, the inevitable map stops happened. Now thunder and lightning had appeared farther up the valley and they were starting to feel spots of rain. Out came the waterproofs and they were suddenly moving forward through a downpour. Gregor was starting to worry about the group ahead. But, he reasoned, there were only two teenagers in that group, and the other four were twenty-something adults. Just the same, he wished that they were not so far ahead.

The rain persisted with intermittent heaviness for an hour or so, and slowly the thunder faded into the distance. But Gregor really doubted that the shortcut across the lake was fordable anymore. As he approached, they saw before them that their journey was going to need to be three to four kilometres farther. Gregor stated that they would have to walk on. He received no reply and wondered if the enthusiasm had finally been dampened.

It was getting dark when they finally rounded the head of the lake and had the short run into the campsite. They were greeted with enthusiasm by the "German" students.

"Did you manage to cross at the ford before the rain?" Gregor asked.

"Ja, ja, ja," said Rosie, grinning and hugging a cup of hot chocolate. "Vee haff made genug fur sich."

Gregor, Bill and Millie were ushered under a tarp that somebody had rigged up, and were given a very, very welcome hot drink. All of these students have passed, there was an unspoken understanding nodded between the three leaders.

On the following day, there was a steep climb out, ascending the Carrot Creek Trail and then a gentle but long trudge to the trailhead. It was the last day, so the three leaders felt they could walk out with the group. It wasn't quite a lap of honour but as good as. The steep climb was arduous but the three previous days had given an increase in stamina, a decrease in the weight of the packs and, most importantly, a well-founded confidence. What had begun with inevitable self-doubt had ended with a spirit of "can-do." This, Gregor contemplated, as he puffed his way up the hill, was what all teaching should be like. No participation ribbons here, just successful learning outcomes because lack of success meant that somebody went hungry, became dehydrated, too wet or too cold. Gregor's heart suddenly sank when Millie stopped the group and pulled out her map. Gregor had a foreboding.

"How far?" Rosie asked, forgetting for a moment that she was a German.

"Not far. We should be out in half an hour."

Gregor knew that was not true. More likely two hours. It was the classic mistake, the "Are we there yet, Dad?" from the back of the car. It was a question that should never be answered.

There's many a slip 'twixt cup and lip, as the saying goes. Now there were a group of people prepared for thirty minutes more work and no more. He knew that they had looked at their watches and that they were about to be disappointed. But there was nothing he could do or say that wouldn't make the psychological situation worse.

"Stop believing in these F------ useless maps!" Gregor muttered to himself.

An hour came and went. They had just come off the top of the climb and were levelling out so the worst was behind them, but Gregor knew that this was the T.E.D. time, the "Tiredness, Exhaustion, Death" period that climbers experience after the peak is conquered and they are on their way down. Of course, this was unlikely to have been so devastatingly dramatic as that, but nobody wanted a pulled muscle or twisted ankle at this stage. So, Gregor did what Colin probably would not have done; he stopped the group. He insisted that everybody take 10 minutes to eat and drink, then he explained that, unusually for him, he was going to walk in front and that nobody was to walk ahead of him.

As they strolled the last couple of kilometres, Gregor wondered if by "taking charge" he had undermined the purpose of the journey. He noted that Bill and Millie were now trudging rather than breezing along cheerily. He was concerned that he might have overstepped the mark. Suddenly, there was a shout of joy from behind him. Somebody had spotted the end and the top half of the mini-bus from behind the wall.

That night after the business of unpacking, Gregor and Colin spent some time together. Gregor told him about his actions of the day and asked him if his actions had undermined the spirit of the trip and offended the other leaders.

"You see, Gregor, I have modelled my professional and personal life on gut, instinct, common sense and experience. Often we do not know why we decide to do what we did but, if we are as experienced as you obviously are, then the decision was the right one. It may not have been the right one for the group at the time. WE will never know the answer to that. But it was the right one for you. Your intuition gave you the information that you probably could not articulate at the time. I think that it wasn't based so much on what the group of young people needed but rather on the needs of Bill and Millie. After all, they are ten years older than you, a lot less fit, relying on maps that do not work, and ignoring good advice to move more quickly. You said they were very quiet on the last little stage. I suspect that it was not because of your decision but rather because they were exhausted. You know, tiredness can also bring clarity. They were probably brooding over their own little errors on that last kilometre. Why don't you ask them?"

Later that night after a beer or two, Gregor sat down with Bill and Millie. Before he could get a word out, they were apologizing to him for the loon delay, the map stops and the error in telling the students that they were nearly there. Gregor slept the sleep of the innocent that night. He would have lain awake tossing and turning had it not been for the wisdom of Colin Dalhousie.

"So learn from this and understand true values. I who
tell you have wintered into wisdom."
- Beowulf

CHAPTER 26

THE WISDOM AND GENIUS OF COLIN DALHOUSIE

One never really knows when one realizes that one is in the presence of greatness. Is there a moment in a crisis when the hour has cometh and one suddenly realizes that so has the man? Or is it just noticing the little things that she or he does along the way? From the Flower Ridge experience, Gregor felt that Colin Dalhousie was a genius in the outdoors.

Gregor was sat at home one night. He had put his children to bed. He and Mae were enjoying a glass of wine and talking about working with Colin. By this time, Gregor had attended a dozen or so trips with him. Some of them had been based in Outdoor Centres, but most of them had been on expeditions.

"You know, Mae, I think that Evans Lake Outdoor Centre was a real eye opener."

Evans Lake is an outdoor centre near Squamish, in British Columbia. The Grade IX students of Eldertree School went there one November. It was a good week. The ninety or so teenagers had behaved like ninety teenagers. They were foolhardy and courageous, cautious and risk averse, both emotionally strong and suddenly weak; they were young people who had thought they had found their way in life. They thought that they knew better than the adults, yet secretly in their heart of hearts they realized that they didn't. They were insecure. Of course they were. They were where we have all been. They were teenagers. Gregor enjoyed working with them, but on the last night of the camp, he had a temperature and the beginnings of a flu.

As the students and staff piled into the big hall for a last night of skits and frolics, Gregor found himself a niche at the back of the room where he could sit and nurse his illness. "The night drove on with songs and clatter" as Robbie Burns would have it. It came the time when the staff knew they were going to be asked to do something, to perform some act of dubious taste that might humble them into making a fool of themselves.

The young Master of Ceremonies was warming to his task.

"Who's next?" he asked the crowd.

The chant went up.

"Dal-housie, Dal-housie, Dal-housie!" Ever louder, ever more rhythmically.

Then the call for silence.

"So what do you want him to do?"

Various suggestions were put forward, some of them inappropriate. Finally, they settled on the fact that he was to suffer "Death by Fly." Colin appeared flamboyantly at the front of the stage in keeping with the occasion. He heard the decision, scratched his head in Stan Laurel fashion, jumped off the stage and dramatically pushed his way through the crowd to where Gregor was sitting. There he paused, looked up and reached for the spider's web in the corner. He grabbed the dead fly, returned to the stage, pretended to swallow the fly and died dramatically, slumping to the floor with Shakespearean aplomb. It was singularly impressive to all there, amazingly drop jaw stuff to the sickly Gregor.

How could a man with all the responsibilities that Colin had register a cobweb in the corner of a room with a fly in it? The students had not been easy to manage on this camp, the activities had suffered heavily through bad weather. Settling at night had been an issue; indeed, Colin had been up late on each night counselling students. He should have been dog-tired. He should have had no inkling that his acting career would demand that he "Die by fly." Yet somehow, somewhere in that amazing mind of his he had registered the trivialities of a fly dead in a web.

There was a further stunning example of this on the trip. A baggage bus arrived and all students' and teachers' bags were thrown aboard to be transported back to school. There was no rhyme or reason or order to the packing; a chain of students was formed and the bags were literally thrown aboard. Colin somehow found himself on board the baggage bus back to school, so by the time students and teachers arrived back on campus, the bags were unloaded in the playground and the bus had gone. Gregor searched in vain for his bags in the pile but they were nowhere to be seen. Gregor did not like to approach Colin after all his work. It seemed selfish and self-centred, but he did so anyway.

"Sorry, Gregor, I separated the teachers' and leaders' bags. They are over there."

Sure enough, Gregor wandered over to a picnic table and there were the adult bags. There were no names, no old travel tags, no individual indicators on the bags, but they were all there. Colin had registered a dead fly in a web and distinguished separate bags in an indistinguishable pile. Gregor spent the drive home mulling over what he had witnessed during this memorable week.

On another occasion, Port Hardy, the northernmost settlement on Vancouver Island, was the starting point for a hike into a beautiful part of the island. Colin lead the group northwards through flat, undulating country past an ancient deserted settlement. Cape Scott has an unmanned lighthouse that was worth the visit and a wonderful beach nearby on which to camp. The large group of teenagers, twelve in all, were lead by Colin Dalhousie with the female presence of Erica, the school nurse. Gregor, as ever, was there. He was leading from the back as usual. They had climbed a local peak, walked out to see the lighthouse and were ensconced on the long strand of a beach for their last night. Nathan Fitch, a 15-year-old student, took a bad turn in the early evening. He slipped into unconsciousness. The school nurse was on a walk along the beach. So, Colin sat the unconscious boy up and began to massage his heart.

"Anything I can do?" Gregor asked.

"Yes, you can go and get Erica. And Gregor, be quick, we could be in trouble here."

Gregor had never heard Colin speak with such emphatic directness, so he moved quickly. By the time Gregor and Erica arrived back, Nathan was conscious. Colin waited a while and then quizzed him on his own. Nathan had not revealed that he was on medication. Colin was annoyed that his parents had not seen fit to enter this on his medical form, but that was a story for another day. On the following day, they were all going to have to walk out of there. Judgment as to Nathan's fitness was going to have to wait until the morning. Gregor went to bed with the uneasy belief that Colin was more medically aware and more attuned to the situation than the medical professional.

Morning came and after a confab between the three adults, it was decided that Nathan could walk out on his own but not carry his pack. Gregor's own pack was huge but Colin's pack was massive. The two of them had to split up Nathan's tent, sleeping bag, clothing and food and add it to their own packs. The time came to leave. Colin and Gregor watched Erica lead off the group, which was in high spirits to be heading home. Gregor waited until the last minute before reaching for his pack. He helped Colin into his bag with some difficulty. He was awed by what the wiry but wily man was going to carry for that sixteen kilometres. He then, with some difficulty but with the aid of a nearby rock, managed to get his pack onto his back. He trembled a bit and almost lost his balance. He had a moment of butterfly-inducing nervousness when he doubted that he had the strength and fortitude to complete this overburdened hike. But he watched the back of Colin begin to move up the beach. He tried to follow and in the process felt the restrictive nature of the beach beneath his feet, the slipping of his boots as he moved forward. For a moment he caught his breath and thought that the task ahead was beyond him. But in front of him was the determined movement of the older man. Older by a decade at least, yet strong and fit and filled with old school grit, Colin was inching his way into a rhythm. Gregor could not, in good faith, do anything but follow such an example. So, he breathed and focused and one foot went in front of the other.

He was relieved when they were off the beach and the trail stretched before them. The group had long since disappeared ahead of them. Colin and Gregor were left alone with their thoughts, their focus and their strength. No words passed between them. In truth, Gregor was grateful for the silence because he really believed that he would not have been able to string a sentence together if he was required to. Such were the demands that were being placed on his body.

The morning proceeded with footfall and focus, frown and fever. Sweat dripped from their brows, the occasional grunt escaped their lips. Eventually, they heard voices in the near distance. Rounding a corner in the trail, they were suddenly upon the group who were finishing up their lunch stop. Exuberant energy, vibrant verbosity and bantering bonhomie were the order of the day.

"Where have you been?"

"We've been here for hours."

Gregor remembered the tired despondency that had been prevalent from some members of the group on the first night when it had rained and blown a bit. He reflected on how quickly teenage moods were down in the dumps and then suddenly high on the hog. He thought also about the self-centred nature of the age, which was blind to the weight and perspiration their teachers were carrying. Erica gave nought but a tolerant grin, a benign smile which suggested to Gregor that, although the adult, she was subject to the whims and wherewithal of youth as well. It would be wrong to say that the lunatics had taken over the asylum—unkind to a degree—but the tail was definitely wagging the dog. Erica the nurse was having to go along with the teenage tide because she, in fairness, did not really know the group. She would have been reassured if the two teachers had been able to keep up with them but had the good sense and character to understand that this was not possible. So she did the responsible thing and organized the group to leave. They were happy to do so.

Gregor and Colin took off their packs, reached for their water bottles, drank deeply and reached for the trail mix. Colin stood up, stretched himself off, placed his pack on a rock, braced himself and hauled it onto his shoulders. Gregor felt a shaking in his legs. There was a quivered trembling of some unknown muscle in his shoulder area as the pack came to rest in the hollow of his back.

"We go now," Colin puffed his cheeks, turned on his heel and strode forward.

Gregor followed. Metres slowly disappeared behind them, kilometres stretched before them. The afternoon drove forwards slowly. Some time just before 5:00 p.m. Gregor heard the shouts and hollers of the group and knew that soon a corner would be turned and the bus would be seen. Sure enough, round the last bend, they were immediately upon the bus, the crowd and the noise. Colin and Gregor eased off their packs and sat on them.

"When are we going?" Jason said directly to Gregor.

Gregor frowned, closed his eyes and rubbed the furrows on his forehead but did not answer. Jason gave up and turned to Colin. Colin reached back and rubbed his shoulders with deliberate emphasis, a less than subtle attempt to evoke some realization from his young inquisitor. Eventually he spoke.

"Mr. MacCrimmon and I are going to brew up a cuppa tea, maybe even boil up a bag of chilli, maybe even have a nap. You are in a hurry to leave, Jason. How are you going to speed things up?"

Nathan was obviously unused to having his schedule unmet, his time constraints being suddenly subject to the needs of others. But he learned quickly. He did not answer but turned on his heel, spoke quietly to one of his team members who opened his pack and brought out his cooker. The two of them were soon boiling water, searching out mugs and tea bags and rummaging around for dehydrated food. The example was soon followed by the rest of the group who organized the loading of the packs onto the roof of the mini-bus. Gregor continued to lie on his back, crossed his legs, folded his arms, pulled the brim of his hat over his eyes and watched. Colin did the same but smiled and winked at him.

Before very long a steaming mug of sweet tea was being thrust into their hands. An aromatic newly-hydrated feast was given to them and the two men mustered the energy to sit up and drink and eat. Feast over, Gregor and Colin were on their feet, checking that the baggage was secure and loading the students into the mini-bus. Before setting off, Colin turned around in the driver's seat to speak to the group.

"Over the last hour, true leadership and cooperation has come to the fore. The beauty of learning in the outdoors is that decision making is important. Bad decisions can be costly, good decisions can save time and effort. You need to know that had Nathan not shown the initiative to cook and make us tea just now, then we would be pitching the tents and spending another night out. There is no way that I would be driving now if I had not had rest and sustenance over the last hour. That would have been irresponsible and put us all at risk. You came together when it mattered. Not only will we catch that ferry but we'll have time for a Dairy Queen stop on the way."

Colin saw the grins and smiles, turned around and drove off.

"Before that sudden journey, no one is wiser in thought than he needs to be."
- Venerable Bede

CHAPTER 27

BADGER PASS

Foot and Mouth Disease in Britain had curtailed hikers and visitors from walking in the National Parks. The British Duke of Edinburgh Gold candidates had been, therefore, unable to get out on their practice expeditions on Dartmoor. Health and Safety being what it was, they were not allowed to make the trip to the Rockies. So at the last minute, Gregor and Colin's summer plans were thrown for a loop. Gregor felt confident enough in his skill set to approach Colin and ask if he would like to go on a Rockies expedition anyway. Colin said that he would. So, Gregor asked two other guys if they would like to come along. One was a young Kiwi gap year student called Jason and the other was a thirty-something P.E. teacher called Tyler.

Gregor planned and booked campsites for seven nights and eight days. Some of the ground they would cover would be familiar to Colin and Gregor, some would not. Gregor organized the passes to Banff National Park, booked the campsites and talked to Colin about borrowing the Eldertree School bus and equipment. Uneventful Dairy Queen stops on the way and, yet again, the continental climate kicked in favourably and they were blessed with sunny weather. Gregor had built in a rest day at Flints Park campsite halfway through the trip, a time to sit back, hang around the campsite and peacefully drink in the scenery.

Gregor had always loved the high places most of all, yet he was not really a rock climber or a high risk taker in either sense of the word. So, he always found himself fearful of the really high places when he was alone. Thus he had missed out on many climbing experiences because of his proclivity for solitary travel. He was excited for this trip because there would be four of them, including the incomparable Colin. Jason was a keen Kiwi. He had once sat down with Gregor and asked him about how long it should take to complete the iconic Vancouver hike, the Grouse Grind. Advertisements called it "Nature's Stairmaster." It was 2,800 feet of altitude gain from base to peak. It was well marked and well cared for with many wooden stairways crafted onto the trail. On summer weekends it was crowded with the "fit on a mission" people and groups of naïve looking tourists, the occasional one sporting high heels. Gregor had explained to Jason that a good goal was to try to complete it in one's age. Colin was 51 so should try for 51 minutes; Gregor was 46 so 46 minutes.

"How old are you, Jason?"

"Eighteen."

"Aha." Gregor smiled impishly.

Jason was well prepared for his eight-day hike. Colin was particularly impressed with his trail mix concoction known in New Zealand as "scrogum." Tyler had spent a year teaching in Japan and had purchased a wonderful camera when he had left. Tyler was what Gregor had always imagined a Canadian to be before he himself had come to Canada. He was a phenomenal ice hockey player. His family had a family cabin. He was athletic, resilient and adaptive, and he said, "Eh" a great deal.

After a night spent at the campsite in Banff's Tunnel Mountain, they were packed and ready to head out to the trailhead. Colin had his large hiking pole, a fixture of his every trip. Indeed, had it been notched for every outdoor experience that it had ever been on there would have been no wood left. Tyler and Jason seemed to be happy to fit in. As they had been doing for years, Colin took his position at the front and Gregor at the rear. Gregor had felt guilty about this a few expeditions previously and had offered to take a turn at the front so that Colin was not always the point person. Colin had declined, stating kindly that he preferred Gregor to be at the back because he saw and heard things there that would be useful to the group dynamic. Gregor had not known what he meant until Colin had reminded him of the Jon outburst on Flower Ridge.

They walked forward, youth sandwiched by age, an energetic filling embraced by two slices of experience. It was a leisurely stroll. Gregor had planned the trip to be a scenic, appreciative walk in the park rather than a hard driving yomp. Frequent stops were happening. Tree cover was prevalent but by no means were they shrouded by a forest. The ground was almost always open enough to see any view that came their way. The peaks were close and rugged, the distant peaks were always drawing them forward. The sun beat down. Occasionally it danced along the ridges and mountain tops, mixing with the blue of the sky and the green of the growth. The varied colours cast some spectacular moments. On one such, Tyler had stopped and asked Gregor if he would mind reaching into his pack for his camera. A short rummage and Tyler was snapping away happily. As they moved off, Gregor replaced the camera in Tyler's pack.

After the third day, Gregor was removing Tyler's camera for the umpteenth time, when Tyler came up with a suggestion.

"I think that it would be a good idea if I were to carry my camera pinned to my chest. That way we are not stopping and fiddling about too much."

"Good idea," Gregor said.

They progressed slowly towards Flints Park. By now, Jason had overdosed on scrogum and was on the hunt for somebody who wanted to share their trail mix. Colin was all too happy to share his. Gregor was not surprised. He believed that Colin could survive on a handful of birdseed for days on end. Tyler was overdosing on taking photographs of birds, close ups of squirrels, detailed studies of wild flowers. Tyler had commented to Gregor that the reason that he had buried his camera in his pack was to avoid binge photographing. He wasn't complaining. Occasionally Gregor noted that he was walking with the lens cap off, even more prepared for the sudden appearance of a stunning view or some wildlife in action.

The trail became wider and more winding. The tree cover thickened but kept its distance about two metres either side of the trail. The four of them rounded the corner and were brought up short. They were confronted by a large grizzly bear about thirty yards ahead of them. It took no command for them to stop in their tracks. Tyler already had his camera up and was snapping away readily. Colin was talking gently to the bear like he was reassuring a child. Jason was creeping closer towards it. Colin told him to go no farther. The bear paced back and forth across the trail several times. He huffed and puffed his irritation at the intrusion then abruptly disappeared into the woods. Slowly, the group mustered their way past the spot where the bruin had been feeding. As they passed they saw the dark outline of the creature in the shadows in the trees. They had gone about 100 metres when they turned and there he was. He had returned to his dinner table and was happily re-ensconsed back in the berry patch.

Later that morning they found themselves in a wide valley with not much tree growth, low shrubbery and a small river tinkling its gentle way. They knew that at some point in the day they were going to turn right and make the long, steady ascent up to the ridge atop Badger Pass. The trail was tending gently in that direction. Eventually, they found themselves at the foot of the climb. There was a clear view upwards to the typical moonscape of a high mountain pass. Harsh winters and cold summer nights meant that very little grew there, and when it did it was stunted and close to the ground. Alpine flowers hugged sheltered nooks and crevices for warmth, gripped desperately to the shallow soil sucking every little nutrient they could get for their short season of blooming splendour.

"It's so wild, so beautiful, so unearthly," commented Jason in awe. "We're the only people here."

"Not quite 'only,'" Colin said, pointing upwards to the ridge. "I think that we'll find some rock climbers up there. There's a pile of backpacks on the ridge there, which they may have dropped off."

They all strained their eyes to see, their palms over their foreheads against the sun.

"I can't see anything," Tyler commented.

"Nor me," murmured Jason.

"I can't see anything either but they're there," stated Gregor confidently.

"How do you know they are there if you can't see them?" said Jason in disbelief.

"I know they are there because Colin said they are there," confided Gregor with a grin.

Gregor smiled at Colin, Colin smiled back, the other two shook their heads.

An hour or so later, they were nearing the top of the pass. There was a shout from Tyler.

"There they are! I count four of them."

Sure enough there were four coloured backpacks in a neat row on the top of the ridge. Jason heard a shout to his right and spotted a multi-coloured climber hanging off a cliff face.

Colin had never been an "I told you so" kind of guy but then he didn't need to be as long as Gregor was travelling with him.

"I told you so," Gregor smiled at the other two.

Slackjawed, they looked across at Colin who was immersed in getting the last drops out of one of his several water bottles. He appeared to be concentrating deeply on a particular drop that was clinging to the side of the bottle in desperation. His face gave nothing away. He wasn't being modest. He knew that he had just preached a sermon and that he had converted two more unbelievers.

They reached the ridge. They eased off their packs for a break from the arduous ascent. Jason ate more of Colin's Canadian scrogum. Tyler played with his camera. Gregor lay on his back, put his hands behind his head and fell asleep. They were all having a wonderful day. They had wondered at the scenery. They had wondered at their own accomplishment but, most of all, they had wondered at the phenomenon of Colin Dalhousie.

"Young Lochinvar has come out of the west,
Through all the wide border, his steed was the best."
- Walter Scott

CHAPTER 28

THE WEST COAST TRAIL

Gregor and Mae and their two children looked to be happily settled living in North Vancouver. Life had pattern and stability. The children were happy at school. Both were involved in school and community sports. There had been uncertainty when they had arrived in 1991, but now Gregor was legally Canadian. He was confident at work. He intended to stay at Eldertree School as long as they could tolerate him. There seemed no reason for change. He had always tried not to put a foot wrong, or bludgeon and stampede his way forward, but rather to plod steadily. He was not likely to be the world's most innovative teacher, but he was not averse to applying innovation when it came his way. He was not the bull in the china shop who created chaos wherever he went. He travelled softly through his working life. Perhaps his Welsh mentor back in the day was correct, he was never going to set any river alight, but then flaming rivers were not healthy rivers, were they?

There was one major accomplishment that he had not achieved, which taunted him. He met many Europeans in his travels and when he mentioned British Columbia, a large percentage of them asked about the West Coast Trail, particularly when they had discovered that he did some work in the outdoors. It was to Gregor's chagrin that he had never done it. He resolved to remedy this.

Two days before he was due to start his walk he caught the ferry over to Victoria where he had arranged to stay with friends. They had very kindly agreed to drop him at Port Renfrew at the beginning of the hike. He had heard horror stories of when the West Coast Trail had become the "Wet" Coast Trail as befits a pathway in a rainforest. The sodden mud had meant that the walk had become a wade and a ten kilometre hike had become a one kilometre mud bath. Happily, this was the beginning of a glorious summer. He knew that the trails were dry, and that he was fit enough for the ups and downs of the ladders and the sand on the beaches that he would have to traverse. He was eager to get going.

Gregor had experienced thick temperate rainforest before. He had seen many rugged coastlines. However, he doubted that he had ever seen them so close together. As he walked through the cedar, Douglas, hemlock and arbutus tree stands, he heard the crashing of waves beyond the undergrowth. He imagined that it was a different planet, a world away from where he walked. Gregor's thoughts were for a moment back on that Australian beach. Maybe 10,000 years ago when the last ice age had slowly drawn its ice cap and glaciers northwards and the land stretched and rebounded from its frozen grave, there was a Gregor who looked down on this very same sight. Gregor was not a botanist or a geologist or much of an "ist" at all, but he had an imagination. He had nobody to talk to so was able to put his own reality on that past. He could make it as ideal as he wanted it to be. Surely that was what a walk was all about, was it not? Recreation meant re-creation, did it not? A time to step out of the life of strife in which all human beings find themselves and strengthen mind and body for the return. He heard the sea crashing closer. Suddenly, he emerged from the trees and descended to a beach.

The littoral was wild and wide. Rocks and seaweed, tide pools and bird life. He thought of the native proverb, "When the tide is out, the table is set." Sure enough, all life and death was here. Oystercatchers using their needle like beaks to dig beneath the sands, mingled bird cries. Somewhere off the shore were a variety of leviathans scouring the surface for evidence of a seal or simply filtering ponderous pathways through an ocean rich in plankton. Somewhere in the forest there were large mammals, all with an eye for the main chance. Gregor had already come across some bear scat and observed undigested "tangle" amidst the intact berries. Surely, he thought, that is not a very efficient system; there must have been so much that was still nutritional deposited on the beach there. Yet the system worked, the weak died and the strong survived.

Seventy-five kilometres, Gregor reflected, is not a long hike over six or seven days, but he saw how it could be arduous with rain and the added ponderousness of walking on the sand. Thankfully, the beach was not too dry so it did present a good grip underfoot. However, he could still see how long hours spent on it would tear at energy levels. The artificial stairs were all solidly hammered into cliff edges, incongruous constructions in this feast of natural sights. They required extreme focus and care to climb with a heavy, unbalanced pack. They were short drops, but they were enough to cause serious injury or death if one were to take a tumble.

Gregor was walking along an edge—an edge of the beach and an edge of the forest. He was about thirty feet up when he heard the hiss of exploding water. He looked out to sea and there were two whales about fifty metres away, easing their undulating bodies fluently to the north. He stopped and watched. He reached inside his pack for his binoculars and focused in on those magnificent creatures. He had about 100 metres to go before he had to descend to the beach. He was unable to keep pace with the duet in the water, but he had the best view of all from above. But, as chance would have it, he descended to the beach as two other grays were journeying on through. He walked along the low tide line parallel to them for some fifty metres or so. Gregor was walking with the whales, which was probably more environmentally sound than swimming with them. He took a deep breath and sucked in the scene as if by doing so he was preserving it forever. It was a sight he would never forget.

Gregor had always been an enigma to many of his family members and friends. He could be gregarious, the life and soul of many an event, yet he could disappear for days on end. Sometimes there was a physical absence, but most of the time he simply retreated within himself. He became a solitary presence in a crowd. He was never lonely for he was perfectly happy with his own company. On camping trips he always tried to judge whether the people in the next tent wanted company or not. Was that singleton two tents down from his site alone because he wanted to be alone or could they share a brew and a blether for a while? He had pitched his tent and was boiling his water when a woman in her early forties breezed into the campsite ahead of three teenage children. Flurry and flourish, she had them putting their tents up as she went to the creek to get some water to boil. Gregor had no hesitation in striking up a conversation with the woman.

"Are these your children?" he asked.

"Yes they are. We are down from Edmonton. Their father couldn't get away from work, so he was happy for us to do this trail without him," she responded.

"You look like you're enjoying yourselves."

"Yes, we are!"

And she was off and organizing. A little bit later, two men and a woman came into camp. They hadn't been long settled when they approached Gregor. One reached into her pocket and brought out a hip flask, offering him a drink. He took a short slurp and gave it back to her. They were all from Washington State and had completed many expeditions together. They were good company.

As he continued his trek up the trail, Gregor had the experience of the boat ride over the swirling turbulence of the Nitinat Narrows. He had the wonderful seafood and chips bought from a vendor on the beach. He had spent a wonderfully moving night at the Tsusiat Falls where the stars had been out in force and, not for the first time, Gregor wished he had a greater astronomical awareness and knowledge. But he had sat on a rock next to a young man who seemed to have a propensity for intensity. In other words, just the sort of person one needs in this situation. He did know his stars and was able to point to dippers big and small, Arcturus, Castor and Pollux, the famed Gemini. Yet again, Gregor promised he would remedy this gap in his education at the first opportunity after he returned home. He also knew in his heart of hearts that he was equally likely to fail in the attempt as the demands of family life returned.

The last night of the trail had come all too soon. Gregor found himself early at the campsite. The three Americans were there before him and, as usual, had gone briskly and efficiently about their business. It seemed to be a well-oiled machine. He was sitting around chewing the fat with them when the mum from Edmonton arrived on her own. She unpacked and got her own tent in order and water on to boil. One by one her children appeared. They looked exhausted.

The two boys did not even remove their packs but flopped down on the pebbles and closed their eyes, mouths agape and nothing left in the tank. The girl went one better. She did get her pack off and her tent out ready to be pitched but soon she too was out of things. Meanwhile, Mum was busying herself with packets of soup and dehydrated chilli con carne. She had two pots nearly at the boil.

"Can I give you a hand?" one of the Americans asked.

"No, no, we're fine, thanks. I've just got to get some food into my kids."

So she hustled and bustled and, eventually, cajoled them awake, sat them up and gave them bowls of soup and plates of stew, a high energy dessert and a cup of hot chocolate. They were hardly rejuvenated but made slow movements to do the washing up. They were slothlike in their tent pitching. They were struggling to get their food up the bear poles. And yet all the time, their petite, wiry mother was buzzing around helping them to help themselves. Finally, all were settled and the adolescents were bedded down for the night. There was little to no chance that there would be any teenagers making too much noise in the wee sma' hours. The Americans offered her and Gregor a dram from their seemingly endless supply of whisky. She told the story of her life on the farm outside Edmonton; how she was used to hours of work that were both early and long, and late and long. She said she was proud of her children but would never allow them to surrender the work ethic that she was born to. The whisky came to an end and they all turned in.

Gregor slept in. He didn't hear the Washingtonians leave. He was not surprised at that because they were always considerate of their fellow hikers. But Gregor was surprised that the teens had been able to slip out almost unnoticed as well. But they all had.

It was 10:00 a.m before he was able finally to get himself on the road. The trail became flat and gentle as it neared the trailhead. He saw three hikers coming towards him along the straight path now shrouded with a deciduous bower. He heard snatches of their conversation and realized quickly that they were Italian. He wished them good luck as they walked past. He noted their fresh, lively steps, their energetic enthusiasm and was envious. He did, however, feel that he would not have liked to have travelled from north to south; he had done the trail the right way. A smell wafted back to Gregor as they moved away from him. At first he could not place it then he realized that it was the smell of freshly cleaned laundry, the fragrance of "Bounce."

Gregor reached the trailhead and mentally congratulated himself. Then he did what all Brits do when they complete an exercise: he sought out a café. He was ushered to a chair in the corner of this glassed-in exterior with a view out to sea. There were the Americans. At the far end of the room were the Edmontonians. Despite the time of day, Gregor ordered all that was fitting for a breakfast. While he waited, he went to his new American friends and told them how much he had enjoyed their company. He went over to the Edmontonians and offered his congratulations at their achievement. The mum beamed her appreciation.

"None of my friends' mothers would have done this," the girl said. "None of them would have dared it on their own with three children. None of them has the courage, determination and sheer toughness to have been able to do this. Oh, and none of them would have had the love."

Her brothers smiled and nodded their agreement. Gregor felt a lump in his throat and turned away.

"Out of the mouths of babes," He murmured to himself.

The bus ride back from Bamfield to Nanaimo was another scenic panorama. There had been such a plethora of images and experiences over the last week that Gregor was having trouble making sense of them all. As he dozed on the ferry after a substantial White Spot supper, he reflected that it was great to see all of that natural beauty but, inwardly, it was probably more about the restoration of his faith in humanity.

"There is one art of which people should be the master: the art of reflection."
- Samuel Taylor Coleridge

CHAPTER 29

OF MICE AND MEN

There was a boy in Gregor's homeroom class in London called Bellion Maurice. Gregor held his homeroom registration every morning in Mrs. Sheila Jefferies' typing classroom. When the children entered they sat down behind the typewriters so that Gregor could see very little of what was going on. He had remembered the approach of Sheila when she had discovered that this neophyte was going to be encroaching on her sacred space. Gregor had seen her advent coming from the far end of the staffroom. It looked to him like a sort of controlled apoplexy if there could be such thing.

"Young man, young man, I need a word!" she said.

"Old woman, old woman, I need my mother," was what Gregor thought about saying, such was the dread that he experienced.

"On no account are your children to touch the typewriters," she stormed. "This must be made clear to them from the beginning." Finger waving recrimination in anticipation of a coming fault.

Now after years of experience, he would have told her that that was a pie in the sky expectation and that they weren't going to be there long anyway. If she wanted to enforce the difficult, nay the impossible, then she would have to be in there with him. Back in those days, his salad years, he was afraid of everything.

So, he settled into his morning routine. He called their names: "Louise, Agiapal, Sherveen, Theo, Bellion," and so on. On his fourth day in his homeroom, he was calling the names as usual when he heard a deep-seated sob coming from behind one of the typewriters. He could not see who it was so stood up and walked over.

"What's up, Bellion?" he enquired solicitously. At which point the young man sobbed more deeply and finally burst into wailing tears. There was now no chance of an answer because he couldn't talk. Gregor returned to his seat at the front of the classroom. Louise, who always positioned herself next to his desk, shook her head and smiled. Gregor had taken one look at Louise on his first day and saw a streetwise cynicism, an understanding of human nature beyond her years.

"I know what's wrong with him," she said.

Gregor's interest was piqued.

"What's wrong with him, Louise?"

"His last name is 'Bellion,' his first name is 'Maurice.' All week you've been calling us by our first names and him by his last. You need to apologise."

Gregor felt his colour rise. Could it be that he had belittled this teenage boy inadvertently?

"Maurice come up and speak to me," Gregor said in his gentlest, most kindly voice. "I'm sorry I didn't know."

On the following day, Maurice was late for school. Gregor was now worried that he was going to get a parental visit complaining about the young teacher's bad behaviour towards their son. He was concerned that Maurice was now scarred for life and no longer keen to come to school. But, Maurice arrived twenty minutes late. Gregor noticed he had been crying again.

"Why are you late, Maurice?" Gregor intoned in a mock grumpy manner. "Dog ate your homework eh? Eh? Ha ha. No worries, son, I'll sign you in."

"You know why I'm late," he replied sullenly.

Gregor denied this vehemently and insisted he knew nothing. Then Maurice explained. Gregor listened and became more and more uneasy as the story unfolded

Gregor owned an ancient Morris 1300 that was held together with toothpaste and mud. It seemed to be terminally ill. Gregor cared little for its outward appearance. He hoped that it would start up in the mornings but always mentally crossed his fingers as he turned the key in the ignition. On his way to work in the morning, he always pulled over at a Newsagents shop to pick up a newspaper. On this particular morning somebody had pulled in front of him to park. Gregor had to reverse slightly to get out. He had heard a slight clunk as he edged backwards but could see nothing behind him.

"You ran over my bike, didn't ya?" Righteous indignation, indeed.

At break time Gregor went out to see Maurice's bike, and sure enough there was a mangled front wheel. Of course, Gregor paid to have it mended. It would have been nice to say that after a rocky start, Gregor and Maurice had patched things up, laughed about past demeanours and got along like a house on fire. But that was not the case. There was always an air of stand-offishness from Maurice Bellion. Similar to Inspector Clouseau's fraught relationship with his boss who developed an unfortunate tick because of his unfortunate encounters with Clouseau's careless and carefree attitude, Maurice never forgave his homeroom teacher for his bike and his surname.

Marshall often disappeared from school for days on end. As a keen young teacher, Gregor had tried to follow up with the parents, but it was to no avail. No note would be forthcoming; often the phone call home was unanswered. It wasn't as if Marshall was a star athlete in some elite programme. Gregor had asked his class to hold up their right hands one day and Marshall had held up his left. Gregor had played a game of catch with a tennis ball. IF the ball was caught then they could go out to break, but only when it was caught. Marshall was the only one left and Gregor was frustrated because it did not look like he would be getting his morning cup of coffee. No matter how gently and directly Gregor threw the ball Marshall always dropped it. Maybe Marshall could have been a top musician. Nobody would have begrudged him time out of school if he had been having a piano lesson. He wasn't. Gregor had heard him sing. He wasn't a singer, either. No, these weren't the reasons that Marshall wasn't at school.

On the Friday, after he had been absent for three days, Marshall was back. He stood in front of Gregor's desk, beaming.

"Marshall, Marshall welcome back. You look fresh and ready for action. What's that you've got there?"

"I have cupcakes for the class. May I give them out?"

"Of course you may. Marshall is coming around with his cupcakes, so make sure you thank him and that no mess is made. Sticky-fingered keyboards will be punishable by a visit from Mrs. Jefferies."

Cupcakes were given out and Gregor was munching away on a caramel and chocolate sugary number with a dusting of white icing. It was delicious. In between mouthfuls, Gregor called Marshall up to the desk again.

"Soooo, Marshall, mmmmm, where have you been for the last few days?"

"Well, me and my mum got diarrhea. Just as well we have two toilets in the house because we were in and out of there all the time. Yes, a shitty few days to say the least. 'The world falling out of our bottoms,' as my mum kept saying."

Gregor looked at his cupcake in disgust and hastily put it to one side.

"Were you feeling better when you made these?" Gregor said, pointing to his mashed up offering.

"No, not really, but it was something to do 'cos we were getting bored sitting on the toilet all day."

The rest of the class had eavesdropped into the conversation. They were vigorously throwing their cupcakes into the garbage bin at the front of the class.

They filed out of the classroom.

"Have a good weekend, boys and girls."

Miraculously on the Monday, nobody reported that they had been sick on the weekend.

One day late in the school year when the weather had taken a turn for the better, Gregor was sat in the staffroom at lunchtime. He had eaten his sandwich and was lazily reading the paper when Jim opposite him asked if he knew that Tony Hancock, the comedian, was buried just down the road in Cranford. Gregor had not known that but was immediately flashed back to the blood donor sketch from years before. Ken, the head of the Upper School, was in the group. Ken was a ferociously competitive hooker with a short fuse. Gregor had occasionally propped for him on the Saturday. He was always wary that World War III was going to start in the front row because Ken liked to slip his bindings and deliver upper cuts to the opposition. Gregor was not a pacifist, not anti-donnybrook in any way, but he would rather have just played rugby.

Johnny, the headmaster of the florid complexion and the high blood pressure, appeared at the door even more rubicund than usual.

"Ken and Gregor, get down to the playground immediately, there's trouble."

Off they rushed. On arrival, there was a circle of boys and girls formed around two boys who were in a scrap. It was more bluster than blows, so the two teachers easily pulled them apart. That wasn't the real problem. The real problem was that a young man in the middle was obviously not a part of the school population. He was in his twenties, tattooed and skinheaded, and ostensibly had come in off the street as a peacemaker. Having set aside the two miscreants, Ken went up to the outsider and asked him what he was doing on school property since he was so obviously not a part of that community.

"I was just—" was as far as he got. With one blow to the face, Ken knocked him out cold.

Gregor was dumbstruck. He looked at the crowd of teenagers and across at Ken. A girl screamed.

"What do we do now?" said Gregor, expecting Ken to call an ambulance.

"Pick him up," Ken said.

Together they picked the stranger up who was now moaning and rolling his head.

"What are we going to do with him?" Gregor was alarmed.

"We'll put him outside school property."

They dragged him backwards across the playground, through the school gates and propped him up against a wall.

"What do we do now?"

"Do?" said Ken nonchalantly. "We go and finish our coffee, that's what we do."

There was something about living and working in the London Borough of Hounslow that appealed to Gregor. Friday afternoons were the best. The gym was free after school and a group of teachers piled in there for a game of five-a-side football. Gregor was too glaikit and ponderous to have any chance of enjoying the eleven-a-side version on an open field. But here with walls to pass to and limited space for everybody to move, he was in his element. They always played until 5:30 p.m. which gave them time to shower and get over to the Queens Head which opened at 6:00 p.m. There he enjoyed the wit and cynical wisdom of Derek, the head of English and the urbane humour of Simon, the Cambridge-educated head of History. Gregor always left after an hour, thinking any longer would impact his rugby game on Saturday afternoon. He thought that he was really serious about bettering his rugby but now in the 21ˢᵗ century that seriousness would have translated into no alcohol on the night before a game.

On the Monday morning after the weekend, they were slowly filtering into the staffroom with an air of Monday Blahs. The Reverend Jonathan Williams, a very, very Welsh chaplain, looked particularly down.

"What's up padre?" jollied Jim Maguire as he poured himself a cup of coffee. "Sunday not the highlight that it should have been in your profession?"

"A verrry, verrry sad weekend in our house, boyo. Look you, a favourite aunt of mine died suddenly. She's going to be buried on Saturday so I have to ask for Friday off. Terribly, terribly sad."

Jim's demeanour changed to one of sympathetic concern. He put his arm around Jonathon's shoulders.

"So sorry to hear that, my friend. Let me know if I can help out with you classes on Friday."

So it was that all week, people were coming up to the Reverend and offering him their thoughts. Gregor was watching this and while outwardly sympathetic, he could not overcome his inner cynicism that suggested Jonathan was milking his grief from all and sundry. It came about that the funeral was to be at 2:00 p.m. on Saturday afternoon in the town of Neath.

"Huge funeral. Absolutely massive, Derek. Bronwyn was much loved in the community. The town is devastated."

The following afternoon Gregor played his game of rugby. He was looking forward to having a pint after the game and watching the highlights of the England v. Wales game that had taken place in Cardiff that afternoon. He was sat in a corner of the bar with his front row buddies, Paul and Dick. The game was back and forth, both sides swapping scores. Late in the first half, the Welsh went over for a much-needed try. The camera panned across the jubilant crowd. Gregor had to do a double take for there in the thick of it, one arm draped around a fellow countryman, the other with a pint raised in triumph, red Wales scarf askew around his neck, was the Reverend Jonathan Williams who only a short time ago had buried his auntie in the town of Neath some distant drive away. There he was at Cardiff Arms Park celebrating a Welsh score with his mates.

As Gregor entered the school on the Monday, he wondered if anybody else had seen what he had seen. It was obvious from the buzz and hilarity in the staffroom that they had. After bantering back and forth, Gregor asked the question.

"Sooo, where is he?"

"That's the beauty," guffawed Jim. "He's stuck in Neath because the uncle needs him to stay and comfort him. He phoned in and took an extra day off!"

The bell went and the chuckling throng went off to teach.

"Initium est dimidium facti (Once you've started you're halfway there.)"
- Latin Proverb.

S C O T L A N D   A G A I N

When Gregor was 17 years old in 1969, he had to attend cadet camp at R.A.F. Consett in the county of Durham. It was compulsory for students at his boarding school to do some time on a Friday afternoon in the Combined Cadet Force (C.C.F.). It was basically drill on a tennis court, the occasional excitement when they had the chance to fire a gun at a target. The trip to R.A.F. Filton near Bristol where they were taken up in a two seater chipmunk and flew over the Bristol Channel and back again was the best part. R.A.F. Consett was to be the last hurrah of Gregor's time in the R.A.F. cadets. Gregor could not wait to get out of the prickly rash-giving uniform. Gregor could take these experiences or leave them. He was not going to join the military, so he endeavoured to fly under the radar even when he was not up in an aeroplane.

Gregor decided to celebrate his last camp by not going back to school with his fellow "airmen" but by having his bike with him. He would go by train to Edinburgh and bike up north where he would meet the rest of the family for their annual Scottish holiday. But before that they all had to get through camp. Gregor was somewhat startled to discover the presence of R.S.M. Christian on the bus heading north. Regimental Sergeant Major Fred Christian was a retired soldier from the Parachute Regiment. He had not achieved his rank in that most elite of regiments without being as tough as old boots and being an excellent judge of character.

Therefore, where Gregor was often able to background his presence by hiding in plain view in front of some of the teachers who strutted their stuff as officers, there was *no* hiding place from the R.S.M. He had once singled him out in the ranks as being a skiver. The fact that he did so with a smile on his face did not reassure Gregor. He had believed that he had remained unnoticed. He was now very nervous every Friday in expectation of a dire consequence from that smirk of weeks previously.

The bus journey to Camp Consett was long and boring. Conversation with friends and familiars soon died. It is pretty difficult to engage too long with people whom one has already spent so much time. Cards and books came out. Gregor always became car sick if he read or had to put his head down to play a card. So, he pulled off his sweater and used it to cushion his head against the window. If sleep came that would be fine. If it didn't he could make plans for his trip in his head. Sleep came quickly.

There is something inevitably eccentric about the officer class in the British military. They are either all action and practical, people one would want at one's back in a battle. There are others who have a plum in their mouths and likely the plum stone for a brain. Gregor pinpointed the latter who stood before them in the Assembly Hall at Consett to welcome them. They had all been instructed to stand silently to attention when Flying Lieutenant Hyphen-Name stood before them. He did have the most glorious moustache, Gregor admitted to himself. It was long and thin. It protruded in a line to a point about six inches from either cheek. It had to have been waxed if it was to hold its shape. Gregor, who was frequently thinking of sex in those days, wondered how any self-respecting girl could have the slightest interest in somebody who cultivated the most anachronistic style. But Gregor was a child of the 1960s so it was all Sergeant Pepper, tie dye t-shirts, long hair and attitude. The oration had started to drone. It was all about the speaker's service in the R.A.F., how teenagers all needed to be broken before they could be built up and moulded into men.

"Now then chaps, for example, I am going to put one of you on the spot here and test your character. I am going to ask one of you to come up to the podium here and talk for three minutes about the word 'If.' It shouldn't be too difficult for you to do. Well educated, well brought up, don't you know? Any volunteers?"

There was silence in the hall. Gregor slumped lower into his seat. He was in the third row in the middle. He was thankful the cadet in front of him was tall. He sat up straight with naïve innocence on the back of his neck and, no doubt, an eagerness to please patently evident on his hidden features. Gregor was confident that if he also rested his head on his chest he would also remain unnoticed. Suddenly, he caught the remarkable shape of R.S.M. Christian striding down the aisle to the front of the hall. There he was, chest puffed out with windy pride, a chest that was emblazoned with medals on an immaculate uniform with knife edge creases. His boots were mirrored and glittering. Even the limp-jawed officer stepped back from the podium. He recognized greatness when he saw it.

"Sergeant Major, you have the floor."

Christian saluted with precision and marched up onto the stage and stood before the audience. "Thank you, Sir."

His eyes searched the room. Gregor realized with horror that he was searching for somebody in particular in the crowd. Suddenly, Gregor felt his steely gaze upon him.

"Private MacCrimmon, march up here at the double."

Gregor's mouth opened in abject terror. There was a flock of butterflies suddenly active in the pit of his stomach. He had a sudden urge to visit the toilet. But he had no choice, other than humiliation, but to step forward into the aisle and march up there. Gregor surprised himself by leaping to his feet and brushing past the bemused but relieved cadets in the row.

"You have the podium, MacCrimmon," Christian said, stepping aside. "Remember, the topic is 'If.'"

"Yes, Sergeant Major."

Gregor gripped the sides of the podium, looked at the sea of faces before him, looked again at his knuckles and saw that they were growing white with the tension.

"You have three minutes to talk about 'If' starting now."

R.S.M. Christian clicked on a stopwatch.

"Errr, 'If' is really a very little word."

Silence. Nothing further emanated from either Gregor's mind or his mouth. He shifted from one foot to the other, he ran his hand through his hair, he looked down and rubbed his furrowing brow. Eventually, the silence was too much for R.S.M. Christian.

"Let me start you off," he said, turning to face the audience. "If me aunt had testicles she'd be me uncle. Over to you MacCrimmon."

Something came over Gregor. He realized that, barring a call up for an unforeseen war, he was never going to put on a military uniform again.

"I don't care any more," he muttered to himself.

He gripped the podium again, raised his head and looked at the faces of his fellow cadets.

"*If* R.S.M. Christian had not hauled me up here I would be sat in my seat thinking about my upcoming holiday in Scotland. If I was still sat in the middle of you on row C, I would be a happy man. But happiness is a fly that flits *if* it is not caught and used quickly. Who knows how many 'Ifs' you and I are going to be faced with in our lives. If I had not come to this school I would never have met R.S.M. Christian. Just imagine what a tragedy that would be if we would never have met the Sergeant. We would not have had the benefit of his testicular wisdom. We would be wandering through life aimlessly wondering whether all our aunties were uncles, indeed we would be confused about our parents, our grandparents, our brothers and sisters. Indeed, we may well be confused about the gender of R.S.M. Christian, not of course that he may be our aunt or our uncle but whether or not he has balls. I can say this for certain, gentlemen, that if all of those medals represent the courage that we think they represent then this is a great man. *If* this man's fitness and tough as teak demeanour are what we think they are then this is a great man. *If* we did not feel that he cared for us greatly and that he would have our backs in a crisis then we would not be where we are today. *If* you believe that this man is a wonderful judge of character young and old, this is a great man. Finally *if you believe in the strength* and goodness of R.S.M. Christian I would ask you to stand to attention and salute him now."

Gregor stood back from the podium, stood to attention and saluted smartly. There was hesitation in the crowd before him but eventually several stood and others followed until they were all standing rigidly to attention. Gregor turned away from the podium and, without meeting any possible gaze from the R.S.M., marched briskly back to his seat. He sat down and looked at his feet. The officer had returned to his seat and was speaking. Gregor was immersed in his own thoughts and heard not a word.

"Shot at dawn," he thought to himself. "Brief interrogation. Marched out, blindfolded and shot. That's what will happen to me."

They were marched out of the hall by some trainees and shown to their quarters. Gregor unpacked carefully. He noted that his schoolmates were silent.

"Probably don't want to be linked to me in any way," he thought.

They had an hour to kill before supper, so most simply lay on their beds and chatted quietly to their friends. Gregor busied himself, not because he had things to busy himself with but because busyness distracted him from when the gavel would fall. Sure enough, there was the unmistakable sound of Christian's boots approaching. There he was standing at the entrance of the dormitory.

"Private MacCrimmon," he roared, "A word outside."

Gregor swallowed. "Yes, Sarn't."

He laced up his boots, put on his beret and marched out of the dormitory. He found the R.S.M. having a cigarette at the edge of the playground.

"Were you frightened when I called you up, MacCrimmon?"

"Absolutely bloody terrified, Sergeant Major," said Gregor.

He blinked at this, smiled as if to himself. He gathered his thoughts. His eyes winkled impishly.

"Most of those things you said about me are untrue except for one. I do have balls. I may not be a great judge of character except on one occasion. I made the judgment that there was good stuff in you Gregor MacCrimmon and I was proved right today. Dismissed."

And he turned away, still smoking his cigarette, and marched off towards the Sergeant's mess.

Camp Consett was over. Gregor had shot his gun. Gregor had been on an arduous day hike with his peers, meeting the teachers in charge at an idyllic rural Northumbrian pub. Now he was lined up with Squadron Leader MacEwan-Mason to get a train warrant to get him to Edinburgh's Waverley Station. It was odd to him to be standing there in a queue with a teacher whom he respected so much. Through his experiences at school he found it hard to imagine that his teachers would ever have to line-up with the hoi polloi to buy something as banausic as a train ticket. Of course, when Gregor became a teacher he would experience from the other side what it was like to have a nine-year-old look in amazement when Gregor was discovered in a supermarket grocery shopping. To most children of that age, a teacher was an alien being who was put in storage at the end of the day and released in the morning to give forth of their wisdom. Yet there he was, this most humane of teachers, standing with his teenage student, perfectly at ease with the great unwashed.

The ticket was bought. Gregor stood there with his bike and panniers ready to travel through the ticket barrier. The Squadron Leader stood there, too. He had said nothing to Gregor in the line. Gregor himself had been too frightened to strike up a conversation, so there had been an uneasy silence from him and a relaxed aura surrounding his teacher.

"Have fun on your trip and be careful, MacCrimmon."

"Yes, Sir. Err, thank you, Sir."

He smiled, raised his hand, turned and walked away.

Gregor managed his bike into the guard's van, found a compartment and settled himself at a window seat. The train lurched its slow start out of the station. Gregor settled in to glory in his aloneness, to look out of the window as the remnants of Newcastle were left behind and he found himself looking out at the fields of rural England and the brown swell of the North Sea. The weather cooperated and the sun glittered off the sparkling scenes as they edged, then sped, towards Berwick and the Scottish Border. "O'er the border and awa" as the song would have it.

Gregor reflected on how ill-prepared he was for this bike ride. He had no idea where he was going to spend his first night. He *did* have all of the equipment he needed for cooking and shelter. He *did* know that there were enough hours in the day to be able to bike out of Edinburgh and make some headway towards the Highlands. He had no timeline other than he had promised his Gran in Aberdeen a visit. That was for the future, he was careless of that commitment for the moment.

The train slowed and edged into the familiar old facades of Waverley Station. Its arrival never failed to produce a relaxed sigh of pleasure from Gregor. He retrieved his bike from the guard's van and walked it up the steep hill out of the station. He turned right at the top and soon merged in the hustle and bustle of Princes Street. Wary of the traffic but eager to be on his way, he had a quick glance at the Scott Monument. He peered up at the castle and down at his bike. There was a great deal to be seen in this beautiful city, but it could wait for a different time. He mounted his bike and entered the traffic flow heading northwards. It took him some time to reach the northern suburbs of the metropolis. It was with a sigh of relief when he finally reached the city boundaries and looked back at the "Welcome to Edinburgh" sign that was now to his south. The structure of the Forth Road Bridge and its railway twin with its very distinctive shape next to it, the old and the new, loomed in the near distance.

The uphill part of the bridge caused Gregor to sweat and the downhill part on the other side caused him to chill. The crosswind was gentle enough to cause little problem but forceful enough to occasionally cause him to have to correct his line of progress. He had reached the other side and had started his movement up the M9, when there was a siren and blue flashing light behind him. At first he thought that the police were giving chase to a car that had been so obviously breaking the speed limit when it had barreled past him a few seconds previously. He was surprised, therefore, when it pulled in front of him and stopped. It had blocked his way but, nothing daunted, he had watched for a gap in the traffic, pulled out and overtook it. Yet again there was the siren and the blue light and the police car overtook him. It pulled over but this time a policeman got out of the driver's side of the car, put his hand up and ordered him to stop. Gregor had no choice but to do as he was bid.

The policeman was not happy.

"Did ye think ye could outrun us?" The accent was obviously from the Kingdom of Fife.

"No, no, officer. I thought you were going after somebody else."

The other policeman appeared from the passenger side door. From behind his peaked cap, he looked Gregor's bike up and down.

"I hope that there is nothing wrong with my bike," Gregor stammered. "I had it checked over recently and it seems perfectly roadworthy."

"Naething wrang wi' the bike. An awfy lot wrang wi' you," said the driver.

"Dae ye know ken the bikes are forbidden on the motorway?" said the passenger policeman.

Gregor reddened as he always did when addressed by authority and he knew he was in the wrong.

"I'm sorry, officer. I didn't know. Ummm, how do I get off the motorway?"

The officer looked sympathetic. "We'll follow ye. Tak the firrrst exit."

And so it was that after the police car had led him off the road and Gregor had waved his thanks. Noting that the wave was not returned, Gregor found his way to the A9. He pushed hard on the pedals and in the late afternoon, pulled up outside a tea shop. He entered to the ringing of the bell on the door. He found no customers and nobody behind the counter. There was a noise behind the plastic curtain strips and soon a little old lady appeared. She was slightly stooped, wore a tweed skirt with an apron and sensible shoes.

"Well, laddie, whit can I dae fur ye?" she said.

"May I have a pot of tea and a Mars bar please?"

"Awa' outside and sit in the sun and I'll bring it out."

Gregor found himself on a bench beside the road. He took in his surroundings. There was little to tell anybody that where he was sitting was a café. There was one small sign that separated it from being an old stone house. There was a well-cultivated flower garden attached to the south end. To the north was a view of the Highlands. He doubted that he would make it there this evening. Maybe a foothill or a gentle upland but not the full-blown Drumochter Pass effect that he knew was to be a long, tiring uphill ride. His tea arrived and was placed on the bench next to him.

"May I join you?"

It was not really a question. She nipped into the building and brought out a chair. For somebody so obviously late in life, she moved surprisingly quickly.

"Well now, tell me about yourself. Off for a wee bit of a ride I see."

So, Gregor talked about his time at school, his camp at Consett and his visit to his relatives in Nairn and Aberdeen.

"So, how long have you lived here?" he eventually asked.

"All of my life. I was born in this house," she said.

She then told her story. Her father had been the local postman, her mother had worked the house and garden. The garden had been several acres back then. They had grown vegetables and sold them from their front door. It had been a simple life, monetarily not rich, but rich in love and laughter. She had attended the local school and later travelled farther to the secondary school. There she had met the love of her life. Three days before the outbreak of war in September 1939 she had married him. After a week's honeymoon on the Fife coast, he had joined up to fight. He never returned from Dunkirk. It was a short but loving relationship. It had produced a son. Now in 1969, he was gone from her as well. Gone to seek his fortune in New Zealand. She sighed.

"Have you seen him since he left?"

She sighed. "Three years now he's been gone. I hear from him, of course. He's working on a sheep farm on the South Island. He says he's fine and happy."

"Will you visit him?"

"No, I'll nae dae that, laddie. This is the only world I've known and it's the only world I'll ever know." She jumped up suddenly and grasped the teapot. "Mair tea?"

"I should be on my way but—why not? Yes, I will."

Pleased, she disappeared into the shop and Gregor got out his map.

She returned. "You should put your map away for the night. Stay here. You can use my son's room and I'll cook you a better supper than you can cook for yourself. You've had a busy time o't. You look tired. I've enjoyed our chat and I would be happy for it to continue. Please stay."

Gregor licked his lips. His legs were tired, it was true, but—staying in the house of a complete stranger? He conjured up an image of Hansel and Gretel in the forest but quickly put it out of his mind.

"Do you smell that?" she asked.

"Yes, I do."

"That's your bacon and eggs cookin'. Come awa' ben and settle yoursel' in. I'll no tak no for an answer. First, follow me around the side of the hoose wi' yer bike and we'll go in."

Gregor followed. She opened the garden shed. She moved some tools. He placed his bike safely inside. He removed his panniers. She locked the door and in they went. It was a meal fit for a king, let alone a starving cyclist. Lashings of bacon, three fried eggs, baked beans, black pudding, potatoes and as much toast as he could eat. Gregor ate ravenously. Maggie, his new friend, tucked in to a much, much lesser portion. The dining room was the living room. It was low-ceilinged, had a fireplace and a mantel that was covered in pictures, more of her son than her husband. Her wedding day had pride of place, however.

Dinner over, Gregor washed the dishes despite the protestation that "'Nae man daes that." Gregor explained that it was a new world and she finally gave up with a smile. She lit up the fire "Not because we need it, ye ken, but it is hamely." She reached across to an ancient drinks cabinet and emerged with a half-consumed bottle of Glenfiddich. She only ever opened it when she had guests and had had the bottle for six years, she explained. Not many guests at all then. She disappeared into the hallway and came back with a photograph album.

"Ye'll earn your night o' rest by listening to an auld wifie talk about her past," she smiled mischievously.

It was not difficult for Gregor to become engaged in the reminiscence, as he found it fascinating. The black and white pictures leapt off the page at him. There she was, wee Maggie, with her satchel of books, walking up the street with her mother to the school. There again her new husband and her on honeymoon at Burntisland on the Fife coast. The old motor cars, the large vegetable garden, the pictures of her friends.

"Who's that?" Gregor asked as yet another picture of the same young girl kept recurring.

Maggie sighed. "That's my best friend, Nan. All through school we were inseparable. She was a bridesmaid at my wedding. I miss her."

"Where is she?"

"She married an American airman and went off to the U.S.A. I never heard from her again. She spoke Gaelic you know."

"Did she not write?"

"Aye, aye, she did write but I never received her letters. Then one day about 10 years ago I received a knock at the door. There stood a strapping young man with beautiful teeth, well-groomed hair and a smart suit. His name was Sandy and he was American. He came in, we had a cuppa and a chat. He explained that he was Nan's son and he had a package for me. Nan had died of cancer the previous year. She had made Sandy promise that he would visit her old friend within a year of her death. After he had left I opened the letters for that is what they were and speculated why she had never sent them to me. They were beautiful, well-written stories of her new life in the New World. She had moved to Upstae New York and become a farmer's wife. Her life had been full and happy until one day the tractor rolled over and killed her husband. Had it not been for her son and his friends and his schooling she would have returned to Scotland then. She had not sent the letters because I would have written back and the homesickness would have been too much for her and she would have come home. I think that this was a tragedy and I am sorry for it."

They finished their dram. Despite his resistance Maggie poured another.

"A deuch an' dorris afore bed," she explained.

The breakfast was equally as splendid as the supper. As he retrieved his bike from the shed, Maggie pressed a package of sandwiches on his hand and a piece of paper and he was away.

"That's my address. You'll pay for the hospitality by sending an auld bodach a postcard on occasions?" Her eyes twinkled.

"Sure and all, I will."

"Aye, I ken you will because that is who you are." She reached up, pecked him on the cheek. "Get awa' wi' ye afore the neighbours start wagging their tongues."

Gregor cycled well that day. He was soon in the hills. Rising up through Dunkeld and Pitlochry, Gregor knew that he was going to face an uphill battle. Blair Atholl and Killiecrankie were gentle slopes compared to what was ahead. The first drops of rain came as no surprise, the skies had darkened soon after he had left the café. Gregor hated riding in his waterproofs. He would just as soon have allowed his bare legs to get wet and suffered the consequences of being soaked but he had heard the mantra "Cotton kills in the hills" while on outdoor trips with the school and taken it very much to heart. So he stopped and donned his wet weather gear aware that it was also going to restrict the fluidity of his movements on the bike. The rain came down like stair rods. Just as it did so, the wind got up. So now Gregor was biking into the rain and wind and with a long way to go. He stopped and sought shelter in a wooded area, hoping that the deluge would weaken. He managed to make himself a cup of tea with his little cooker and ate Maggie's cheese, onion and pickle sandwiches. He did notice an easing thereafter, or maybe that was wishful thinking brought on by the sandwiches, but there was nothing for it but to continue on his way.

The wind did not cooperate as much as the rain had done, but he was making slow progress. About 4:00 p.m. it came on heavily. Gregor's legs and back were crying out for rest. So he found a copse situated between the road and the railway, slipped down the bank and found himself a flattish base near a flooding burn. Gregor smiled ruefully at the knowledge that he had plenty of fresh water with which to cook. He could have done without the water all day but he was certainly grateful for it now. He found shelter for his cooker behind a rock, sat on a rock opposite and brewed a kettle from which he added to the food and the teacup. It looked like it would be a wet night, but he had at least found shelter from the wind. There was something very comforting about the proximity of the railway line. Sure enough as he crawled into his sleeping bag that night the clatter of a train reminded him that he was never very far from warmth and comfort in this little stretch of wilderness.

He was a reluctant riser from his tent in the morning. The rain still battered down on his tent. He, however, managed to get his sleeping bag packed away dry. The tent was sodden and there was no possibility of drying it. He packed it away as best he could and pushed his bike up the hill. He mounted and headed northwards. The wind and rain were still against him as was the slope, but he had no intention of travelling quickly. He was quite content to push forward no matter how slowly. He did not count how many kilometres he was covering per hour; there would have been no point. Dalwhinnie was his goal and anything farther would be a bonus.

It was sometime after lunch that the road became gentler and the wind seemed to ease. The slopes of the hills on either side seemed to be closer and their tops to be nearer. The road was also bending slightly more eastwards. Around the next corner was the hope of a sign and the next and the next, an interminable longing for a mile marker was upon him. Gregor's legs throbbed, his lungs burned, painful chaffing was starting to become a problem. Then the sign appeared: "Dalwhinnie." There was no "Welcome to Dalwhinnie," no "Home of the Famed Dalwhinnie Whisky," no "Britain in Bloom" victory parade. It was just "Dalwhinnie." But Gregor did feel welcome because Gregor would have felt welcome at any little nook of habitation at this point. He pulled into the garage. He walked in and bought himself four Mars bars and a bottle of Coke.

"Miserable day," he said by way of conversation to the waterproofed middle-aged lady at the cash desk.

"We like it," she replied with no hint of irony.

He had turned a corner on his trip both literally and metaphorically. Now the rain had eased but the wind hadn't. Now the wind was behind him and he was heading downhill to Newton More and a campsite and, he hoped, a shower.

The psychological effect of the wind at one's back can be huge. Gregor flew down to Newton More with a song on his lips and a light in his heart. He saw the campsite nestling by the river and the railway just before the entrance to the village. He swept over the bridge, veered to the right, turned in just before the village sign. He looked around the campsite, which was fairly empty, and picked himself a spot a little bit back from the river and the railway. It was dry when he pitched his tent. He hoped that the rain would hold off and that the wind would continue so that the sodden canvas had some hope of drying out. It was the fickleness of fatigue that had changed the wind into a friend from being an adversary. He was able to rummage around the site and found a little bit of a shower block, unspectacular though it was. He ventured his towel and wash bag and headed off to give it a try. It was not as warm as he would have liked but it did get him clean. After he had towelled himself off, he stretched out in his tent and found some dry gear. He was able to find heat and lay in his sleeping bag in the afternoon, happily reading his book.

The following day, Gregor headed down the road to Kingussie. This little village was going to come to hold a special place in Gregor's heart. Two years or so later, Gregor was to live with his grandmother in Nairn and work for the Nairnshire Laundry. His Monday morning route as a van boy for Donald Mathieson would take him up through Aviemore, Carrbridge, Boat of Garten, Grantown-on-Spey, Nethybridge, Kincraig and so forth. Donald and he would spend the night at Columba House B & B on the hillside on the Inverness side of the village. Gregor would not go to the pub with Donald, who loved to spend his Monday evenings hanging out in a local hostelry with the network of friends he had built up over his years in the Laundry. But that was down the road in a few years time for Gregor. Down the road for him now was Aviemore. He found himself turning right just before the famed ski resort village of Aviemore and heading towards Cairngorm and Loch Morlich. He pulled in to a campsite just after the Coylumbridge Hotel.

July 20, 1969 was a date that Gregor would remember for the rest of his days. In subsequent visits to this very campsite, he would remember buying the *New Scientist* magazine and numerous newspapers on the following day. Gregor would always remember that he was resting his weary head in this campsite when man first landed on the moon.

"One small step for man, one giant bike ride for Gregor MacCrimmon," he had thought on the day after as he headed out of Aviemore towards Grantown-on-Spey and upwards to Tomintoul, the highest village in the U.K.

As a child, Gregor had loved the story of *The Lost World* by Arthur Conan Doyle. It was a tale of a high, isolated plateau in South America that had suddenly been thrown upwards, isolating the animal population. It had become a throwback, peopled by prehistoric dinosaurs, a raison d'etre for Professor Challenger and his expedition. Gregor could never ascend any plateau without thinking of it as being a lost world of sorts, a place of isolation above the world of the hoi polloi and the great unwashed. He imagined that a winter spent in Tomintoul would be a place of splendid isolation, a white wilderness of chill and bracing cold with cosy cottages huddled around each other for comfort and warmth. Neighbours would be real neighbours, ever welcoming and helpful. The local pub would have an open fire and seats for the regulars, a dart board, a pool table and perhaps, sadly, a juke box.

Gregor knew enough about life to know that one man's idyll was another man's trouble. He had read once that nobody saw a piece of art in the same way. The *Mona Lisa* might be the smile but one can never put oneself into the eyes of another human being. So there would have been local youth in Tomintoul who could not wait to get into the adventure of the Boer, First, and Second World Wars; to escape the mundane and the routine. Having seen those horrors they probably could not wait to return to their little village on the plateau and never leave it again. Gregor had also read about the spirit of "sehnsucht," the "seeking to see" of explorers that became the sword with the double edge. One side couldn't wait to get into the wider world and see what was out there, wheras at the same time experiencing an overwhelming desire to return home. There they would arrive, and joyously greet, and jovially celebrate, and after a few days would experience the overwhelming desire to be away and exploring again. Like Tennyson's Ulysses always roaming with a hungry heart never able to be still and settled.

Gregor arrived in the middle of the village and its large green and its surrounds of trees. He saw the wonderful stone houses, the old hotel, the museum and the gentle tranquility of the scene. It brought up in him a feeling of ecstatic joy.

The Lecht road which skirts the Cairngorm National Park and leads past the ski hill was and is in Gregor's opinion one of the most beautiful in Scotland. Gregor accepted that he might be biased because it lead him into the county of his birth. Aberdeenshire is really a most diverse county. It has a rich farming tradition in the north, it has the fishing ports of Fraserburgh and Aberdeen. Since the 1970s it has had the oil industry. It has the Peterhead Prison. It has the royal connection with Balmoral and the so-called Royal Deeside, which includes so much that is beautiful on the banks of the Dee. Braemar, Banchory, Aboyne, Linn of Dee, all nestled beneath the grand rugged peaks and plateau of the Cairngorm National Park. Scots Pine stands, heather sometimes blooming and many different sights just as intriguing. The wildlife of deer, ptarmigan and grouse, squirrels and eagles, a plethora of different views inspired Gregor to believe that there still was hope for the wild places in this very crowded island of Great Britain. There were castles, too, not just for the royals but also Colgarff, an isolated garrison baronial-style stratagem constructed to prevent any repeat of the '15 and '45 rebellions. The Jacobite Risings of the 1700s had instituted a cultural purge that only just fell short of ethnic cleansing. It was an attempt to destroy the clan way of life by proscribing the Gaelic language and forbidding the kilt. It may be argued that they almost succeeded with the first but failed miserably with the latter judging by the number of kilts that appear at English weddings these days. Gregor's favourite campsite, however, was in his favourite town, Ballater. It was there that he was headed.

The sun kissed the land as he rode out of Tomintoul. There were enough cotton wool-shaped cumuli to suggest that the weather would remain fair but that there would be interludes of shade and shadow. Gregor resolved to stop every 30 minutes or so even though his teenage instinct was always to push on towards completion. This day was to be cherished. Little glens, burns and broom, the nooks and crannies of the hills were not to be rushed.

Savouring the smells of the heather, Gregor was stripped down to his shorts and sleeveless shirt. He looked like a throwback to the early 1900s. He could have been a poster boy for *Scouting for Boys*, the old Baden-Powell bible that was filled with such useful advice as battering underwear with a rock to make it clean. Gregor had dipped into bits of the book when at school and had learned among other things that sex was bad for boys! Gregor had wondered when reading this at what point in one's life sex became good. Presumably if it was always bad then human beings were doing wrong by perpetuating the species. Gregor had sought answers to this at school but they were not forthcoming. Sex talks had been from the biology teacher who dispassionately introduced the subject by explaining that he could teach the "plumbing." Presumably this meant that there was an emotional side to the "business" as well but no teacher in a boarding house in the 1960s was going to broach that. Gregor and his fellow boarders had held out more hope when a lady arrived in a tweed suit and brogues to further explain the mysteries of something they did not understand. The seriousness of the topic had been lost when the lady climbed onto the dining room table and explained while kneeling on all fours that this was how Peruvian women gave birth. Gregor and his buddies had really wanted to know what was causing them to stay awake at night and why their eyes were drawn inevitably to the shapes of pretty girls as they passed on the way to class at school. To this there was no answer. Gregor turned his thoughts and eyes back to the panoramas before him.

Each bend in the road seemed to produce some new spectacular panorama, craggy peaks with their minatory dominance, the occasional green field carved out of the heather, eventually the Lecht ski hill. Gregor parked his bike amongst the buildings and detritus of the winter resort. There was nobody about. Cabled t-bars swung gently in the breeze. Lifts on either side of the road, fenced off areas and runs that were so short compared to the ones that Gregor had experienced in Europe that Gregor wondered how it would have been worth it. To drive to the Lecht or Glenshee, the other ski hill to the south of them, for a day on the slopes and then drive out again, would require a real passion for one's sport. Yet here was this business clinging to life, ineluctably optimistic that the snow would come and with it the people. It seemed to be a fragile premise for success. The occasional car passed as he was nosing around, but none of them stopped. Gregor returned to his bike and continued downhill.

Colgarff Castle came into view. It was perched on the side of a hill. It's position was suggestive of the confidence of the time. It was not strategically placed to withstand siege or attack. There was no moat, no ditch, no real attempt to have the high ground with all enemies below. Sure, there was what passed for a keep, but far from being an inner sanctum the keep was the castle and the castle was the keep. No, Gregor thought, this castle was built to subdue a population that had already been subdued. This was here to assert a presence, stamp an authority that was already ascendant. There was no need for this other than lordly arrogance. On he rode to the village of Colnabaichin where he turned right for Ballater rather than straight on for Aboyne. Now the rural aspect of the road was more tree cover, mostly deciduous, the verdure was more verdant, the burns had joined hands to form a river, the views were closer but no less interesting. The road was narrower and windier, more undulating than forever heading downwards. Gregor needed to be more aware of traffic ahead and behind because most of the time they were unseen until they rounded the bends. Soon, he emerged at the Bridge of Gairn and was able to turn left and make the short ride into Ballater.

Queen Victoria and Prince Albert brought notice and a railway to the small town of Ballater. Gregor loved the grey granite stone buildings that led into the town. Wealth seemed to ooze from every pore. Yet Gregor could not understand where the wealth came from. No factories seemed to be there. Certainly there were hotels and tourist shops, cafes and bakeries, the odd restaurant, but no heavy industry, no woolen mills. Gregor was at a loss. Gregor craved fudge.

Gregor always craved fudge on his travels. At any other time, the sweet, sugary tablet quickly over-sweetened him so that only one piece would do. As he walked into the newsagent, peopled with magazines and books about royalty, Gregor saw the familiar packets of home-made fudge on the counter. He bought himself a couple of newspapers—two because the headlines and stories were all about the moon landings. Such occasions were those where he would keep them as souvenirs of an historic event and his campsite at Coylumbridge. He picked up his bag of fudge and paid for his purchases. He left the shop and walked his bike the few short steps to the village green where he found a bench next to the war memorial and vacuumed up his sweet treat and the stories in the paper. Gregor could think of nothing better to do than to get to the campsite, pitch his tent and set up his sleeping bag and mat outside his porch and laze away the rest of the afternoon reading, and writing in his journal. He walked his bike off the green and towards the golf course at the south end of the village, which he knew was next to the river and the campsite.

Gregor enjoyed his guilty pleasures but after a repast of beans on toast he decided to assuage his guilt by walking out of the town and climbing the hill of Craigdarroch. This he knew would give him a spectacular view of both the town and the River Dee. "The Hill of The Oaks" was exactly that: a gentle walk upwards through a deciduous woodland. Gregor saw more people coming down than going up, possibly because of the lateness of the hour. Although 6:00 p.m. was not late at all when in the north, darkness was but a short interval in the play of daylight.

Gregor noticed how easily he climbed. Long days in the saddle had strengthened his stamina and his legs although he noticed that he was using different leg muscles while climbing. Gregor understood what his rugby coaches had called "game fitness." One could train and run as much as one liked but there was nothing like playing a match, competing for every ball, pushing in every scrum and following the play around the field. It was that one was not thinking about one's fitness when climbing Drumochter Pass but one was thinking about getting to the top of the hill, watching for every nuance in the view, craning one's eyes to see the beginnings of Loch Ericht or the edge of the next village. This should not have been news to Gregor Mitchell MacCrimmon but there was always a side of Gregor that remained gullible and naïve. It endeared him to many but frustrated more. As he descended and walked back to the campsite, it was time for Gregor to head to Aberdeen and knock on his Grannie's door. She was expecting him. He knew that he would be greeted with a soft bed and a substantial supper. He would be spoiled. He had forgotten when the rest of the family were arriving in Nairn but presumed that he had a few days leeway before he would have to head off to the "Brighton of the North" as that small town on the Moray Firth was affectionately, albeit incongruously, called.

Ringing his Gran's doorbell in Aberdeen was always pleasant. She came downstairs from her upstairs flat, slim, trim, well turned out and freckled.

"Come away in, Gregor, and let's get you a cuppa tea. You're a strappin' loon and no mistake," she said.

Well spoken Doric but indubitably Aberdeenshire none the less. Gregor had spoken like his Grannie until the age of eight then morphed into an English that was middle class and bland. The jury was out as to why the Aberdeenshire dialect had come to be called the "Doric." After all, there was little that was Greek about it; indeed it had more French words in it than anything else. "Corbie" for "crow," "ashette" for "large plate" were surely the French words "corbeau" and "assiette," bastardized certainly but a seeming fit nevertheless. One possibility for the "Doric" moniker went back to the period of Scotland's enlightenment when Edinburgh had been christened the "Athens of the North," so the suggestion was that the language of the countryside was rural Greek therefore Doric. Whatever it was, Gran had opened the gate and was leading him and his bike around to the back where there was a strip of walled garden in which he could safely stable his horse.

"Up the stairs with ye. Were you needin' a bath? Plenty of hot water. Let's have tea and a biscuit first."

Gregor had yet to speak, there was no edgeways with which to get a word in. He was ushered into the cosy, well-lit lounge with its photographs and pictures. Gran liked to paint and occasionally did so on ceramic, so there was a scene of an Austrian church with an alp in the background on a tile-topped table onto which Gregor's tea and biscuits were to be placed. Photographs of her children were on the mantlepiece. Pride of place was a young man, a teenager, slightly built, handsome in his boyish way with an intelligent twinkle in his eye and humour in his demeanour. This was Gregor's Uncle Billy dressed in his R.A.F. uniform, possibly nudging his 20th birthday but not much older. Gregor knew that he had not made it to his 21st birthday because he was shot down and killed over Italy in late 1944, a tragic Christmas memory for a mother who had already been widowed in 1929.

"So, tell me about your trip. Is there a Highland lassie that's kept you from your Grannie for so long?"

Gregor recounted his travels. Rarely had he had such an interested audience. There were questions at times but they were rare. There were nods of understanding, smiles of wisdom and all the time the focus and concentration which, Gregor knew, made the speaker feel as if he were the only person in the world during those moments.

Gregor took his bath and left his dirty clothing outside the bathroom as requested.

"Can't have you turning up in Nairn and presenting that Grannie with work. **She's** far too grand for **that**," Gran had mischievously smirked.

He emerged from the bathroom feeling like a new man. Judging by the delicious smells coming up from below, he was going to be feeling like a newer man still in a few moments. Supper was wonderful.

"I'm away to watch the news and you're away to your bed, are you not?"

Gregor nodded. The good food, the warmth of the room and the generosity of his Gran had worked their magic. Gran had noticed his drooping eyes and chin.

"Early rise, early breakfast, early train for you, laddie. Can't have you keeping that auld besom in Nairn waiting for you any langer. Awa' you go."

Gregor had found himself outside the front of the front door of the flat ready for the short ride to the station.

"Nane o'your soppy kisses and saft English words, awa ye go or you'll miss your train. And tell that faither of yours I'm expecting him next weekend."

Nairn was another story.

PART IV

SERENDIPITY

*"Do not follow where the path may lead. Go instead
where there is no path and leave a trail."*
- Ralph Waldo Emerson

CHAPTER 31

EUROPE

"You spent your summer in Florence? You dirty bastard," giggled Giles when he had asked Gregor on his return to college in September about his summer. Giles Allen played on the wing for the college rugby team. Invariably, he buttoned his shirt up to his neck.

"Who am I today, boys?" he said in his Pembrokeshire West Walian accent.

"We know. You're Gerald Davies," was the hackneyed answer from his old school friend, Ryan Paul.

Gerald Davies was a Welsh rugby icon, probably the best winger in the world if one was Welsh. Indeed, probably one of the best wingers in the world if one *wasn't* Welsh. It was just that one never ever admitted that in front of Welshmen, particularly Giles Allen.

"I mean in the city of Florence in Italy, not a woman," the frustration at his friend's ribald attempt at humour had worn thin very quickly.

Gregor had entered Newhill Teacher's Training College in September of 1972. It was perched on a hill to the south of the dreaming spires of the city of Oxford. It had nothing to do with the prestigious university but had all the perks of playing in some of their college sporting leagues. Gregor had sought out the college rugby club and immersed himself in the training nights and the games. He liked the fact that he was not studying P.E., but English and History, while most of his friends were in the P.E. programme. He loved the fact that he was a resident on campus. He was determined to stay there for his three years. The bedsit commute from the city every day was not for him. No, up late in the day, turn up at the café for breakfast and saunter over to hear Frankie Braithwaite or Molly Tillings deliver their history lecture or attend an English seminar or two. Gregor supposed that he could call himself a mature student, having had two years out in the work force prior to attending the college. He was not fresh out of secondary school but to call him "mature" was a bit of a stretch. He still had the air of glaikit gullibility that he had possessed when he had first attended boarding school those many years ago. But he could certainly pretend maturity when his younger friends slumped into sexual innuendo.

Gregor still loved his rugby with all the passion that he had invested in it at school. The highlight of the college fixture list was their annual game against Pelham College. It was a fixture that always drew a crowd. Pelham were too strong, they had a couple of players who were playing for top class clubs in London. In the week before the game, Newhill had trained very hard. Their coach, Graeme Halifax, an ex-rugby league player who now taught P.E. at the college, assumed his role and berated his charges with a Northern no-nonsense banter that included telling the centres that they were "soft centres," a la the chocolate box variety. He also told the wingers, of which Giles Allen was one, "My grannie can run faster and she's been dead for 20 years." He referred to the forwards as the "Clydesdales." When he was running and scrummaging them until Gregor could hardly hold his head up, Halifax would stand there with his whistle shouting, "Keep going. I'm not tired yet!" Everybody hated him on training nights and loved him the rest of the time. Halifax was a bluff northerner with a heart of gold.

Gregor could not sleep on the night before the game. He suspected that many of his teammates were in the same boat. He managed to eat a large breakfast and hold it down. He was able to find his teammates and persuade some of them to go for a walk. There was forced banter from most of them. All looked tense and nervous. Gregor imagined that this was what it must have been like when they were about to go over the top in the First World War, except here they were supposed to be doing it for pleasure and nobody was expected to die.

During the last half an hour before the game, there was a line-up outside the toilets. Their captain stood them up 20 minutes before the game and led them in a slow warm-up. Jan van Merken was a tall blonde twenty-seven-year old Dutchman, a mature student who really was mature; he captained the side from the centre. Everybody respected him because he was fearless. There was a scar on his left leg where he had had a pin inserted after a car accident. It was long and wide, a metal support for his shattered femur.

"Underdogs, boys, nothing to lose. You're all as fit as butcher's dogs. They're arrogant. Strutting peacocks all of them, not fit to tie up your bootlaces. Deep breaths and let's get out there and get into them."

So it was that they clattered out of the changing room, careful not to slip on the tiled surface. They were greeted by a wall of noise. It wasn't the Arms Park, nor Twickenham or Murrayfield, but it was the biggest crowd that Gregor had ever played in front of. In the first few minutes of the game, Barry Milne, the flanker from Bangor in Northern Ireland, made the most of a gap after a scrum near the opposition try line and went over for a try. The game went by quickly for Gregor. He remembered that Pelham had a penalty near the halfway line. It was a well-practiced looking move that went hopelessly wrong. The ball was dropped and sat alone on the ground. Gregor found himself on it, if not in a flash, then unopposed. He had an unusual amount of space in which to run. He ran about 15 yards and heard a familiar Welsh voice to his right.

"Gimme the ball, gimme the ball!"

Gregor delivered the perfect pass and Giles Allen went over in the right hand corner. The rest of the game rushed to its conclusion. The whistle went and the underdogs had won. A bit of a speech from both principals and the cup was presented to Jan. Hands were shook, backs were slapped, a sea of Newhill scarves and smiles escorted them to the changing room. They entered and sat on the benches. Nobody spoke, nobody smiled, nobody hooted and hollered, they just sat and stared. Gregor felt a huge wave of relaxed, satisfied exhaustion pour over him. Heads were down. Out of the corner of his eye, Gregor caught movement as a figure moved into the centre of the room. There he stood before them all with his shirt buttoned up to his chin.

"Who am I today, boys?"

With that the dam broke, jeers and cheers, hoots and hollers, water bottles thrown at him, discarded bandages pelting him. It was the beginning of a night to remember although it became a night of forgotten memories. All Gregor remembered was that he was not successful in his pursuit of female company but he did have a pocketful of girls names with notes like "Come and see me when you are sober." Gregor didn't care. He had a hangover to nurse, a headache to drug and a tender stomach to grease.

On the following morning, rather sad and forlorn, Giles Allen arrived in the cafe, long hair a mess, complexion wan, the runkled clothes of last night hanging off his frame, shirt hanging out and buttons not matching. He grabbed a cup of coffee and sat opposite Gregor.

"So, tell me about Florence."

"Huh?" Gregor looked up. His dishevelment and dishabille was little better than that of Giles'.

"We're hung-over and you want me to reminisce about my trip to Europe??"

Giles shook his head. "No, not Europe, not even Italy. Just Florence, or Firenze as it is known, I believe."

"How did you know that?"

"I heard it last night."

Gregor shook his head in disbelief. He sat back. "OK."

Soon he had forgotten his hangover and had launched into a description of the famed Italian city, the red-tiled roofs, the museums, the narrow streets, the culture and history. The pizza was "the best thing since sliced bread." Gregor chuckled at the incongruous analogy. Opposite him were features that were hanging on his every word so much so that the fry ups that sat in front of them both remained barely touched.

"Did you bring back any guidebooks? Something I could read?"

"Well, yes," Gregor said. He had barely completed the phrase but noticed the intensity of the eyes before him.

"Can you get them for me?'

"Yes, I suppose so."

"Like, now?" Giles' eyes were intense and wide.

Gregor sighed and got up. "Back in 5 minutes."

"Thanks!"

Gregor dragged his sorry body up the stairs to his room in the residence, opened his desk drawer and found his guide to the Uffizi Gallery and some assorted postcards he had brought back as souvenirs. He locked his door and returned to the cafeteria, which had started to fill up. The usual students who had stayed around for the weekend and then some ghostly apparitions who were his teammates appeared. Gregor swore that Jan's blonde hair had turned white over night. Giles was sat at the table and his plate had been cleared. He was pouring sugar into a fresh cup of coffee.

"Got them?"

"Here they are."

Giles snatched them away with unseemly haste and started to peruse them intensely.

"Uuum, thanks," he said, without looking up.

At that moment the café doors opened and a woman entered. She was dressed in jeans and a white top. She was of slim build with long black hair, her complexion was tea-coloured. She was beautiful. Gregor had never seen her before. He knew that because he would have remembered. She began the long walk across the cafeteria. When he could take his eyes off her, Gregor noticed conversations and laughter dying, eyes turning, jaws dropping open. Gregor was surprised at the smile of recognition and more surprised that she was approaching his table.

"You must be Jill's friend, Gregor." She reached out an elegant hand which Gregor stood up and shook.

"Er, um, I don't know any Jill."

She chuckled and put one hand up to her mouth and the other on Giles' shoulder.

"I am Rosetta and I am from Florence in Italy."

"Please, please join us," said Gregor.

She sat down next to Gregor, reached across to "Jill" and briefly touched his hand. Giles' face was a picture. He was "struck with wonder all too dread for words." The little, fleet-footed Welshman was smitten. Gregor rose from his seat, made his excuses and left. The couple barely noticed him going. He pulled up a chair next to his teammates.

Barry Milne suddenly looked up and in his Northern Irish accent said as he pointed across to Giles and his friend, "Who is he today, boys?" They gave him a smirk and a guffaw and went back to eating and talking.

Later in the day as Gregor was lying on his bed alternately dozing and going through his thoughts of his trip to Europe, he thought about how much travel changes a person. At the beginning of the summer he had caught the ferry from Dover to Calais, and boarded a train for Salzburg. There he had set himself up in the local tourist campsite and walked the city. He had ascended to the castle and had had himself a pastry and a cup of the richest hot chocolate he had ever tasted. He had looked out over the hills and imagined them alive with Julie Andrews dancing her way through her alpine floral spread. Gregor had decided that he would take a bus to the German border, cross over and visit Konigsee and Berchtesgaden, Hitler's mountain lair. Gregor had enjoyed Professor Wright's 20th century history lessons and had resolved to see for himself one of the abodes of the century's greatest villain. That would be an interesting subject for debate. The 20th century's greatest villain? Was it Hitler, Stalin or Mao? At that time Pol Pot had yet to make himself known.

The bus pulled up at the Austrian/German border and the border guards got on board and began asking for travel documents. This was a surprise to Gregor who had had to surrender his passport to the officials at the campsite. He had ID but no passport. However he didn't foresee that there would be a problem. One guard was making his way to the back of the bus, checking as he went. He reached Gregor.

"Ihre passé bitte."

Gregor showed him his Youth Hostel card. The guard barely blinked.

"Nix pass, nix Germany," he said.

Gregor was escorted off the bus, and he fumed his way back down the road towards Salzburg. He had been looking forward to his historical visit and now his day was wasted. All that was left for him to do was to walk back towards Salzburg until the next bus passed him. He sat down beside the road and noticed a sign about 100 yards farther up. On reaching it he discovered that it was a trailhead. A pretty little path led upwards to several short little peaks. Gregor decided to go for a hike. The day was sunny and he had nothing to lose. Off he went.

He had travelled about a mile when he came across a sign. It was a short, innocuous insignificant piece of woodwork that announced in German that this was the German/Austrian border. Gregor walked across and he was in Germany. He stepped back and he was in Austria. He spent a happy, childish three minutes skipping back and forth between the two countries chanting "Germany—Austria" as he did so. Then he decided to continue his walk on the German side for a while, after all there was no "verboten" that he could see on the sign. After 30 minutes or so in Germany he decided that discretion was the better part of valour and retreated back to Austria, loped down the hill and eventually found a bus to take him back to Salzburg.

Another night in Salzburg and Gregor decided that he would try to hitch a ride to Italy. Accordingly he set off towards the Brenner Pass. He had no idea whether hitching would work in Europe like it had at home. Sometimes he had waited a long time and sometimes not. Sometimes he had judged his position on the road badly and had had to walk a long way to get himself to a junction where traffic had to slow. This was what he did in Austria. He waited for about 15 minutes and a middle-aged married couple stopped. He was directed to put his pack in the boot and ushered into the back seat.

"Danke, danke," was all that Gregor could say.

He really had no idea why he was bowing while he was doing it but hoped that they weren't insulted. At least he hadn't clicked his heels together and given a Nazi salute. Gregor had a smattering of German because his father had had a love of the language. So he had dictated on certain days that they should only speak German at the dinner table. This was a little bit strange, but Gregor had developed a love of the sound of the language. Unfortunately, father's interests were in fishing and skiing so the language became limited to only a narrow range of vocabulary. So, Gregor sat in the back seat of the car feeling that the least he could do for this kindly couple was to try to make conversation with them in their own language. Eventually, he thought he had found the words, so he rehearsed them, briefly muttering to himself. Then he thought he had it.

"Entschuldigen sie mich, haben sie forellen auf Osterreich?"

He was very precise and slow in his pronunciation so that he would be clear. He saw husband and wife look at each other quizzically and thought that they had misunderstood, then the husband answered.

"Jawohl, wie haben forellen auf Osterreich."

Gregor smiled and nodded and exclaimed loudly, "Danke, danke sehr."

He was then silent for the rest of the journey, smiling happily into the mirror and getting reciprocating smiles back. They dropped him at the north end of the Brenner Pass. He retrieved his pack, shook their hands and bowed again though he had sworn not to. They moved away, completed a U-turn and headed back into the Austrian Tirol.

Gregor had wondered why his question had elicited such strange looks. He had been walking for about half a mile and he suddenly stopped dead in his tracks. It wasn't that his German had been faulty, it was just that he had made such an outrageously silly introduction to these good people. He had asked them simply whether or not there were trout in Austria. He could have asked their names, talked about the weather, told them where he was from. He didn't. Instead he asked them if they had a type of fish, a trout, in their country.

"Bloody silly idiot!" he said aloud. "Dummkopf!" he added for good measure.

Gregor entered Italy with a bias. His excuse was that he was young and naïve and he had a terrible propensity to stereotype. In Austria and Germany he had stereotyped at the German border. He had stereotyped the pleasant Austrian couple who had been kind enough to give him a ride. So now he was ready for terrible driving and incomprehensable opera, for gondoliers and ice cream, for art and artists. Of course he was wrong. There were cultural differences it was true, but he was coming to terms with the fact that the world was a small place. The irony was that he had to travel a long way to learn how small it was. Gregor enjoyed Venezia, splendid buildings and magnificent café atmospheres. He camped at a campsite outside the city. He preferred Florence but he could not put his finger on why. Maybe it was because of the campsite above the city. He never did make it to Rome and when asked why, he couldn't answer. He never regretted not visiting Rome. He was, however, sorry that he had not known that his uncle was buried in a war cemetery at Forli, which was not far from Venice. He would have visited his resting place. He would never forget the photograph of the man, barely old enough for the name, who was resting on his Gran's mantlepiece. Gregor left Florence and hitched north and homewards as quickly as possible.

So when Gregor returned to college and the jokes and barbs of his rugby friends, he was determined to keep his tales of his European trip to himself. He was, therefore, somewhat gratified that Giles Allen was having his own European cultural experience albeit it of a different variety. During that year, Gregor and Giles had been smitten, one by the city and the other by the girl.

Gregor had become an Europhile on this trip so the next summer he headed off again. After earning a bit of money on a construction site, he caught a boat from Harwich to Kristiansand on the south coast of Norway. Gregor was unsure of the physics behind the depth of water and its propensity for turbulence. The North Sea is a shallow sea so, Gregor guessed, easier to disturb than an ocean. He knew that oceans could be wild and dangerous in really bad storms but believed that it was harder to waken a sleeping giant than a mischievous imp. To Gregor, when he made the crossing from England to Norway, it was very much the mischievous imp. On boarding he had asked one of the crew what the crossing was going to be like.

"Choppy," he said.

As the ship progressed out of the lee and into the full flow of the open sea, Gregor had thought that if this was "choppy" then he was in the presence of an axe murderer. The ship rose and ducked, shuddered and rolled. Walking through to the saloon was foolhardy without hanging onto a rail. Soon, green looking men and women were reaching for sick bags. Gregor himself felt the need to get onto the deck for some fresh air. He forced the door open against the buffeting wind and glowered into the blackness. Wind and rain were driving him backwards. He stood holding the rail and trying to ride with the motion of the ship rather than fight it. About two yards upwind from him was an anorak shielding somebody tall and lean. The hood was a cowl. The hunched demeanour suggested that it contained somebody who was not very happy with life. Suddenly, something other than wind hit Gregor's coat. He looked down to his sleeve and saw the remnants of somebody's lunch. Meat and two veg had arrived courtesy of the upwind anorak. A look of hopeless apology appeared from inside the covering. It was a silent plea for forgiveness. A pathetic raising of the hand was all that was possible by way of apology. Gregor saw that the face that had appeared from behind the hood was easy to forgive. It was that of a blonde, blue eyed Viking and, more importantly, it was that of a young woman.

Gregor smiled his lack of concern about the mess to the forlorn figure, waved goodbye and went back inside to find the toilet to wash off his sleeve. The toilet area was a crowded mess. People were huddled in the cubicles. There were piles of vomit on the floor. Gregor dodged them, found a sink and washed off his sleeve.

The saloon bar was deserted, apart from two people chatting to the barman and nursing a couple of beers. Gregor ordered a beer and somehow managed to get to a seat in the corner without spilling too much. Gregor managed to doze for most of the night in the bar. He noted that the sea became notably calmer early in the morning and guessed that they were now in the lee of Southern Norway and soon in the shelter of Kristiansand Harbour.

The landing and entry into the country were easy. Gregor walked up the hill outside the city and was greeted with a spectacular view over the town and the water. The storm had abated. A light breeze toyed with the conifers beside the road. Gregor sat on a rock and drank it all in. He was going to continue his walk along the road for a while. When he became tired, he would stick out his thumb. He stood up to walk on, noting that a car was coming up from the town and driving far too fast. He watched as it zoomed by and then was surprised when its brakes were slammed on and it was reversed back to where he was standing. A young woman leaned over from the drivers seat and said something to him that he did not understand. Gregor pointed to himself and said, "English." She responded with perfect accentless English, "Would you like a lift?"

This was unplanned but he decided to accept and have his planned walk farther down the road. Ilsa from Oslo was twenty-three years old. Gregor introduced himself and told the bare bones of his story.

"Why did you pick me up? I wasn't hitching."

"I felt that it was the least I could do after what I did to you last night."

A slow dawning came over Gregor's face as he recognized her from the previous evening.

"Yes, I was the Viking Vomiter. I am so sorry about that. I hope that you got your jacket cleaned up OK."

"Yes that was no problem," Gregor said, smiling at his memory of the disgusting state of the toilets.

"I am going to Oslo but I am guessing that you probably don't want to do the whole journey today. Let me know where I can drop you."

Gregor got out his map. "Would Tvedestrand be OK?"

"Certainly," she said.

The conversation continued. She had been in London conducting some business for the small shipping company that she worked for. She had left her car with her uncle and aunt in Kristiansand, which explained why she took some time to get on the road after the ferry ride. Her parents had retired and were now living in Lillehammer so she shared a flat with her sister in Oslo. Gregor was welcome to visit them there when he eventually arrived in the capital city.

She pulled over on the outskirts of the town, scribbled her address and phone number and waved goodbye. Gregor walked into the small town and became a tourist. It did not take him long to realize how expensive everything was. It also dawned on him that to find anywhere that sold alcohol let alone a pub of any description was going to be difficult. He did find a grocery store and bought himself some food to cook during the evening. The tourist information bureau directed him to a campsite and Gregor made his way there with little difficulty.

Camping in the trees by a wooded bay on a sunny evening, Gregor cooked his chilli and rice, brewed a tea and spent an hour or so on his back, looking out to sea and across the bay. He was thinking what a beautiful country Norway was and then thought a little sadly that it still must have problems. He had noticed on the streets of Tvedestrand that there were drunks but no alcohol in view in the shops. There was no pub that he could see. Every society has issues, but he had seen so much that was clean and good and friendly. He was reminded of a gross example of racial stereotypes that he had read. A group of children in Europe were asked in school to write about elephants. As Gregor remembered it, it went:

The German children wrote about the dental health of elephants. The French about the love life of elephants. The British wrote about the hunting of elephants and the Norwegians wrote about Norway and the Norwegians.

He laughed as he remembered it but his experience had not demonstrated any such self-centredness. The few people to whom he had talked had asked him about his life. One young woman in a café in Tvedestrand was so enamoured of Gregor's Britishness because of what

Britain had done for Norway during the war. Gregor explained to her that he had been born some seven years after the war's end so he could claim no credit at all. She explained that she had been born a decade after V.E. Day but, of course, memories are atavistic and a Norwegian Christmas tree in Trafalgar Square remained a gift of gratitude from the Norwegian people every year. Gregor did not have the heart to explain that the word "quisling" had found its way into the English language. It meant "traitor" and was named after Vidkun Quisling who had aided the Nazis in WWII. Gregor later discovered that it was also used throughout Scandinavia in the same way. She probably would not have blinked if he had mentioned it.

Gregor got himself ready for bed but before he crawled into his sleeping bag, he perused the map, found that he was just beside an "A" road (red on the chart) and decided he would walk or hitch that on the morrow. It would take him closer to Oslo. It hugged the coastline. He loved the idea of walking through intermittent forests and coming across quaint little bays. If he became tired he could always stick his thumb out.

Gregor packed up in the morning and was on the road by 9:00 a.m. He was a little bit confused because the "A" road that he was sure he was on was not tarmac but dirt. He checked and rechecked his map several times but became convinced that this was the right route.

The day started warm and became rapidly warmer. Gregor bounced along quite happily but by midday the heat was starting to slow him down. He had consumed plenty of water. He found a shady nook by the side of the road and consumed some bread and cheese and some nuts. At this point, Gregor was surprised he had seen only one car. He decided that he would start to hitch after lunch. So he trudged on and on and on. Finally, he heard a car approaching from behind so he stuck his thumb out and turned to face it. He manufactured a face of beatific innocence, butter would not have melted in his mouth. The oncoming car was full. It flashed by with mum and dad smiling and waving and the children in the back doing the same. This should have cheered him but it didn't. Such a display of enthusiasm for another human being suggested to him more than anything else that he was alone; that he was a rare piece of fauna to be ogled and pointed at and maybe even photographed.

"What did you see on your road trip?" Grannie may have asked when the children had returned to their house in Oslo.

"We saw a lesser spotted British tourist," Henrik would have chimed up with glee.

"Daddy said that it's very rare," Olaf would have added.

"I wanted to stop and feed it," Little Lise noted with sadness, "but Mummy said that it is wrong to feed the wildlife because it encourages dependence."

Gregor was quickly coming to realize that he was going to have to walk the whole way and was deep in thought when he leapt out of his wits because a car had snuck up behind him and hooted. A beaming face stopped the car and got out.

"Want a ride?" the driver said in English. Gregor did not hesitate. He pulled his pack from his back and the driver flung it into the back of his truck.

"I am going to Oslo?" The question implied that he was willing to take him the whole way if he wished.

"Yes, please," Gregor heard himself saying.

They had been travelling for about eight kilometres when Gregor asked, "How did you know that I wasn't Norwegian?"

Fridthjof laughed heartily. "Because no Norwegian would hike along this road."

"But it's an 'A' road," said Gregor.

It turned out that a red line on the map did mean an "A" road but as Freddie, how he liked to be called, stated, "An 'A' road does not mean a busy road."

Still, they had seen no further traffic and still the road was dusty, sandy and ill-maintained.

Oslo is a lovely city. At the campsite, the host was explaining to a camper that "Oslo was not Paris." Gregor had never been to Paris but he knew that to be true. Oslo was northern, Oslo was quaint, Oslo was almost a village, Oslo had its ski jump, its memorials to long dead Norwegians of whom Gregor had never heard. Gregor loved "The Idea of North." This became a book by British author Peter Davidson. He had explored north and northern peoples through the eyes of poets like W.H. Auden and artists like Edvard Munch, a famous Norwegian it is true. To Davidson, based in Aberdeenshire, the North of Britain had a ruggedness that was not present in the rather effete south. He expressed admiration of the blunt statement that appeared on the main roads of the U.K. that explained all in the phrase, "The North." The language and dialects of the North were more pragmatic, more down to earth, harsher and less aesthetic. The North could be a hard life, the south could not. That was his inference.

Gregor was due to leave Norway on the Bergen to Newcastle ferry in a few days. He had long ago planned that he was going to take one of *the* great train rides of the world. From Oslo to Bergen, he had been told, was a journey that was never to be forgotten.

He was excited that morning to be mounting the train. He had had some regrets about leaving Oslo. He had never made contact with Ilsa and her sister. He had pondered over that neglect but then rationalized it as he always did in these situations. Ilsa was a pretty girl and nothing was designed to put off a Gregorian contact more than that. Had she been a rough and ready guy, raring to show him the pubs and the night life of the city then he would certainly have called him up. But calling her up would have been too embarrassing for Gregor, she would have thought that he was calling her for all the wrong reasons, that his phone call was based exclusively on lust. It had never occurred to Gregor throughout his teenage years and after that a young woman might *actually* want to spend time with him. Such was his lack of confidence in that sphere of life that he wasn't hurt by it, he was just gullible and naïve and moved away from situations that he found so minatory. The other regret was that he hadn't made it out to the famed ski jump area of the city. Holmenkollen had been on his list of places to visit but he had been seduced by the parklands and the streets of the city and it had just passed him by.

The train departed with minimum fanfare. Gregor had made sure to snag a window seat. It wasn't long before they were outside the city limits and heading slowly westward. It was an overland crossing, so Gregor did not expect bays and beaches, but he knew to expect mountains and patches of snow. Sure enough, they were soon amongst the most spectacular of mountains. Rugged rocky ridges, high hanging valleys, colls and cirques. Bare and brown higher up, green and lightly treed lower down. He was looking forward to passing through Voss, a little alpine ski resort where he had skied as a child. He remembered living in the youth hostel with his brothers while his parents had had the luxury of a hotel. He remembered the texture of the snow being different from what he had experienced in Austria and Switzerland. It was colder so there was less moisture in it. He remembered the lightness and fluffiness, which was never the case in Scotland. He remembered the distinct Norwegian brown cheese that had been part of the youth hostel breakfasts. Indeed, he had brought some with him so that he could time his lunch break as they were passing through the village. All places look different in different seasons. As they pulled into the village, Gregor had no recollection of anything. He craned his neck to see anything that seemed familiar, but there was nothing. It had been a few years, of course, and views from the self-centredness of youth take on a different lustre when the salad years are nearly over. He wasn't disappointed by what he saw, but he was reflective as they pulled out and on to Bergen.

Gregor preferred Bergen to Oslo. It was smaller, of course. Do smaller towns have more intimacy? Gregor pondered this philosophy and came to the conclusion that intimacy and anonymity were the two edges of a double-edged sword. Gregor would come to enjoy living in a big city with its indifference to his fate. Here he thought everybody may have an unhealthy interest in everybody else's business. Still, and all the old buildings were fascinating as was the old wooden museum on a hill about the town.

After Gregor had embarked on the ferry, he walked up on deck to look back at the city. Gregor's experiences in Europe had been tasters really. He had not immersed himself in any particular culture but he had sampled a few. He knew that he would likely return some day; after all, the little island that he called home was really part of Europe despite the fact that his mother insisted that it wasn't. Yes, Gregor would visit Europe again in the future. After all, Giles Allen now seemed to spend more of his life in Florence than in Milford Haven. Gregor resolved to look up the Italian for, "Who am I today, boys?" It was ironic that Giles had fallen in love with a European before he had ever visited while Gregor had visited several times and his only intimacy had been vomit on his jacket!

"Firmness is enduring and exertion is a character I always wish to possess."
- Robbie Burns

CHAPTER 32

SCHOOL DAYS AND SCHOOL WAYS

When Gregor was learning to be a teacher and mastering the art of not setting rivers alight, he was dispatched to various schools in the Oxford area. His first school had been a primary school in Abingdon. It was in an old building. Mike Evans, a late middle-aged Welshman, was the only man in the school. Gregor speculated idly when he was being introduced to him why it seemed to be his fate in the profession to be accosted by the Welsh at every turn. Maybe they were just natural teachers or maybe Wales was such a lousy place to live that they were fleeing, a mass exodus as the waters parted in the Bristol Channel, opening up to the promised land. It was said that one could take the boy out of the valley but one could never take the valley out of the boy. Certainly he had met more patriotic Welshmen, almost jingoistic in outlook, outside Wales than in. But Gregor was the same was he not? He was grateful that England had opened its arms to him at a young age, but he would always remain a Scotsman. He would cling to his culture like a drowning man.

Mike introduced a rather timid Gregor to his class of eight year olds. They seemed a sweet, pleasant little bunch. A little curly-haired redhead took it upon herself to introduce him to the aquarium and to introduce each of the little fishes to him by name, explaining in some detail why they were christened thus.

"That's Neptune, he's king of the fish. We have been learning mythology and Neptune is also Poseidon, you know." She chuckled and pointed, "See that one there, the fattest of the goldfish? He is called 'Lunch" because that's what Mr. Evans wants to do with him. We have to protect him from our teacher."

Gregor cracked a smile. He could see and feel that these children looked up to their form room teacher. The classroom had a very pleasant ambience. The children were calm and relaxed around their equally calm and relaxed teacher. On his first day in the school, Gregor simply had to relax, observe and take notes. On the second day he was asked to mingle and get to know the children. He had availed himself of the limited space in the staffroom at lunchtimes. He was welcomed by all of the teachers there. He was careful to not take a cup or seat that was so obviously the reserve of somebody who had been there for a long time.

On the third day, Gregor's big day, he was to teach for the first time. He had tossed and turned the whole night. He had asked Mr. Evans what he should teach them.

"Whatever you want, bach, just 'ave fun doing it."

So, Gregor had mustered up a math lesson that included making shapes, naming and measuring them. He had found a story that he decided to read to them. It was the fable of the tortoise and the hare with the motto of "slow and steady wins the race."

Mr. Evans was there to support him during the math lesson. The children enjoyed the gluing and the sticking. Gregor prepared well and provided plenty of paper, glue and rulers. He managed to get some reasonable cubes and pyramids from the children. He remembered almost too late on the night before that straws and string would make a great difference so he had dashed down the hill from the college, spoke to John, the landlord of The Fishes Pub, who had given him plenty to see him through the morning. Even so, Gregor found himself overwhelmed. He was helping Eric thread a piece of string through his straw when there was a wail from the far end of the room. Gregor jumped up and the carefully threaded string unthreaded itself onto the floor. The problem was that Tyler was manufacturing paper pellets and blowing them at the girls. Juliet had caught one in the eye and was, naturally, upset. By the time Gregor had pacified the fracas, Eric, who was waiting for his string to be threaded, was hiding under the desks pretending to be a troll and leaping out disrupting the groups that had been working quietly. Gregor did what he had been taught to do in such situations, he stopped everything and got the children together for a talk. Some semblance of normality was restored and some recognizable shapes began to appear. An engineer may not have recognized them as cubes and pyramids but Picasso certainly would.

Gregor must have looked distracted when he eventually made it to the staffroom for a short break. The other teachers gave each other knowing looks. There was no other man in the school than Mike Evans. The head was a severe looking, slightly-built woman who frightened adult and child alike with the merest glance over the top of her glasses. Nobody approached Miss Judith Grotting without at least a sharp intake of breath. Gregor sat there for the most precious five minutes of his life. The bell went and he returned to the classroom where he was happy that the children began every lesson after break with silent reading. It was a well-practiced regime that Gregor frankly hoped could carry on for the rest of the day so that he could somehow recoup his energy. Twenty minutes was the limit, however, and then the children were into their handwriting notebooks, which Gregor hoped would also be easy. He spent time at his desk pretending to read his book. Mr. Evans had a rule that when the children read for pleasure then the teacher had to do so also. But really Gregor was going over his afternoon lesson, planning each step as meticulously as possible. He had some questions for Mike but he was nowhere to be found. No problem, he would find him in the staffroom at lunchtime. After he had dismissed the children for their lunch break, Gregor immediately headed off there. Mike was nowhere to be seen. Gregor asked the friendly looking Jennifer Bowsprit, who was knitting a scarf for her nephew, where he might find him.

"In the King's Cross Pub, Gregor," she said. "He goes there every day."

After school and a successful afternoon's teaching, Mike debriefed Gregor.

"Righto, bach, 'ave you any questions of me?"

Gregor hesitated. "Just one really," he said.

"Ask away."

"How come you go to the pub every day?"

It was Mike's turn to hesitate.

"Er, that's where my mates have their lunch. And—umm, 'ave you been in our staffroom? You're a Scotsman, aren't you? Have you heard of John Knox?" Gregor nodded. "Go home tonight, drop in at the library and see if you can find any John Knox quotation that might be appropriate. I'm saying no more."

The college bus arrived at 4:00 p.m., and Gregor boarded. He had been sat for about 10 seconds and was sound asleep, only awaking when the driver shouted at him to get off as they were back at college.

Four weeks later, Gregor was a bag of nerves. John Savage, Doctor of Education, was dropping in from the college to give him his final assessment. It was an afternoon lesson that Gregor had prepared with meticulous attention. It was all about mammals. He was going to teach the children all about what mammals were; vertebrates, sucklers of their young and so on. He would then divide the classes in teams. They would be given a set of pictures and asked to identify the type of animal in the picture. It would be a fun-filled experience. Mr. Evans and Dr. Savage would observe. Gregor introduced a surprisingly nervous looking doctor as he entered the room. He raised his hand in greeting and went to take a seat at the back. Mike Evans sat down next to the noble doctor and the lesson proceeded apace. Gregor had only been going for about 10 minutes when John Savage raised his hand, made his excuses and moved to leave the room. Gregor realized too late that he was heading to the art cupboard storeroom and not the exit of the classroom. Mike raised his hand to head him off but was unnoticed. The children too realized that he had made a mistake. Everybody in the room expected him to emerge as quickly as he had entered. After all, it was a storage room with no room to swing a cat or even a mouse. No much-respected college lecturer could hang about in there for long without realizing his mistake. Dr. John Savage did not reappear.

Meanwhile, Gregor was back in full flow, waxing lyrical about his family and other animals. Young Josh Adams put his hand up. Gregor nodded him to speak.

"My mum wouldn't be happy if you called her a mammal," he said with righteous indignation on his face.

"She'll be fine with it, Josh, believe me."

Josh looked doubtful.

Gregor's enthusiasm, his warming to his subject, was now starting to manifest itself in vigorous movement. He was becoming so enthralled at the sound of his own voice that he had not noticed young Annie Wade who had knelt down to pick up her pencil. At that moment Gregor made a speedy rush to the other side of the room in an attempt to engage a group of three boys who were distracted. He tripped over Annie and was suddenly falling headlong towards the aquarium. Little fish were coming up to meet him. He hit the aquarium with the full force of his right shoulder and it teetered over against the wall and shattered on the floor. Mike quickly stood up and ushered the children away from the broken glass and the more distressing sight of the dying fish. A shriek and a moan went up from the children. Gregor's hand was bleeding but he was desperately trying to gather up the squirming fish and spoon them into the sink. It was a desperate life-saving gesture that was doomed to failure. The janitor was called. He arrived with mop and bucket, dustpan and brush. The class was evacuated to the playground where Gregor and Mike pushed them on the swings, twirled the roundabout and supervised the children in an extra playtime. Eventually, the janitor came out and told them it was safe to come back into the classroom.

The fish had all died. Mike took the time to sit the children in a circle and talked about life and death and accidents that could happen. He talked to them so kindly and calmly that the children became peaceful and settled, ready for the end of the day.

"Any questions?" Mike said, looking around the upturned faces. He nodded for Pavel to speak.

"What happened to that man, Mr. Evans?"

"What man, Pavel?"

In the chaos, both Gregor and Mike had forgotten about the disappearance of Dr. Savage into the art cupboard.

"UUUUmmmm, I expect he went back to college," Gregor said. "College lecturers are very busy men, you know, Pavel."

At that moment there was a creak and the door of the art storage room opened. A very sheepish Dr. Savage appeared. He reddened when he saw them all sat there.

"Ooh, I thought that you had all gone home," he said.

He hurried across the room and out the door. Mike fiddled intently with his right ear lobe as he always did when he needed a thought to come. Gregor found something fascinating in his fingernails that needed dealing with. Mike decided not to comment.

"Now then children, get your hats and coats and your bags and let's get you out to the front of the school. You will have lots to tell your parents. It's been an exciting day, hasn't it?"

Dismissal happened. Gregor's head drooped as he walked back to the classroom to pick up his belongings. This was the end for him. Teaching was proving too much. Even before today's disaster, he had been exhausted by the demands of the job. He was running to keep up, now he thought he was going to be run out of college. Inevitably, he had failed his teaching practice. He would be on the next train home and walking up his parents' driveway with his tail between his legs and a different future ahead of him.

Mike Evans looked at him and put his hand on his shoulder. "When the bus comes to pick you up, send it away. My wife makes meat loaf on Thursdays. There's enough for three. We'll get you back to college afterwards," he said.

"But, but—"

"But me no buts, bach. You're coming home with me."

So, Gregor sent away the bus and found himself in Mike Evans' old mini and heading out of Abingdon to the little hamlet where he and his wife lived. The cottage and garden were homely and welcoming.

"This is Gregor," Mike said to his wife when they arrived.

"I'm Mary. Welcome Gregor, I 'ope you've brought your appetite. Come in, come in. Sit you down yere and I'll get the two of you a drink," said the kindly woman.

She was gone and back in a trice carrying two glasses and two bottles of beer.

"Mike's told me a lot about you. Good teacher, he says," she said.

"Not after today," Gregor said in a sad, feeling sorry for himself kind of voice.

"Stop that nonsense, accidents happen," Mike said impatiently.

So they sat down in the little dining room and Gregor demolished a plate of meat loaf, mash and carrots with lashings of gravy. More beer came his way and he was soon at his ease.

They laughed about the day. Gregor's lips were now loquaciously loosened by the alcohol. He paused in the full flow of one of his stories with sudden realization.

"One thing that worries me. What happened to Dr. Savage in the store cupboard?"

Mike laughed, "I shouldn't worry about that, I've seen it all before. People go into teaching, discover they are not very good at it. In his case he's terrified of children so he left and did his 'Piled Higher Deeper,' his doctorate. They leave teaching and go off to college to teach teachers how to teach. You'll get a good report from him because you have rapport and you relate to children. Dr. John Savage relates to dustcovers and books and NOT human beings. IF he gives you a bad report, send it to me and I'll put him right. By the way did you ever find an appropriate John Knox quotation?"

"Yes, I did," Gregor said, looking sheepishly across the table at Mary. "Was it something about 'a monstrous regiment of women'?"

Mike laughed heartily and Mary smiled her approval.

"Don't worry about Mary. She approves of me getting out at lunchtime and getting some male company."

It was the wrong side of midnight by the time Mary and Mike dropped Gregor back to college. He had been baptized into his chosen profession. Pity that the baptismal waters had caused the expiration of much loved fish.

"Short few hours sleep for you, my boy, and you'll be back at it in the morning. See you then," Mike said.

This was Gregor's first teaching practice. His second one was at The Grange Secondary School in Aylesbury in Buckinghamshire. It would be his first experience of teaching teenagers.

ROSLA had become an acronym that haunted Gregor at the time of its introduction and had given him bad dreams. He found himself waking in a cold sweat in the night with images of a rampant chaotic classroom, chairs being thrown, boogers being flicked and acne being squeezed. There was no storm drain in sight down which the whole sorry image could be flushed. In September 1972, the British Government raised the age of leaving school from 15 years old to 16 in England and Wales. It seemed that the 'Raising of the School Leaving Age' (ROSLA) was passed deliberately to thwart Gregor's attempt to become an effective teacher.

The Minister of Education no doubt had a dart board in his office with a picture of Gregor dead centre at which he threw darts regularly, accompanied by the mantra, "So you want to be a teacher? Then teach this!" He'd throw a dart into Gregor's forehead and return to his witches cauldron. Now there were a group of 15 year olds who thought that they were leaving school and then suddenly they weren't. They were already teenagers with an instinct for rebellion but, unlike most teenagers, they now had a cause that mattered deeply to them personally. In the previous year they had anticipated leaving school and getting a job but their jail sentence had been extended. There was no appeal.

Aylesbury in Buckinghamshire is not a rough part of England. It's a medium-sized town with good employment and not much heavy industry. Gregor was one of the last to be dropped off on this second teaching practice. His mentor teacher was Mr. Tony Redman, a young P.E. type of jocular disposition and throwaway remarks. Gregor sensed that he was not going to get the calm and gentle awareness of Mike Evans but then, he figured, Tony was not teaching eight-year-olds. Tony welcomed him and took him to his classroom. He reached into the pile of papers on his desk and handed Gregor his timetable.

"Any questions?"

"Eer, no, not at the moment," Gregor said.

"I'll introduce you to the kids when they come in. You can watch me for the first day. Then tomorrow you can get your feet wet," said Tony.

The bell went and Gregor heard the bustle and hustle in the corridor. A sea of blazers, ties and white shirts pushed and shoved its way into the classroom. Gregor sat at the front next to Mr. Redman's desk, his hands resting in his lap. Eventually, all were at their desks and Gregor looked up to see all eyes on him. He was determined to look around the room and meet the gaze of a student here and a student there, rather than looking down. He noted the smirks and grins, the elbows in the ribs of their classmates. He reflected with concern that he was only some six or seven years older than they were. How he wished he were older, maybe with a grey hair or two. He wished his eyes were shrouded by his Stetson, that he had a day's growth of beard, that he had a cheroot in his mouth that he was about to light by striking a match on his boot. He wished he had the look of a man who had seen life and death and war and tragedy; a man for whom fate held no surprises.

He wished he was the man with no name. If he had adopted a thousand-yard stare he knew it would become a source of more amusement. He wished that he was Clint Eastwood. Instead, he was Gregor Mitchell MacCrimmon, a name that struck bravery into the most timid of teenagers.

Gregor stood as he was being introduced and raised his hand by way of greeting.

"Would you like to say anything, Mr. MacCrimmon?" said Mr. Redman.

"Yes, I would just like to say that I am looking forward to working with you and getting to know you."

He sat down. Gregor would like to have said that his foray into his first secondary school experience was a good one. He worked fine when Mr. Redman was with him in the classroom but, as soon as his mentor teacher stepped out for a few minutes, things changed. At first little fidgetings happened then questions.

"Ave you got a girlfriend then?"

"Do you have a car?"

And so on.

Gregor was usually skilled enough to get them away from the personal stuff but couldn't get them to focus on the 20th century history that he was trying to teach them. Still, he muddled through the first few days without too much of a disruption. As Mr. Redman put it to him on the Thursday after school when Gregor was worried about something that had happened in class that afternoon, "Did anybody die? No? Well that's all right then."

But Friday afternoon loomed heavily on Gregor's horizon. A double block of English with the ROSLA group. Gregor was distraught and sleepless on Thursday night, distracted and unfocussed on Friday morning, and a pale, twitchy tangle of messy emotions—none of them positive—by lunchtime.

"What's up?" The red hair and moustache of Jim Maguire sat down opposite him in the staffroom. He had noticed Gregor's "deer in the headlights" demeanour.

"I have to teach *Romeo and Juliet* to the ROSLA group this afternoon," said Gregor.

"Ah," Jim said, nodding in sympathy. "Bribery and corruption can work, mate. Promise them that you'll show them the movie if they behave. You know, the recent one with Natasha Kinski. They'll like that. There's sex in it."

Brian Hardy, the physics teacher, joined them. He frowned and looked across at Gregor. "You look like death," he said.

Jim explained the situation. Brian pondered for a few moments.

"Well, nobody really succeeds in teaching too much on a Friday afternoon anyway. The kids won't learn and you are tired from the week. Not much I can suggest here. Maybe open the door, throw some raw meat in, close the door and run."

Jim put his eyes to the heavens. "That's not helping," he said.

"No, it's not, is it?" What are you both doing for the weekend?" he said, quickly changing the subject.

It wasn't a help for Gregor but, of course, Brian's cruelty was really a kindness. Nobody expected much of him. He was on his own and he would just have to get on with it and then it was the weekend, a game of rugby, a few beers and back to it on Monday. No sweat, only a couple of hours out of his life and he was free.

At 1:00 p.m. the condemned man rose from his seat, took one last gulp of his coffee and exited the staffroom. He heard them before he saw them. He entered the room to find two boys play fighting on the long table. They looked up and paused. There was a sudden silence in the room.

"Good afternoon boys and girls, my name is Mr. MacCrimmon and I am here to teach you *Romeo and Juliet*. Would you give out the books for me please?" he said, handing a small, acne-covered individual a set of books. He was immediately set upon and the books were strewn across the floor.

"Shakespeare's plays are meant to be acted or watched but not read. But I thought that I would give you some understanding of the plot. Have a seat and we'll make a start."

The hubbub continued unabated. Gregor decided to do what he always did when faced with a difficult situation: he gave up. He sat at the desk, reached into his briefcase, brought out his newspaper, put his feet up on the desk and began to read. At least, he pretended to read. But really he was wondering at what point he would have to step in. After all, at this point the texts of *Romeo and Juliet* were being used as ammunition. The Montagues and Capulets had divided themselves into two teams, one boys and one girls and they were hurling the books at each other with laughter and the occasional obscenity. Gregor eventually decided that he had to make a stand and did just that. He stood up turned to the blackboard and started talking to it. After a couple of minutes the noise subsided and he became conscious through the eyes in the back of his head—which were issued to all trainee teachers—that the students were taking an interest. He did not turn around but explained the plot line of the play, how it had been made into a musical, and so on and so on.

"E's cracked up," one student said from behind him. "'Ere mate—what ya doing?"

Gregor turned around.

"Doing? What am I doing? I'm, uuuh, teaching my lesson. There's no point in teaching it to you because you won't listen but I am obliged to teach it nevertheless so I am teaching it to the walls, the board, the doors, the windows and any other inanimate object because they give me far more attention than you lot."

There was a hush and they all sat down. Gregor stood before them.

"You've been cheated, haven't you? You were all ready to leave school and then suddenly you weren't. Life suddenly dumped on you from a great height. Well, it dumped on me too 'cos I don't want to teach students who don't want to be taught. But we have to be in this room together and we have to see each other through the next few weeks together. So, what are we going to do? Well, I'll tell you what I would like to do for the rest of the afternoon. I'd like to sit here and listen to you talk about anything you want to talk about. No strings, no rules, nothing. You talk. I'll listen and try to learn."

Gregor would have liked to describe this as being a seminal moment in his relationship with this bunch of unfortunate teenagers. He would have loved to have them eating out of the palm of his hand, hanging on his every word, but sadly it was not to be. As far as he succeeded with them, the unwritten law was that they were in the room and he was in the room for *that* two hours. Occasionally one of them came for a chat but it wasn't about Shakespeare. They were good fun as people, Gregor reflected on his last lesson, it was just that he would rather have gone for a pint with them than been responsible for teaching them. Gregor was grateful that his supervisor from the college had not attended on Friday afternoon. Mr. Redman came in on occasions, saw what was happening and accepted it for what it was. Gregor's experience at The Grange in Aylesbury was one that he would not have missed for the world.

Woodstock is an idyllic Oxfordshire village. This was to be Gregor's third and final teaching practice. At the end of the street stand the portals which are the entrance way to Blenheim Palace. This was home to the Dukes of Marlborough and the birthplace of Winston Churchill. Gregor found himself in the village to do his final teaching practice at Woodstock School. It meant that the bus would drop him off first and pick him up last. Gregor was ecstatic at this because he believed that he would be able to avoid taking work home with him at the end of the day.

After the Grange, this village secondary school was a dream. Gregor taught a bit of history, a bit of English. He had learned the hard way that children like the visual, so he had sought out the help of the Audio-Visual aid man to help set up slide shows and movies. Phil Stillman had, by reputation, been a wonderful classroom teacher. He had built up an expertise that had allowed him to step aside from the classroom and become the man who ran all the projectors and recorders and such in the school. Gregor felt sorry for Phil because he had gone from this much-respected guru and much-loved personality around the school to a backroom boy. Inevitably, when people searched him out in his backroom he was never there. When they wanted something done, there was always a delay. Thus, his name went from being Phil Stillman to "Still Philman" over a period of about six months when he first took over the job. Gregor, however, was never let down by Phil who was only too happy to pander to his AV needs and quickly.

Gregor was proud of himself because he had managed to pull off something of a coup in his history teaching. He persuaded his history lecturer, Dr. Frank, to come to the school as a guest speaker. Frank was a leading authority on the Second World War with the added bonus of having fought in it. He had survived the D-Day landings on June 6, 1944 and chased the Germans back to Germany over the next 11 months. Gregor managed to persuade him *not* to tell his stories of his other conquests in Germany. His tale about the German frauleins who were making babies for Hitler and found it hard to get out of the habit may well have gone down well with the students at college but was inappropriate in the context of Gregor's teaching practice.

The day came for Dr. Frank's visit. He had met with Phil and was ensconced in the very up-to-date theatre and ready for action. Phil handed him the remote control, very sophisticated for the time, and Frank introduced himself. He told a little bit about what it was like in wartime Britain with rationing and bombing raids on the big cities and the constant threat of invasion after Dunkirk and the fall of France. He talked about the "phoney war" or the "sitzkrieg" as the Germans called it, the "sitting war." That was the period after war was declared and nothing seemed to happen. It was the lull before the storm. Then he talked about the training prior to D-Day, the knowledge that something was about to happen but also the mystery and uncertainty about where they were going. He talked about the time that they were asked to write a letter that would be forwarded to their loved ones in the event of their death. Gregor noted how that statement really hit home to his young audience.

So then it was time for Dr. Frank's slideshow. Gregor noted that Phil had disappeared. They were on their own with 80 or so teenagers. Frank pressed a button and the blinds edged their way down so that they were all in darkness. Frank pressed another button and the lights came on. Frank introduced the first slide and pressed a button. No slide appeared, but the blinds went up.

"Sorry about that," he said.

Frank came from the "let's reinforce failure" school of thought—the thought that suggests that if one presses the button frequently at pedestrian crossings then the light will change quicker. So, now Frank with determined emphasis pressed harder on the button and the blinds came down again. He waited until they were stopped and with renewed emphasis pressed a different button and the lights came on. Thereafter came a moving panorama of ups and downs, ons and offs, until Gregor spotted one of his pupils, Edwin, making his way to the front. There was a quiet few words between Edwin and the good doctor and the slide show began and went onwards without a hitch.

You could hear a pin drop while Frank went through his slides. There were original pictures of wartime posters, photographs of burning buildings, pictures of a young Frank grabbing a ride on the top of a tank and so on. Finally, he came to an end. Edwin flicked the lights on and the blinds up. The applause was loud and long and Frank stood back, head bowed but eyes beaming.

"Thank you indeed. You have been a wonderful audience. I had forgotten how great it is to be teaching in a school again. Give Edwin a round of applause, for without him we would still be dashing forth between light and darkness every 10 seconds or so."

Loud cheers were unleashed for Edwin who bowed modestly and sat down.

"Are there any questions?"

Ben had his hand raised and was eager to ask.

"In the constant movement, the heat of the battle, did you write home much?"

"You have to remember that the letters were censored, so I didn't write home much at all. I did send one letter right at the end to my girlfriend. The war was just over and we were going home soon. It was a short letter. It just said 'BURMA.'"

Ben looked quizzical. Gregor put his head in his hands. He knew what was coming. He was powerless to stop it.

"What did BURMA mean?"

"BURMA meant 'Be Undressed & Ready My Angel.' It was an acronym. You all know what an acronym is, don't you?"

Gregor jumped up and walked briskly to the front. He stood in front of Frank. He thanked him profusely for coming in and producing such a wonderful afternoon's entertainment, called for another round of applause, shook Frank's hand and escorted him through the throng that was now standing, clapping and cheering.

As Gregor expressed his thanks and said goodbye to him at the entrance to the school, he must have looked a bit ill at ease, so Frank turned back to him as he was unlocking his car.

"You know, young Gregor, you need to relax a bit more around these young men and women. Give them more credit for their maturity and their intelligence. The 'BURMA' piece was for you rather than them. Being away from those that you love in a state of heightened intensity is bound to increase one's need for physical love. You have the potential to be a great teacher as long as you cut away the little bit of prudishness that is a part of your character.

I enjoyed myself today and because I did your students did also. It's not astrophysics, young fellow. Thanks for including me. I'll see you back at College."

He was in his car and away.

Gregor had learnt wonderful lessons on all of his three teaching practices and they had all come in the most unlikely of circumstances.

"You have let loose the bull and you now complain that he gores you."
- Mirabeau on the French Revolution.

CHAPTER 33

CHILDREN AND NATURE

Gregor, in a long career, found himself getting frustrated by how children were relating to nature but more than that how adults were restricting children from nature. He had always believed that the younger one was, the closer one was to the natural world. It was being in school, college, an office building, all of those things which were the business and busyness of life that took young people away from the natural world. Gregor had noticed over the years that the slightest drop of rain had produced a bevy of children at his desk pleading to be allowed to stay indoors at break time. He had grown up with peers who didn't care what the weather was like, they wanted to be out and about playing sport or creating tunnels and forts in the woods. One of the many straws that was about to bring about the breaking of the camel's back was the delegation of parents asking—almost demanding—that teachers "organize" play time. Gregor had then thought back to the family trip to London when they were young children. To his father it was all about the culture, traditions and history of Empire; to one of his brothers it was all about collecting lollipop sticks for something that he was making at home. He had remembered reading that children were never playing when they were "playing," they were preparing themselves for adult life. Gregor was not passionate about much in his profession but it was likely that he would leave teaching if the powers that be ever asked him and his colleagues to "organize" play time.

So, Gregor pondered this when he was taking a group of nine-year-olds for a walk in the woods. It was unfortunate on this occasion but he was burdened with parent volunteers. Gregor was leading as they clambered over rocks ascending a dry riverbed. He suddenly heard a squawk behind him. It was Josh's mother, a parent who had expressed concern that young Josh had leapt from one rock to another with the gay abandonment of youth. The worst that could happen was a fall and maybe a fracture or a sprain. But Mum had squealed because of her mother instinct. Gregor could, he supposed, understand that, except that he was privy to the knowledge that she was pregnant with twins by a father other than that of Josh. She was preparing a flit, leaving Josh and his father to their own devices. Not only was it a flit but it was one to the other side of the world. She was going to inflict almost irreparable damage on her child, the tragedy of abandonment, the sudden depriving of a mother's unconditional love. Yet here she was worried about him falling off a rock! To Gregor's simple brain it made no sense whatsoever.

Then there had been the shriek from the back of the line. Gregor had rushed back, expecting the worst. All that he found was Enrico who had seen a toadstool that frightened him. Gregor wondered if it might be a real phobia similar to his own fear of snakes. However, there was then the panicked group at the front who had run into some innocent harmless flies. Gregor decided that it was that he, Gregor MacCrimmon, would be the rare adult to give these children any outdoor experiences. Far from preening himself, he was deeply saddened by the fact that these children had such structured lives that they did not get outside with their buddies, never turned over a rock on the seashore on their own, were unaware that a nettle stung and that wild flowers were beautiful. Should he blame the parents or should he blame wider society? It mattered not. It was an unassailable fact. Suddenly, Gregor resolved to do something about it. If he had been lacking in passion before, slowly, by degrees he was finding his raison d'etre in the profession. Teaching children in the outdoors was to become a passion, almost a mission.

Later in his career, there had been the Grade 9 student who had arrived next to him as they were walking up a logging trail on an expedition in Canada. Rory had passed the time of the day with Gregor, which was pleasant. Then he observed, "You're tired, Mr. MacCrimmon."

Gregor wasn't, so asked, "What makes you say that, Rory?"

"Because you're sweating," Rory said.

As he trudged onwards, Gregor thought about the equation that associated sweat with fatigue. Gregor had always been prone to sweat. On a summer's day he couldn't do his shoelaces up without a bead appearing on his brow. He understood how fit or unfit he was. What he didn't understand was how a Grade 9 boy did not understand that sweat had nothing to do with tiredness. On his return to school, Gregor discovered that Rory was one of several boys in his grade who avoided physical activity at all costs. He could not ride a bike, was driven everywhere and did not play any sport. Perhaps this explained why Rory was exhausted on the first night of his expedition. It was probably the first time in his life that he had really exerted himself and, to Gregor, this was tragic.

So, Gregor often found reassurance in the holiday expeditions. They restored his belief in the facts that there were still young people who could get outside, could put themselves through a physical trial and could reap the rewards of their labour through seeing beautiful sights. They could crawl into their sleeping bags at night and sleep that most restful of reposes caused by healthy physical exertion.

CHAPTER 34

FOREIGN TRAVEL WITH SCHOOLS

Gregor had been lucky over his years in teaching to have been involved in foreign travel. He organized one such trip from his school in Lincolnshire. He and a couple of colleagues were to take a group of ten children on a walk on the West Highland Way in Scotland; not exactly foreign but foreign enough if one was from a deprived inner city area. They loaded the roof of a mini-bus with all of the camping gear and Gregoir recruited two colleagues, Mick and Billy. They headed north.

The West Highland Way has an interesting beginning at the back of a supermarket in the Bearsden/Milngavie area of Glasgow. From there it is roughly a six-day hike to Fort William. It is 155 kilometres long. It takes in some wonderful lowland sights as every step brings one closer to the magnificent scenery of the Scottish Highlands. In those days of the 1980s, Health and Safety was not the bureaucratic force that it has since become. So, if somebody in authority had asked where they were going to camp on their first night, nobody would have been able to answer. Gregor, however, knew that wild camping was permitted in Scotland so was happy that flying by the seat of his pants was the plan. As they walked steadily outside the city limits,

Billy took off in the mini-bus to scout out a campsite for the first night. The plan was for him to suss out an appropriate area and set up a welcome for the rest of the group as they headed towards him. If there was time, Billy was to walk back down the path to meet them and ease any loads from children who may be struggling.

Eventually, they were walking towards Loch Lomond. As they neared the village of Drymen, Gregor spotted the unmistakable blue of the school mini-bus parked in a field just away from the path. Billy's tuneful whistling could be heard approaching so the tired bodies knew that their first day was coming to an end. It wasn't an ideal campsite. The farmer had been happy to let them use the field but there was a herd of cows present and they were inevitably curious. There was also no running water although they had planned for this with large containers that Billy had thoughtfully filled up. The mess tent was up and soon the healthy smell of unadulterated cholesterol was frying away merrily. The cows nosed around until shooed away by Mick and his stick. All the adults were somewhat taken aback when Sean came to the staff tent later that evening when the three adults were having a cuppa tea and a review of the day.

"I would like to be friends with a cow," Sean announced.

This caused looks of alarm from the adults who knew that Sean was a potential sex offender. Tragically, that prediction was not a signal for preventative intervention, so subsequently Sean found himself going through the court system having hurt several people on the way. Gregor was always uneasy in his conscience about that because he felt that the signs were so obvious that there should have been a better system in place to steer Sean away from such behaviour. For the moment, however, their main job was to stop Sean becoming too friendly with a cow.

There are two sides to Loch Lomond. The west side has the road, which weaves its way along the bonnie banks through the quaint, albeit touristy, community of Luss, up to the railway village of Crianlarich. By this point the road has left the northern tip of the loch behind. The east side, however, has only the path, so there was no possibility of rescue by mini-bus on that day's hike. The goal was to reach Rowardennan Youth Hostel and spend the night there. Mick would take the bus up the west side of the loch, park it up for the night and catch the little ferry across to the hostel. What should have been a pleasant day's walk through the deciduousness of the vegetation proved difficult. Every time they stopped, the West Highland midges, the "no-see-ums," the irritating little bugs that people the Highlands, demanded their pound of flesh. This was such an irritant that young Robert had burst into tears. All had been sprayed with repellent but it seemed that nobody had told the midges that they weren't supposed to like it. To them, however, it seemed to be a Chanel #5 on steroids; they loved it and proceeded to descend and tear chunks out of the hikers. Then as they neared the hostel, Billy, who was chatting aimiably to Gregor at the front of the line, suddenly ran off into the bushes. When he returned he explained quietly to Gregor that he had quickly relieved himself of his lunch. This numinous occurrence was an unfortunate herald of the night to come.

Gregor loved the idea of the youth hostel experience for these students. They would get to mix and share rooms with hostellers from all different walks of life and from many different countries. The adults knew that their EBD (emotionally and Behaviourally Disturbed) children had had limited positive experiences with things that were different; they were naturally conservative and liked only what they knew. There were groups of Dutch, Germans and French in the hostel that night as well as a mixed group of six up from Glasgow. The students were allocated their beds and gathered in the communal kitchen to sample the pasta that Billy, Mick and Gregor were conjuring up.

Despite their hard day of walking, there were students who were pale-faced and distinctly not hungry. In light of Billy's earlier symptoms, the adults were concerned. However, they managed to get the children off to bed with little fuss. Robert was on the top bunk of three. Beneath him were two twenty-something Germans who Gregor had tried to speak to unsuccessfully. They had very little English and Gregor was not about to burden them with his German. He succeeded in telling them that Robert was part of their group and if there was a problem then please wake one of the three of them up.

They were all early to bed that night. Gregor was quickly asleep and almost as quickly awake. It was one of the Germans, looking alarmed, who was shaking him. Gregor went with him back to the dormitory and was shown his bed which was covered in vomit. He pointed up to Robert on the top bunk who was snoring peacefully. From what Gregor could gather, Robert had had the sickness come upon him suddenly, had leaned over the side of the bunk and vomited on the face of the sleeping person below and gone back to sleep again. Gregor apologized profusely and ushered the young man to his own bunk saying that he would tidy up the messed up bed and sleep there so as not to be too far away from Robert.

On the following day they were a pale group, but they were up and walking. It seemed that the short distance to Crianlarich was all that the group could manage. Manage it they did and they booked into the youth hostel in the village.

It was a couple of days later that Mick left the group and drove the mini-bus to Glasgow to hand over to the Deputy Head, Bryn, who was to carry on with the group for the last week. Bryn arrived at the campsite on the edge of Rannoch Moor, promptly lined the boys up and dosed them all with midge repellent.

"No more problems with midges, Gregor." he said finally.

Gregor and Billy nodded wisely but said nothing. Nothing needed to be said because the midges said it all. They feasted royally on the new flavour and then set about the children as a second course. Meanwhile they were making significant progress on their walk. They crossed the moor and reached the eastern head of Glencoe and the Blackhouse Hotel. They decided to camp outside the public bar. Bryn agreed to supervise the children while Billy and Gregor settled themselves for a bit of a night off in the public bar. They were settling into their second pint when suddenly Bryn rushed in through the door and headed for the toilet. He was ashen and grey and it was obvious that he had caught the bug.

On the following day, Bryn decided that he was going to take the bus around to Kinlochleven while the rest of them hiked over the hill past the Blackwater Dam and down to the town of Kinlochleven. They climbed slowly up the path that the Irish Navvies had taken all those years ago when they were building the dam. Legend had it that many died on the way home after a night out at the hotel, falling by the wayside and freezing to death. A night in Kinlochleven and then there would be the short hike over the pass to the Glen Nevis campsite. Gregor was looking forward to getting to the old familiar town of Fort William, which he regarded with a certain amount of affection.

It was a bright, sunny day when they finally descended the gentle hill that led to the busy campsite. Bryn was there with the tents all pitched. He was enjoying a cup of tea. He stood up and shook every student's hand in congratulation. The plan was to give the children some free time in the town on the following day and then drive south. They packed up camp on the following morning and were ensconced in the van after a large lunch of fish and chips. All were there except Billy. Bryn and Gregor were anxious to get going, the boys were getting restless. They waited for thirty minutes. Gregor eventually allowed the boys out of the bus to stretch their legs. Billy arrived full of the joys.

"Where have you been?" Bryn demanded.

"Just had to stop in the pub for a whisky, a wee deoch an' dorris, as they say up here."

Bryn said nothing but shook his head. They reloaded and were away.

On the next foreign trip, Gregor found himself with the same school catching a ferry from Dover to Calais. It was simply a day trip but involved camping overnight in a quaint little village on the Kent coast. Gregor was reassured to find that a quaint little village still existed in densely populated Kent so, as far as he was concerned, this was a good start. Mick had organized the trip this time. Gregor secretly thought that he had wanted to do this, to fine toothcomb the details so that there was not the seat of the pants anarchy that had almost prevailed on the West Highland Way. Mick was too much the gentleman ever to refer to Gregor's organization in negative terms, but it was obvious on this trip that every "i" had been dotted and every "t" crossed before setting out.

They crossed on the ferry with very little drama except that Gregor, Mick, and Penny, the third adult on the trip, noted that everywhere they turned whether that be the outer deck or the indoor cafeteria the boys were there. They didn't have to be. They had been told that they could roam freely as long as they were in twos or threes. Mick had informed the ship's purser of their presence, so if there was any trouble, one of them would be called to report to his office. The boys had money to spend having been "paid" to do chores at school for the previous two months, but they weren't spending it. They were hovering about the staff.

On docking in Calais, they picked up the pre-booked bus, which dropped them in the centre of the town. The boys were now free to dip into their francs they had also been allocated for the trip, these being the days before France had joined the euro currency. Mick gave them instructions to remain in a certain prescribed area and not to go alone. He explained that the staff would be sat at *this* table outside *this* café if the kids needed them.

They did need them. They stood before them, hovering and uncertain. They stepped back occasionally and looked around. The adults were sat, having ordered coffee and croissants. Eventually Penny had had enough and called them over.

"What is it boys? You are free to go and explore. What's the problem?"

"We don't speak any French, Miss," Mark said.

"It's OK. They are used to English visitors. They make money from English visitors. Go ahead. Find out for yourself," Penny said.

They took a few tentative steps up the street. The view from the café saw Stuart reach forward and pick up a piece of fruit from a stall and examine it. He was approached by the shopkeeper who asked him something politely and was ushering him in to the store to have another look. Stuart dropped the fruit like a hot potato and stepped back, terrified. Mick looked across at Gregor and Penny.

"We may have to take charge here for a bit if this trip is going to be the cultural experience we want it to be," said Gregor.

Penny stood up. "You stay here, Mick. Come with me, Gregor." They approached the group. "Are you boys starting to get hungry?" Penny asked. They nodded eagerly. "OK, go and find a place at which you want to eat and come back and get us."

Gregor and Penny returned to Mick and the croissants and watched as the boys began to stroll around the square. Eventually, they noted that they were standing before a store which was advertising "Fish 'n Chips" in English. Penny arose and headed across to help.

"We want to eat here, Miss," said one student.

"Then one of you go in and ask for a table for 10," said Penny.

They all looked at each other but none committed.

"Could you do it for us, Miss?" Jamie said.

"No," Penny replied. "I might come and join you when you are sat at the table, but you're going to have to do it yourself. They're French. They won't bite."

Eventually Stuart spoke.

"I'll do it. Come with me, Jamie?"

Jamie nodded. They all watched.

"The French word for 'ten' is 'd-i-x', pronounced 'deece.'" shouted Penny after them.

The teachers watched from the street as Jamie held up ten fingers and the waiter ushered them to a set of tables that he put together for them. Stuart came out and asked the others to follow him in. Penny went in after they were all seated. They seemed puzzled and angst-ridden, but they were sat down and hungry.

"Join us Miss, please," said Jamie.

"I don't think so. You'll be fine," said Penny.

She turned and began to walk out, stopping to have a quick word with the waiter who nodded wisely. She pointed over the square to where her two colleagues were sitting, he nodded. She turned and waved back at the boys who were now looking terrified.

Penny returned to Gregor and Mick who were now looking amused.

"Speak or starve," was all she had said to them.

On the boat ride back that evening there was excited bravado from the group. They were so relieved to be heading back home that they were no longer hoarding the private space of their teachers. They did head out and explore in groups. Tales and legends were being born and borne about their French experience. The three teachers preened themselves on a job well done but couldn't get over the fact that these were children who were difficult to manage. They had behavioural problems that frequently manifested in tantrums and violence. But when it came to the crunch, they were still children with insecurities. It was a lesson for all that when people, young or old, are removed from their comfort zones, a true test of character comes in the shape of how they adapt to their situation. With a little bit of guidance and a bit of hunger, these children had adapted.

When Gregor arrived in Canada, it was time for *him* to step outside *his* comfort zone.

When Gregor arrived in Vancouver, there was a sudden movement to get him to coach rugby. By this point, Gregor had played the game for some thirty years but he had never coached the sport. He had developed a very blinkered vision of it. Whenever he had taken the field, his thoughts attained a black-holed single mindedness, a blinkered blundering into the dismal abyss that was the front row. What did he know of the elongated, towering second rows except that they likely nurtured their own climate as they leapt skywards in the line-out? The back row was full of the rough and the ready, those who did have a petty penchant for ball carrying but really liked the opposition to have the ball so that they could hit them. The half backs talked too much for Gregor's liking and what they talked about made no sense to him anyway. What went on beyond the fly half was a truly distant land. Centres spoke of "missed passes" and "switches" as if they were off-duty electricians. Wingers shivered and waited, festered and rotted in hopes of crumbs from the rich man's table. As for the full back, well he was *full back*, which was the best place for him.

So, when Gregor was suddenly saddled with the senior rugby team because of the five week enforced absence of their head coach, who was playing for Canada in the 1991 World Cup, he had a terrible panic. So, on the Saturday, immaculately dressed in his blazer, slacks and tie he somehow found himself on the ferry between Horseshoe Bay and Nanaimo and on the green fields of Brentwood School on Vancouver Island. He had little to say to his charges except to do as their coach had trained them to do and do it quickly and with vigour. Eventually Gregor *did* decide to try to improve as a senior coach but didn't really succeed and sought comfort somewhere in the younger grades where he found a niche in basic skills for players who were new to the game.

It was strange then to him that he was asked to go on the biannual senior rugby tour to Australia some 15 years later. He was honoured to be asked and set about making himself useful. He was christened Big Gregor for the trip because his fellow coach for the "B" team was Little Gregor.

Little Gregor was a real rugby coach. He was some 20 years younger than the bigger version. He was still playing the game and therefore was up on the latest laws and flaws. As well he had an eclectic approach to coaching that was outré and somewhat removed from the usual bombast often associated with the proprietors of the coach's tracksuits. Big Gregor had his own stock phrases that were not run of the mill.

"If you pick up mud with gloves on, the gloves get muddier but the mud doesn't get glovier," was one which had required some explanation.

"Don't have hands like feet," was easily understood.

"The touchline never misses a tackle."

These had become his stock phrases.

So, there they were on a plane to Sydney. The senior coaches had laid down the law about how important it was to make sure that their boots were immaculate because the Australian authorities would not allow any remnants of a foreign field to enter the country. Thus it was that they entered the country without incident until it came to the two Gregors who were bringing up the rear of the contingent. The "B" team coaches' boots, Big Gregor and Li'l Gregor, were confiscated to be deloused. Somewhere behind the partitions some Aussie in a hazard suit had to spray Agent Orange and other defoliants onto the offender's boots before they were allowed into the country. The senior coaches expressed no frustration at the delay; they didn't have to because it was written all over their faces. The players could not contain their delight at the coach's dilemma. The culprits hurried onto the waiting bus and said nothing.

Big Gregor made himself useful on tour. He filled the water bottles, got the ice, drank the wine and sang the songs whenever he could. What he could not do properly was play cards. He was picked as a partner in the bridge-like game of euchre and even when he was part of a pair that won a hand, his partner became frustrated because it was not enough for them to win a hand it was important for his partner to understand *how* they had won it. Big Gregor prided himself on being a good tourist. He got along well with the opposition coaches. Li'l Gregor used to disappear surfing on occasions and he would always have a ready explanation as to his whereabouts. BG would delight in an early morning mugaccino sat on a sea-swept, warming strand soaked by the early morning sun with the senior coach, Barry, who was also an early riser. He had even spent hours at the hospital with Rene who had a broken nose. He had tolerated the comment on the following morning when passing Rene and his buddies in a mall: "Mr. MacCrimmon, you look awful."

"That may be true, Rene," Gregor replied, "but at least I have never broken my nose."

An early morning riposte of which he was particularly proud.

Gregor made two rugby tours to Australia with Eldertree School. The head coach, Darren, was so well organized and so attentive to their needs that when he caught Gregor lined up at the Post Office in the Blue Mountain town of Katoomba, he asked him what he was doing. He was sending postcards abroad as was his wont whenever he travelled. Darren reached in his pocket and gave him some money from the tour fund, insisting that nothing was to be bought on tour from the coaches' own pockets.

Gregor left Australia on both those occasions with enhanced memories of the country after his sojourn there in the 1980s. He remembered the tale of the coach from Central Coast Grammar School whose junior rugby team had lost every game of the season. At the team photograph, he was stood at the back so did not realize that the players had purloined every trophy from the trophy cabinet and placed them on the floor in front of them. They looked like they were world beaters!

Also on that tour it was probably one of those occasions when Gregor had been coldest standing on the touchline because the rain came down in torrents, drowning them and freezing them at the same time. They had been improperly equipped for cold weather on their Australian tour.

There had been the people carrier rides along the sands of Fraser Island, the swim in the clearest waters that Gregor had ever seen in the lake there and the frightening sight of large lizards scrounging food as the group ate lunch. Gregor had seen Steve Irwin buggying around his animal reserve in Queensland some years before his unfortunate death.

Gregor left the country on both those occasions with a better affection for it than when he had left in 1982. Even then Gregor had felt that Australians had taught him most about what it took to be a mate, to be a friend, to be a comrade, but it had been the climate that had determined that he could never have settled there. He remembered the flight that took him home in 1982; the plane coming into land at Heathrow and the patchwork quilt of green below him. He had known then that he would have to live in a country that had distinct seasons. So, he was happy to return to Canada after those two trips, happy to have been and very happy to have come home.

On a completely different venture, Gregor was co-opted onto a trip to India. An erstwhile colleague had landed himself a teaching post in Mussoorie in Northern India, so a large group was arranged for a cultural visit over three weeks.

Landing at Delhi was something that was uneventful for the students, after all they were mostly from wealthy families so were used to a lifestyle that involved aeroplanes. However, having to wait for transport outside the airport was a cultural shock. For many, it was the first time that they had seen real poverty, real hardship for the very young and the not so young. Deliberate disablement of some of the victims was evident, a shock to the systems of all westerners. The bus arrived to take them north to the foothills of the Himalayas. There they would ascend from

Dehra Dun to the hill town of Mussoorie. Accommodation was to be provided at the school, Warburton College, for the students and staff. Kevin was the group leader and organizer. Val and Kate were the accompanying female teachers. Gregor had no idea why he had been brought along on this trip other than a friendship with his hiking buddy, Kevin. And the fact, he supposed, that he had actually been to the country, albeit a long time ago. Val and Karen were sound, down to earth, pragmatic types who were extremely adaptable and had a sense of humour to match.

They were met at the school by their ex-colleague, Derek. Derek had been an excellent English teacher at Eldertree a few years previously. He and Kevin had become firm friends. Derek was married to Thalia. They lived in a quaint little English-style cottage on the school campus. After having spoken to the students and handed them off to be taken to their billets, Derek and Kevin settled in to talk about the plans for the next few days. The plan on the following day was for them all to mount a bus and head off to the mountains to experience the largesse of the Himalayas first hand.

All awoke refreshed in the morning, mounted the bus and headed off on a windy, narrow road shaded by a deciduous canopy on either side. They had not travelled far when the bus ground to a stuttering halt, a gronching of gears and a bit of a mechanical temper tantrum. They all dismounted and waited by the side of the road for contacts to be made and a rescue or replacement to come. The bus at this point was full of student detritus, crisp bags, pop cans and such like. Kevin decided that he would take the opportunity to get the students to clean up. So, they poured themselves back into the aisles and worked quickly and efficiently. It wasn't long before they had three full garbage bags neatly tied up and sitting at the front, ready for an opportunity to dispose of them. Derek arrived on his motor bike, saw the situation and took Kevin off to seek help. The other three adults and the students left the bus driver and his courier and walked the short distance back to the school. It was an hour or so before the bus was fixed and they were on their way again. Kevin caught up with the bus later and he asked the driver to wait while he took all of the students off the bus. Gregor wondered why. Karen and Val were bemused. Kevin was not happy at all.

"I asked you all to clean up the bus, not pollute this beautiful environment. To say that I am disgusted is an understatement," he said.

At this point the students were looking confused but said nothing.

"Why would you behave like that? You know far better." Apoplexy was getting close. Gregor, Karen and Val were still confused

"I drove past with Derek and all of the rubbish from the bus was strewn across the road with crows pecking at it. Why would you spend the time collecting it and then throw it out of the bus with total abandon? You wouldn't do that in West Vancouver. Put your hand down, David, I'm not interested in any of your excuses. Get back on the bus."

All were very subdued as the bus continued its slow progress through steep-sided valleys with beautiful green rivers barrelling noisily down the gorges far below. Eventually, the driver found a pull off and they stopped for lunch. Determined to set a better example than before, Kevin issued garbage bags to three students and delegated them to collect all of the lunch debris. Such was Kevin's mood that nobody dared to object. Lunch ended, and they left the picnic site left as they had found it. All boarded the bus and waited to leave. Three neatly-tied garbage bags again sat at the front of the bus. The driver was revving his engine, ready to depart. The courier had just taken his seat when he spotted the bags. He said something in Hindi to the driver, who nodded. The courier opened the door of the bus, grabbed the three bags and hurled them down the gorge into the river, one of them splitting open on the way down. Gregor looked at Kevin, whose mouth was open in amazement. Gregor was aghast. The two women looked at each other with knowing wisdom. The courier dusted off his hands, jumped back on the bus, closed the door and sat back in his seat nodding at the driver to go. Kevin turned to Gregor.

"I guess I owe the students an apology," he said.

"You weren't to know," Gregor said.

At the next stop Kevin stood up and looked around the bus and said, "I'm sorry."

Everybody knew that there was no point in confronting courier and driver about their behaviour. It was simply a different way of doing things, simply a different culture.

There were other occasions of shock and awe on that trip. They included Val lining up at the local bank to get some cash out. She was there for over an hour. She reached the teller. He abruptly pulled down the shutters and went home, leaving her to join another line. Gregor shared with her his belief that the teller would not have done that if she had been a man.

There was the trip to Agra where they were slowed by traffic and were confronted through the bus windows with a shackled bear doing tricks for tourists. Kevin rightly forbade photographs of this disgusting display of cruelty.

There was the affronted and ironic delay of the entry into the Taj Mahal because they had closed it to the public for a visit from, of all people, the Canadian Ambassador. There was righteous indignation from staff and students alike at that gesture.

But there were highlights, too. There was a walk through beautiful meadows and a day-long hike up one of India's tallest mountains. There was a river rafting trip down the Ganges. There was Singapore on the way home.

Ah yes, Singapore on the way home! They were all set up in a high-rise hotel prior to an early morning departure for the airport. Gregor was aware, but not as much as Kevin who had spent a year working there, how strict this city state was about many things. Spitting out gum on the pavements was subject to a heavy fine. Execution was the punishment for drug smuggling. It was a strict but well organized, disciplined society. Gregor and Kevin had resolved not to go to bed on that last night. Instead, they decided to have some fun and get their own back on a group of boys who had been a bit of a nuisance on the trip. Accordingly, they bought several canisters of shaving foam, found a couple of pieces of cardboard, formed a shaving foam sandwich with the cardboard, wedged the thin end under the door where the three were sleeping and jumped on the cardboard. The effect on the other side of the door would have been an explosion of foam. Gregor and Kevin ran off giggling at their mischief and hid in a stairwell before heading off to their room.

Morning came and students and staff were lined up at the checkout desk. Kevin was just finalizing things when the head of hotel security interrupted to show him a Polaroid picture. It was obviously the picture of the sabotaged hotel room. Gregor swallowed. He felt Kevin grab his elbow under the lip of the desktop.

"We just need to spend a few moments establishing the extent of the damage here and who is responsible for this," said the security guard.

"Errrr, no problem," stammered Kevin when it was painfully obvious that there was a problem. He stepped aside and spoke sotto voce to Gregor. "Go upstairs back to our room, pick up the empty shaving foam containers and dispose of them. Got it?"

Gregor's heart was in his mouth but he reclaimed the room key on pretence of having left something behind. He collected about a dozen canisters and, without thinking, walked back along the hallway disposing of them in the various garbage containers along the way.

When he returned to the lobby, Kevin was doing his talkative best to get everybody on the bus and on their way. The women were in the background with knowing looks and fixed smiles. The head of security was talking about possible damage costs and Kevin was agreeing with him and asking that the bill be forwarded to Canada as they really did need to get going.

"Just a few minutes, Sir, we are going through the tapes now and we will soon let you know who the culprits are."

Gregor heard himself start to whistle tunelessly, an attempt at nonchalance that fooled nobody. Kevin was in full negotiating mode.

"Get the students on the bus. I'll deal with this," he said.

So they ushered them away and had an anxious few moments waiting for the bus to move. To Gregor it was an eternity. Kevin arrived at a run and in a sweat, poured himself down next to Gregor and tapped the driver on the shoulder.

"Let's go. We're late," he said.

Gregor could contain himself no longer but muttered out of the side of his mouth.

"Did they find the tapes?"

"No, they are still looking." Kevin blew out his cheeks.

Gregor put both hands up to his face and covered it, massaging his forehead in the process.

"You know, they'll find two causes of concern. When they go far enough into the investigation, not only will they see me and you doing the deed but they will also find me on this morning's tapes walking down the floor hallway dropping off the empty canisters."

Kevin's eyes widened and his mouth dropped open. He shook his head.

"If we get away with this, MacCrimmon, we'll need to have a celebratory pint in the transit area."

They turned to look at Karen and Val who were still smiling but now with a rueful acceptance rather than fear. They shook their heads knowingly.

HIKES

On their return from Australia, Gregor found himself a teaching job in Lincolnshire and Callum went back into the lift industry, fixing elevators in the west country.

"How's the lift business, Callum?"

"Up and down."

Callum and Gregor kept in close touch. So, way before the school expedition to conquer the West Highland Way, Callum suggested to Gregor that they do it as a summer holiday. Accordingly, Callum caught the train up to Lincoln and visited Chez MacCrimmon. They had decided to take the bus to Glasgow so they went down to the National Bus Station with a view to booking up for the following day. There was a line-up for the single ticket seller. Gregor felt a bit sorry for her because long before they reached her she had seemed to be overwhelmed. Finally, they were at the counter and the woman said, "Yes?" somewhat aggressively for Gregor's liking. He knew that Callum would have noted this as well.

"We'd like to catch a bus from Lincoln to Glasgow tomorrow," Callum said.

This was too much for the poor woman.

"This will be difficult and will take some time to arrange."

She clearly expected Callum to give up and move on. He reached under his left arm-pit with his right hand, pulled out his copy of *The Daily Express* newspaper, opened it out on the counter and began reading.

"What are you doing?" said the representative, scowling.

Callum didn't look up but licked his fingers and turned to the next page.

"Moi?" he said, pointing to himself. Gregor was always wary when Callum went into his pidjin French. "I'm just waiting for the arrival of my bus tickets."

The people in the line behind them were starting to shuffle from foot to foot, their fidgetiness would likely turn quickly into full-blown frustration before long. What was certain, however, was that Callum was not moving

Patricia, at least she had a name tag, turned and went into her office area and came out with a paper timetable and worked out the route for the two travellers. After about ten minutes the tickets were ready and she was handing them to Callum.

"There now, Patricia, that wasn't difficult, was it?" he said as he placed them in his wallet.

Gregor has since noted that the attitude and demeanour pf people in the service industry in the U.K. has improved since he emigrated.

The following morning, Gregor kissed Mae goodbye and he and Callum left for the bus station. It was a surprisingly speedy journey with only two changes on the way. They arrived in the city far too late to start walking so booked themselves into a Bed & Breakfast for the night. Their accommodation was close to the start point.

Their journey was blessed with wonderful weather. They made steady progress to the Bridge of Orchy where they decided to have a day and night of luxury in a bunk houset. They did nothing but lie on their beds and sleep and read, apart from a bar meal and a couple of pints locally.

They were both very happy when they reached the Glen Nevis campsite after seven days, pitched their tents and walked into Fort William for a bit of a celebration. It was a wonderful evening of fun and frolics, the highlight of which was running into the groundsman of the local golf club. Very proud of his work, two older gentlemen teased him mercilessly about the state of the course.

"Barren desert of a place, greens are bumpy and brown, mole hills all over the place, can't tell the fairway from the forest. Awfy place to play gowf."

That was the honesty and impish mischief of Scotland. Hiking was a wee bit different in Canada.

When Gregor immigrated to Canada, he was taken under many wings. Kevin was a math teacher and field hockey coach at Eldertree School so his was one of the feathered nooks under which Gregor occasionally nestled. Kevin had decided that Lake Lovelywater would be a lovely place to go for a hike.

"Lovely," Gregor had said with twinkle-eyed humour. The plan was to get over the river at Squamish using the Canadian Geological Society cable, which crossed the fast flowing river with a chair. They would have to find somebody to unlock it but Kevin was confident it would be no problem. The plan was to ascend the steep wooded peak to the Alpine Club cabin and spend the night in the luxury of a simple roof over their heads. Getting the key would be no problem, Kevin explained. But, they would bring a tent just in case. It would be no problem to find a place to pitch it, Kevin decided. Oh and yes, they were going to be bringing three dogs. They would be no problem. Gregor felt ominously that this was going to be such a problem-free trip that it was going to have a distinct lack of challenge so that it was hardly worth going!

On the day of departure, Gregor had picked up a recurrence of an old eye infection. It was herpes simplex, the recurring cold sore that had resulted in him leaving his Indian trip so early on his way home from Australia in 1982. He did not want to climb up to Lake Lovelywater in his current state of health but Kevin's wings flapped vigorously so he was happy to crawl under them yet again and be led rather than lead. So, they soon found themselves in Squamish by the cable car, which was locked. They had no key for it. Gregor breathed an inner sigh of relief but said nothing. He would have been more than happy to turn around, go home and nurse his troubled eye. But Kevin was undaunted.

He felt there would be another way. So, off they drove with no idea where, but into and around Squamish. Gregor covered his face with his hands to stop the bright lights hurting his herpetic eye. Kevin was oblivious. Suddenly Kevin was excited. Gregor noticed that they were pulling up at a helicopter hire firm. He parked and disappeared inside. Gregor was worried. Kevin came out a little crestfallen.

"How much?" Gregor asked.

"A lot and they won't take the dogs," said Kevin.

Sighs of relief from Gregor.

So, off they went and headed towards the local First Nations reserve. Kevin disappeared again. Gregor closed his eyes and went to sleep. Kevin returned and introduced his new friend named Darby.

"Darby will get us across and pick us up in a couple of days."

So they had a convoy. Darby was in his truck with a canoe atop it and Kevin and Gregor following; they reached the river side. It was a couple of hundred metres wide, fast flowing and deep. The plan was to take Gregor and his bag across first. Kevin was then to be picked up with two of the dogs and his pack.

"What about Jethro?"

Jethro was Kevin's own dog.

"It's OK. Jethro will wait for me to come back and pick him up."

All went well. Gregor was deposited safely on the other side. He sat down at the trailhead noting a pile of bear scat nearby. Berry bushes were prevalent along with the prickly devil's club. Kevin was about ten metres from the bank. Gregor was reaching out to help him unload the two dogs when Kevin shrieked. Jethro had plunged into the water on the other side and was swimming across, drifting rapidly downstream as he swam. Gregor and Darby quickly grabbed the first two dogs, and Kevin turned to desperately give chase after Jethro. Gregor battled his way through the devil's club, calling as he ran for Jethro to come. Eventually, Jethro was getting close. By this time he was being shepherded to the shore by Darby and Kevin. He was in touching distance of Gregor when he decided to turn around and head back the way he had come. Gregor lunged for his collar and missed but disturbed Jethro enough that he was pushed towards the canoe and Kevin reached out and grabbed his collar. All were safely on the west side of the river. Kevin was in shock. Gregor had forgotten his sore eye. They mustered enough energy to confirm that Darby would be back at 6:00 p.m. on the following day to pick them up.

Kevin was very silent as they ascended the trail. After about three hours the canopy gave way and they found themselves just below the Alpine cabin. They sat down on a flat rock and took in the most magnificent view of the Squamish Valley below.

"We could camp on this rock. Just think of the view in the morning," Kevin said.

"No we won't," Gregor said.

"Why not?"

Gregor pointed to a sign: "This rock must be kept clear at all times. DO NOT CAMP HERE."

"Won't be a problem," Kevin nodded to give himself confidence.

For once, Gregor put his foot down.

"I am *not* camping on this rock."

Kevin had had a couple of shocks during the day so he did not put up a fight.

"Let's see if we can get into the cabin," he said.

It was a bit of a climb because the cabin was built on stilts so as to rise above the snow. The humans climbed in easily, somehow found a window open because they had not been able to get their hands on the key. The dogs were lifted. That evening they cooked and talked, Gregor found his hip flask and they shared a few drams of whisky. Kevin opened up.

"I thought that we had lost Jethro. I would never have forgiven myself," Kevin said.

"I know," said Gregor.

He resolved not to comment. He sensed Kevin needed to unload his worries and was happy to let him do so. He thought about the old saying that if somebody had the wisdom to speak then others should have the wisdom to listen. Gregor bit his lip silently and let Kevin unload.

They slept well that night but were awoken by the clatter of helicopter blades. They looked out to see the helicopter approaching. It was heading straight for the cabin. Soon it was upon them and landing on the rock upon which Kevin had planned to camp. Gregor said nothing.

"I think that I should listen to you more often," Kevin said.

Gregor almost blurted his "wise" thoughts from the previous night but, well, his lip was going to need stitches if the trip continued for too long!

Lake Lovelywater is like Mystic Lake. It is a wonderful natural amphitheatre with the Tantalus range of alpine peaks above. Pelops and Niobe gnashing their rugged teeth, encroaching on the deep azure behind. Gregor, Kevin and the dogs had the place to themselves. They had the weather and the lake. The climbers had long since headed upwards. A short sunbathe by the shore and it was time for them to pack up and head down to meet up with their transport. There were no adventures with the dogs going back, just an easy coast down the hill and the canoe ride across the water. It was a short, sharp, shocking expedition.

Kevin was to lead Gregor astray on many a different occasion. Over the border and away was the next one.

Mount Baker in Washington State is a ski hill. It is volcanic so its hollows and holes produce sulphurous smells all the way up. There was a group of seven who set off across the border to climb it. Gregor was in the car with Albert the Pole driving when they edged the car forward to the line and the American border guard. Albert was very European in outlook. His rigour was based on the hard skills of the techniques of hiking and climbing. He did not suffer weakness in others too well. He was a "get to the top at all costs" kind of guy, a force to be reckoned with but one to be reined in as well. In the back of the truck was Kevin with his buddy, Todd, from northern Ontario. They reached the border and Gregor and Albert handed their passports to 350 pounds of American uniformed authority. The two Canadians handed their passports to the front to be scrutinized by this walking Body Mass Index. He had obviously sat for so long that his swivel chair had taken on the aspects of a dog that inevitably looked like it's master. These were the halcyon days before 9/11 when border entries into the United States were less subject to intense scrutiny. Nevertheless, there was a redneckian attitude from many border guards. Gregor handed over his British passport. He bit his lip as the comment was passed, "Great Britain? The only person who think it is 'great' is you."

He waited for a reaction. Gregor gave none. Albert handed over his Polish passport. This was too much for the blob of blue jelly

"You are British, you two are Canadian and you're letting the Polack drive?"

Gregor was afraid that Albert was going to say something so was relieved when he offered no response and they were waved through.

J.L. was driving in his jeep ahead of them. Kevin was getting frustrated at his abject refusal to break the speed limit. J.L. was a by the book kind of guy. He knew about avalanches and safety in the mountains so Gregor was glad of his knowledge and his restraint.

They reached the foot of the mountain, walked the trail through the low lying flatlands before the ascent. They started to ascend and before long arrived in a short valley protected by two lateral moraines, one about 50 feet lower than them and the one higher up the mountain that towered above them about eighty feet up. They pitched their tents on the snow and managed it as a base camp from which to assault the peak on the following day. Nobody questioned the fact that they were going to climb it when they could have actually driven to the car park and taken a ski lift up. That said something about the motivation of the group. They wanted to conquer the conquered. They were desperate to say that they were the first to be 156,000th man atop Mount Baker!

The early morning dawned bright the next day. They were breakfasted and ready for the ascent. Kevin and Albert had decided to carry their snowboards up with them with a view to a speedy exit when they had completed their ascent. They trudged upwards enjoying the physical challenge of walking on hard snow. They had been going up for about two hours when Todd pulled up with a pulled muscle. He decided to limp on but soon felt guilty about the fact that he was slowing the group down. He stopped by the side of the trail and made himself comfortable lying on his pack. He said that he would wait for the group on its return. Several of the group were uneasy about this. Albert offered no consolation to him but merely said to the group, "Leave him. We'll summit and pick him up on the way back." J.L took the lead and said, "NO! We came together, we are together, we are going down together *NOW*."

They all knew the logic behind this. It was going to take some time for Todd to hobble down. It would be dark if they had gone onwards and up and then had to manage him down the mountain. Albert shook his head but turned to Kevin.

"Well, at least you and I can snowboard back to the camp," Albert said.

He started to unstrap his snowboard from his backpack. Kevin was caught on the horns of a dilemma but realized that there was no stopping the Pole and thought that the responsible thing to do would be to go with him.

"We'll get back to camp and cook up the supper," he said by way of justification.

J.L nodded in agreement. They divided up the contents of Todd's backpack, rigged him up with two walking poles and began their slow trudge down. They had been gone but a few minutes when Kevin and Albert slipped past them and down out of sight.

It took a lot longer for the hobbled group to descend than it had been for the fit one to ascend. When eventually they found their way into the campsite they were surprised that there was no sign of their buddies and, more importantly to Gregor, no sign of their promised supper. J.L looked thoughtful and tried to cover his alarm. Gregor gulped his anxiety and made a brew of tea and boiled enough water for the dehydrated stews they had bought with them. They were silent as they ate. Gregor broke the silence.

"This is not looking very good is it, J.L? What can we do?"

"At this stage the prudent thing to do is wait. We don't need to be alarmist quite yet. Come nightfall it becomes a different issue."

After supper Gregor crawled into his tent to rest. If he was going to be involved in something desperate he was going to need to conserve his strength. He was lying there going over in his mind what he was going to tell the wives of his two "lost" buddies. He was adjusting his thinking towards the possibility of a tragedy, and he did not like it much. He could lay there no longer. He had to move. All was quiet outside of his tent as he stuck his head out but he looked up to the top of the lower moraine and saw J.L. silhouetted against the sky sitting on a rock with his elbow resting on his knee like *The Thinker*. He was obviously searching a variety of horizons. It made sense to Gregor. The sensible thing to do was to attain the high ground and give oneself the best chance of seeking and seeing. Gregor resolved to climb up and join him, figuring that two sets of eyes were better than one. He was just getting his boots on when J.L shouted down to him.

"They're in the valley below us. They're OK."

Gregor breathed again as if he hadn't breathed since they had gone missing. He started to scramble up the hill but J.L stopped him.

"Wait there. Pack up the camp and then climb up."

Smiles broke out amongst the five of them, relieved at the safe return. Gregor packed up his own stuff and then demolished Kevin's tent, pouring all of his contents into a garbage bag as the two snowboarders had their packs with them. It was sweaty work climbing up the steep bank with his pack on his back and dragging Kevin's bag as well. By the time that he reached the top Gregor was roundly cursing the friends that they had been about to lament. Reaching the ridgeline, they looked down the other side to see Kevin and Albert sat on their packs eating granola bars.

"Hey, Gregor, can you through down my gear?" said Kevin.

"Nothing would give me greater pleasure."

Gregor hurled the plastic bag into space with all the pent-up rage that suddenly swept over him. The group of five then slipped and jumped their way down over the rocks and the snow until they were finally united. It was not a happy reunion. Kevin approached Gregor with a smile of relief and arms akimbo for a hug. Gregor, uncharacteristically, drove forward in the snow and launched himself at him, hitting him in the chest with both arms. Kevin stumbled backwards, tripped and was down. He was surprised and taken aback.

"Don't you smile at me. I thought you were dead, you bastard," said Gregor.

Gregor turned on his heel, picked up his pack and started to head down the mountain. The rest silently followed. As they came out of the snow and hit the gentle trail they knew would lead them to their vehicles, Gregor sensed Kevin pulling up close to him. Soon they were walking together.

"You know, Gregor, Albert was absolutely the wrong person to snowboard off this mountain with. You should have stopped me from going with him."

Gregor kept walking but said nothing. After about five minutes of silence he said, "Would you have listened to me if I had?"

"Er no, probably not."

They stopped in their tracks, looked at each other, smiled and spoke no more.

"Would you tell me please which way I ought to go from here?"
"That depends a good deal on where you want to get to," said the Cat.
"I don't much care where," said Alice.
"Then it doesn't matter which way you go," said the Cat.
"So long as I get SOMEWHERE," Alice added as an explanation.
"Oh, you're sure to do that," said the Cat, "if you only walk long enough."

- Alice in Wonderland *by Lewis Carroll*

CHAPTER 36

A LIFE IN THE DAY OF

In 2008, Eldertree School saw fit to offer Gregor a sabbatical. Accordingly, he was given the last term of the school year off with full pay. He decided that he would return to Britain, celebrate his mother's 80th birthday and head off to do some hikes. He and Mae and one of their children were in Devon for the celebration. Then Mae returned to Canada and Gregor was on his own. On the first day of the last term, some time in mid-March, he caught a train from Bristol Temple Meads down to Penzance on the Cornish coast. His aim was to walk the coastal path as far as Land's End and then reassess his plans.

He arrived in Penzance at about noon and decided that he could not have lunch in Cornwall without it being a pastie. It did not take him long to find a pastie shop, so he bought a couple of them, went outside, found a bench on the sea front and ate them. He had felt a bit of a fraud because the pasties were not those that could have been considered the most traditional, being hot and curried to curry favour. Indian food had become British food, such was the love affair that the Brits had developed for the spices of the subcontinent. Gregor was hungry and when he was hungry not much else interested him. He scoffed and devoured the pasties while carefully eyeing the interested seagull that was perched on the promenade fence not ten yards from where he was sitting. No scraps fell from the rich man's table at that particular lunch date.

After his hasty repast, he loaded up his pack and headed along the seafront towards the quaint little village of Mousehole, pronounced "muzzle." He paused for a few moments to show respect to the Penlee Lifeboat memorial plaque. The eight-man crew had lost their lives while trying to rescue the eight crew members of the stricken vessel the MV *Union Star* in December 1983.

Gregor found himself meandering through the village trying to find the entrance to the path. Eventually, he weaved up behind some buildings and, he suspected, through somebody's garden. He was soon out on a fern-laden path and heading at a steady trudge ever westwards. It was not long before he found an idyllic little promontory on which to pitch his tent. Mindful of the fact that he was above the sea and subject to winds coming off it, he manoeuvred his tent into as sheltered a nook as possible and settled in for the night. As the sun went down, he saw the approaching lights of the Scillonian, the passenger ferry that plies its trade between Penzance and the Scilly Isles. It was slowing down to turn the corner into Mount's Bay.

On the following day he continued his progress along the easily-negotiated path towards Land's End. Gregor loved walking along the sandy cliff edge amongst the ferns and gorse. Being early spring, the area was not peopled yet by the holiday hordes, so it was easy to be far from the madding crowd. He stumbled on little coastal villages and sampled their ice cream. Bays and coves appeared, steeped in long history and longer geography. Not for the first time Gregor regretted his lack of knowledge of the geology and stories of the places he was passing through. One more night of wild camping and he was on the point of reaching the Lizard and Land's End. He had hoped that his arrival at the most southwestern tip on the shores of mainland Britain would be memorable. When he arrived there, it was indeed memorable but not in the spectacular way that he had hoped. It was a monument to trashy commercialism. It was not the black cloud cover that decided Gregor on his early departure. It was the ruination of a wild place through exploitative selfishness. Hiding his disappointment, he was walking through the car park, when he was hailed by a car owner.

"Hey, do you want a cuppa tea?" he said.

Gregor saw that he was brewing up on a camper's stove sheltered by the wall of the car park.

"I would love one," Gregor replied without thinking.

So, Gregor and a complete stranger sat on a wall in a car park on a bleak, cloudy day sipping a cup of thick black tea.

"Sorry, I forgot to buy milk," he said.

"No problem," said Gregor.

It was just the sort of pick-me-up that Gregor needed. He would have preferred Land's End to be a bleak slab or rocky cliff subject to the battering of the waves. Above it should have been the beautiful natural cliffs and vegetation that he had spent most of the last few days walking through. Instead, it was all candy floss and fairground, touristy knick-knacks and sordid gaudiness. So, Brendan from Stoke-on-Trent was a point of very human contact who could not have made his cheery appearance at a better time.

"Do you want a lift?" Brendan said, flicking the remnants of his tea cup over the wall.

Gregor hesitated. "Where are you going?" he asked.

"I don't know. Where do you want to go?"

Gregor delayed his answer. He was here for the purity of the walk, the communing of his treading feet with nature and the purifying of his wonderings as he wandered. Was not the acceptance of a ride a treasonable offence? A treachery to all he had talked about before he left Vancouver? He enjoyed the breeziness of his new-found friend. He could take him away from his Land's End disappointment physically and metaphorically. He needed the distraction.

"I'd love a ride. How about St. Ives?"

As they journeyed through the high-hedged country lanes, Brendan told his story. As a courting couple, he and his wife had holidayed in Cornwall. They had loved it so much that they came down on honeymoon and every summer thereafter. Brendan's wife had died the previous year. This trip was a journey down memory lane in his grief. It was a tribute to her memory. Brendan talked lovingly about his wife. They were both from Stoke-on-Trent, had met at school and been inseparable thereafter. They had not had any children, which caused his bright eyes to suddenly droop in sorrow, but they had had each other and a decade of marital bliss and companionship to look back upon.

"10 years was nowhere near long enough," said Gregor.

"A lifetime would not have been long enough with my Maggie," Brendan said with a catch in his throat.

After that there was silence for the next fifteen minutes or so until they hit the outskirts of St. Ives. Brendan dropped Gregor in the centre of the town and shook his hand, then headed off. Gregor got his bearings and headed down towards the coast and the beach. He had been grateful for the ride and the company. But, he thought, Brendan had been equally grateful. He had been able to open up about his tragic loss. He had been able to do so to a complete stranger. Gregor suspected that he would not have been able to do so to a friend or close acquaintance. A complete stranger was human enough to be a sounding board for his thoughts and cares. A complete stranger would not be around for very long. The ability to open up and betray one's innermost feelings would cost nothing because the two men were never likely to see each other again. It had not been a happy story, but Gregor was strangely uplifted by it. He decided to treat himself to a Bed & Breakfast.

The breakfast on the following morning was the biggest he had ever seen. Bacon, sausage, two eggs, fried bread, black pudding and lashings of toast and butter all washed down with plenty of coffee and juice. He was energized and walking with a bounce in his step and found his way down to the coast and the head of the trail. The weather had cleared from the previous day. He was stepping north from St. Ives and from the depressive drear of Land's End.

There is something about the county of Cornwall that makes it so different from the rest of England. The Cornish coast is different again. What with Tintagel being one of King Arthur's legendary homes, the history of smuggling and the tin mines, it lives up to its name as being a wing—a "cornu"—of Wales. Indeed, the last native speaker of Cornish only died in the twentieth century. Cornish names beginning with "pen" or "tre" are not just place names but have their place in the surnames of the people. Its distance from London was a world away in culture although only 290 kilometres or so physically. Hiking along the cliff paths, descending and ascending into bays and villages, passing the ruins of tin mines, Gregor felt like he was in a foreign land.

The quaint wee village of Perranporth is basically on the beach. It has a campsite next door to a rugby club. Gregor pitched his tent, resolving to drop down to the RFC (Rugby Football Club) on the following day, the Saturday, and watch a game if there was one. There was a touring side from the Midlands in town and they were up for a good time. So, drink was being consumed on the touchline and banter was being consumed on the pitch. If there is anything more merciless than the comments of spectators about the opposition, it is the cheery disrespect they show towards their own players. Comments from the touchline from behind a pint and a sandwich are rarely touched with wisdom. When the "caveman" went on a run he received a storm of laughter and grunting noises from his "friends" on the touchline. When a ball was dropped, a pass went awry or a lineout was lost, there was no mercy shown. Gregor gave the game until half-time. Strolling along the beach he decided to make a pilgrimage to Padstow and Rock. His family had owned a cottage at a place called Tredrizzick near Rock for years so he decided to camp near Padstow and take the ferry over the Camel Estuary for a trip down memory lane.

He took a bus there and found the campsite just above the town. It was pretty empty given the fact that it was early April, but it was open and it had good facilities. Frost came on the first night as if to confirm that any hint of summer was a false dawn. He walked into the village and boarded the ferry. The Camel Estuary had been a place of several misadventures in Gregor's youth. His father had owned a sailing boat, a laser, which was bigger and bulkier than a sailboard but not by much. Gregor had visited Tredrizzick with his old friend from college days, his Dutch rugby captain, Jan van Merken. Jan was keen to go for a sail in the laser so they walked down to Rock to find it at its mooring in the sand dunes by the club. It was not there. They decided to venture over the threshold of the Rock Sailing Club to make enquiries about *Lassie*, for so she was called.

There was only one person in the bar as they entered. An ancient mariner sat in what looked like his traditional seat at the corner of the bar. It was a surprise to find that he was dressed in a blazer and sea captain's hat. Gregor and Jan looked at each other, signalling an inkling of what their conversation would be like as they approached him.

"I wonder if you could help us," Gregor said, almost saluting as he approached his quarry. "Our family laser, *Lassie*, is not at its mooring. How might we go about finding it?"

The "Commodore" was very tired as he spoke. He drawled a bored condescension to them both.

"Many, many high tides here recently. Must have carried it away. Not much I can do about that, chaps. You'll just have to peruse around a little farther. See what turns up. No, of course, it could have found its way over to Padstow. Worth a look over there. Catch a ferry. Nose around the village."

Jan and Gregor walked down to the beach and over to the slipway where the small open-air, twenty-seater ferry came in. Gregor saw that the tide was out and asked Jan whether or not he would like to walk and swim across.

"You know this place, Gregor. Just remember that I'm not a very good swiimmer," Jan said.

It was true. Jan was a P.E. student who was a good athlete. He was an excellent rugby player, a budding cricketer. He loved all sport, except swimming. Gregor shrugged.

"Should be no more than a paddle here and there," he said.

So, off they set. They enjoyed the heat of the sunshine on their heads and legs. They revelled in the cooling waters as they paddled through the remnant pools. As they came closer to Padstow harbour, the river channel asserted itself so they were able to distinguish the river as opposed to the tidal seawater. The swim was about thirty or forty metres but the water was running fast and would likely sweep them downstream a good way before they were across. However, nothing ventured, nothing gained, so they plunged in. Almost immediately they felt the force of the water driving them away from the bank. They commenced a slow crawl towards their goal. Gregor was a better swimmer so kept a close eye on his friend who was beginning to struggle against the current. Jan was spluttering and losing rhythm. Gregor was getting worried. They were about halfway across and were moving quickly downstream from the town. Gregor decided to tread water and bide his time until his friend came closer. He reached down with his feet touched the riverbed and stood up. The water was flowing past him. It was only up to his waist. Meanwhile Jan continued to thrash away. Such was his focus on the job at hand that he did not notice his friend standing next to him. Eventually, Gregor looked down and tapped him on the shoulder. Jan looked up in surprise, stopped his efforts and stood up before he was swept farther away. They both stood next to each other looking sheepish. Quickly they waded over to the other side and were soon ascending the stairs to the town.

"I need a pint," Jan iterated.

There was a yelp from Gregor and he pointed. There on the harbour quay was *Lassie* the sailing boat.

"Well, I'll be buggered!" Gregor exclaimed with glee.

He went over to examine it and found all of its bits intact. They went for a celebratory pint, which was useful for washing down the pie and chips they had ordered. They discussed how to get it over to the other side of the estuary. They had no sails or paddle with them but it was fairly light. The tide was about to come in, so they believed that it would be possible to walk and paddle it over to the dock. They launched it with some difficulty into the water and proceeded to pull it through the current, which was easier because the sand was no longer bare but now covered with water from the incoming tide. They were about halfway across when they were hailed with a megaphone from a tourist boat. They were shocked to hear the voice.

"Ahoy, you two, I have a salvage to claim on that boat," said Captain England, a well-known roguish businessman from the Padstow area.

"How much?" Gregor responded.

"'undred quid should do it," he said.

"I'll give you eighty."

"I'll meet thee at the Rock Sailing Club tonight. Thee 'ad better be there."

So it was that Gregor and Jan found themselves at the corner of the bar with the "Commodore" and Captain England at 7:00 p.m. that evening. There was a real contrast in the rough tanned Cornish sailor with the complexion beaten brown and wrinkled by the weather and muscles hardened by the day to day labour of running a ship. It was obvious to all the company that the "Commodore" was by far the inferior sailor, and yet, here in the presence of the great unwashed, his condescension remained unscathed, as intact as it had been since the day of his birth. He expected forelock tugging and respect and was naïve enough to believe that he was getting it. It was the Commodore's advice that had led to the finding of the laser, it was his experience of the waters that had surmised the only possible outcome. He was King Neptune and the three others were there to worship and kowtow. And worship and kowtow the three men did (with large tongues in larger cheeks).

They settled on ninety pounds and a round of drinks. The Captain spit on his hand and offered it with a shake. The Commodore frowned his disapproval.

"Lets get out of here, boys, and go to the pub," the Captain said.

The Commodore huffed a sigh of relief. They headed down the stairs of the sailing club and into the pub on the other side of the road where Horatio England was a local character and received a welcome full of bonhomie and back slapping good nature.

That was then. Now Gregor was on his sabbatical and doing what one shouldn't do: going back. He nosed around the corner to the old family holiday home in Tredrizzick and found it deserted. The quiet close was quieter than he remembered. He had visited there with friends, with girlfriends, with family and with those who were no more, those who had enjoyed the feel of the sailing boat on the water; those who had actually enjoyed the pompous bombast of the Rock Sailing Club.

Gregor did not wait long there but headed off to St. Enodoc Church, which nestled in the sands within crashing wave distance of the sea, almost sheltered from the almost winds. There he bowed his head before the grave of John Betjeman (1906-1984). He had been the Poet Laureate, probably the first in the TV and radio media age. He had brought his poetry to the people. The powers that be suggested that his verse was not highbrow enough to merit the authority and fame that he achieved; that it was puerile and naïve. That may have been but it had appeal and, surely, appeal was what verse was all about.

Gregor paused in the churchyard for a few moments and then headed out towards the headland. He saw nobody else on his walk. When he turned to retrace his steps to the ferry and the campsite at Padstow, he did not regret his journey down memory lane but was strangely surprised at his own blithe indifference, a realization of how little it meant to him. Tredrizzick had been, after all, a place for family and friends, a summer home that had witnessed seduction and lust as well as love and unrequited love. He had visited there when Mae was pregnant with their first child. He had remembered that that was probably the last time that they had visited the house before his father's death and the sale. But he felt nothing for it now, very little for the memories. He had enjoyed the runs on the coastal pathways, the surfing in the beach at Polzeath. He thought long and hard about his relationship with the people who summered in Rock. There was a "hooray Henry" arrogance about some of them that he had disliked intensely; a spoilt brattishness that omitted a selfishness that had little time for the hoi polloi and uncaring ignorance of the lifestyles of the great unwashed. Gregor pondered that it was probably too reminiscent of his boarding school experience to carry pleasant memories for him. But he did remember with a sigh and a smile the two separate long weekends he had spent down there, the one with Sharon and the other with Christa.

But those trips had little to do with the scenery of Cornwall and the magnificence of its scenery. He was happy enough to leave this place and to head back to Somerset to see his family. He would then head off to Wales for a few days to walk with his daughter in Snowdonia.

Unlike Tredrizzick, Gregor had great affection for Snowdonia. It stemmed from a time many years previously when he and a friend, Richard Thwaite, had spent a weekend trying to cover all of the fourteen Welsh 3000-foot peaks. They had accomplished twelve of the fourteen. They had justified not doing the last two in the belief that that was a goal for a future trip. Now it was many years later and they had still not made that return trip and were increasingly unlikely to. There was a lesson here for Gregor and Richard and it involved something like "carpe diem." Seizing the day, making the most of the opportunity was something that they had not done. Yet, Gregor reflected, summits were not the be all and end all; the weather had been lovely, the companionship had been supreme and the scenic panoramas had been stunning. A paltry little bump of an ascent just to claim conquest had never really been Gregor's modus operandi. Perhaps that lack of drive had been a reflection of his long teaching career, a distinct lack of goal orientation and ambition, a wish to be in the crew but not steering the boat. Whatever it was, as he drove up through Hereford with his daughter, Jessie, in the car, he knew that if there were goals on this trip then they would likely be achieved.

Jessie was a sharp-witted, some might say caustic, young woman. She was very goal oriented. She was academic and determinedly athletic. If she said that the peak was going to be conquered then she would scramble through fair weather and foul, through scree and scarp to make it so. Jessie was tough and resilient. Tryfan was the first goal.

If ever there was a more convenient mountain, Gregor did not know of it. Tryfan was a short drive from Plas y Brenin and at the head of Llanberis Pass. They parked the car near Llyn Ogwen and set off up the trail. It was a steep, rocky ascent with rewarding views towards the coast all the way up. The tradition at the top was to leap from the two named rock pillars, Adam and Eve, by way of celebration. This they both did before descending to the road below.

The following day would be a longer hike, up the Pyg track to the top of Snowdon. This peak is the highest in Wales. Access could be easy or difficult, an easy entrance or an extensive exposure. There was also the train ride. The PYG track was long and gentle with a steep piece to the summit at the end. The day was not wet but it was overcast and getting colder with elevation. Gregor forgot whom he was with for a moment and suggested that they might not bother with the summit. Sacrilege! The figure in front of him deliberately increased her stride as a daughter to father form of retaliation. The summit was reached but there was no view on this day, just a shivering group of train tourists circling a short route around the points of the compass, checking off the tick box of Snowdon. Jessie and Gregor beat a hasty retreat, retracing their steps, trying desperately to resist the temptation of the warmth and welcome of the waiting train. Going downhill was not a MacCrimmon strong point but Jessie was young and had knees, Gregor still had knees but he needed to work hard to preserve them intact. There were hints of ache and pain here and there, which were a warning of aging to come.

Jessie was instantly asleep as they drove back down to the Betws-Y-Coed Youth Hostel where they were staying. As they meandered down the country road, Gregor saw a jet fighter coming up the valley towards them. The RAF were frequently observed exercising their skills up and down the coires in the National Park. Indeed, Gregor had observed a pilot accomplishing a very tight turn below him on the trip. Gregor had had his heart in his mouth as he felt that the pilot was not going to make it. This time the sleeping Jessie and he were head-on with the jet bearing down on them from about 300 feet. There was a quick flash of its lights and it was over them and gone. Gregor was sorry that Jessie had not been awake to witness it but wondered if they had just been the victims of a rocket attack. Had they just been "bombed"? Gregor would never know the answer to that and Jessie would accuse him of imagining things when he told her the story, but somewhere up there was a fighter pilot with an impish smile on his face. He was probably sat over a pint in his officer's mess bragging how he had "taken out" a Nissan Micra.

Driving back through Mid Wales, having started the journey east from Aberystwyth was a pleasant surprise. Like the Borders region of Scotland there is a tendency for travellers to skip the Lowlands in their eagerness to get to the more spectacular Highlands. This is perhaps a mistake. In Wales, people go to the Gower coast for their holidays as they do to Llandudno and Snowdonia in the north. Mid Wales is rolling hills and a little gem of sheep farming and green fields. It was once stated that if Wales were flat it would be bigger than England. Gregor mentioned this to Jessie as they drove through to the east and the Severn Bridge. Gregor's enthusiasm for trivia rarely received an enthusiastic audience. If he was expecting joyous exhilaration at this particular gem of information then he was to be sadly disappointed. She merely nodded and refolded her arms and continued to look out of the window.

Because he had been dragged up Snowdon, albeit not kicking and screaming, Gregor thought that he might attempt the highest peaks in England and Scotland: Scafell Pike in the Lake District, and Ben Nevis by Fort William. Jessie had returned to Canada. His son, Ross, who had been visiting and playing rugby in Bridgewater for a season, had returned to Canada as well, leaving Gregor with his rather suspect car with which to take him northwards. Gregor resolved to try and take in the three peaks of Yorkshire before heading into the Lake District. Whernside, Ingleborough and Pen-y-ghent formed a famous, classic hike. It was no more than a day's round but teams raced on these three hills on a regular basis. They clocked in and out from the café in the village of Horton-in-Ribblesdale. This café probably sold the largest cups of tea in the world. Gregor found his way into the café and asked about who he should see to book into the campsite next door. He was pointed in the direction of the local farmer but, after a futile search, he decided that he would simply risk pitching his tent and seek forgiveness later. Despite being a Friday night, he found that it was almost totally deserted. As was his wont, he sought out the corners, the far reaches of the campsite, places of peace and privacy. It often meant that it was a long distance to the toilet block but, if there was a bush behind his tent then that had always sufficed for his night bladder needs. He pitched and went off to the pub. An hour or so watching the bar fill up and he thought that he had better return to his tent as he was to have an early start in the morning. He had decided that he would not do the round in one day but simply dash up Pen-y-ghent and back in a short burst, then tackle the other two peaks on the following day.

The valley was bathed in late evening sun as he walked up through the village to the campsite. He could not believe the transformation. From being virtually deserted it was now cheek by jowl tentage. Families had set up with their large-porched tents, hikers were settled around their cooking pots. There were leather-jacketed, tattooed motor bikers, there were panier-clad bicycles and their lycra-clad owners. What had been a wee quaint hamlet had transformed into a city after a few short hours. It wasn't difficult for Gregor to find his tent, but it was difficult to reconcile his love of peace and quiet with the loud music booming out from the family to the right of him and the colourful language of the leather jackets to the left. Nothing to be done about it but to do what Gregor had always done in situations with which he was not particularly happy. He edged over and made friends.

He moved towards the bikers first of all, asked them from whence they came, were they members of a club. He laughingly could pretend no interest in their bikes but was certainly interested in what attracted them to the area. Apparently the road passed the famous Ribblehead Viaduct, a glossy calendar picture if ever there was one. This road up to the village of Hawes and beyond was wonderful as seen from a motorbike.

The two children on the other side of his tent had somehow found space to create a small badminton court. They were flicking the shuttlecocks over the net as mum and dad were sat in deck-chaired splendour watching them over open cans of beer. Dad did not look as though he would be flinging himself around the badminton net any time soon and Mum looked like everything she had ever eaten had come out of a frying pan. Gregor went up and shook their hands. They were up from Birmingham for their annual week's holiday. What were they going to do with their time here, Gregor had asked. Drive into Settle for fish and trips, maybe drive up to Hawes for afternoon tea if the weather was good. They loved the area, loved the scenery but grumbled that their fitness wouldn't allow them to become fully immersed in it as they would have liked.

Gregor suspected that there was no point of an early night as the company was likely to have the noises of playing children until the sun went down and the deep biker stories late into the night as they shared their chat. He returned to the three bikers.

"I'm heading up to the pub and would enjoy your company if you would like to come along," he said.

Gregor did not know who was more surprised at the affirmative answer, Eric, who accepted, or Gregor who had asked it. Accordingly, the four of them walked through the campsite. Eric, it turned out, was an art student at a college in Liverpool. Gregor must have looked surprised at this because Eric explained that he was surprised, too. He had decided about a year ago that he would like a tattoo and happened on the local parlour when the other two, John and Wayne, were getting additions to their already extensive collection of assorted inks. He had got talking to them and listened as they weaved their enthusiastic, lavish tales of the open road. So, he had asked if he could rent a bike and join them one weekend. It had only then been a short step to borrowing money from his parents and buying a bike of his own. Now he sought every opportunity he could to get away from his studies and was out on the open road with his new-found friends.

There was a cusp in the evening when Gregor was torn between staying until closing time or heading back to his tent for his planned early night. For once in his life he did the sensible thing and left them to their revelry, explaining his plans for the morrow. All was quiet from the family next to him, which was fine, but he knew that their peace would be disturbed when the triumvirate returned from the pub. They had been pretty lively when he had left them and were unlikely to be less so when they came back. So, Gregor was resolved to sleep but also expectant that he would be woken.

He awoke at 7:00 a.m. the next morning feeling refreshed and wondering why he had not been shockingly awakened by John, Wayne and Eric. There was an eerie silence in the campsite only disturbed by the occasional crash of the doors as somebody entered or left the shower block. Not a sound from the family next door and only the faintest of snoring from his new friends' tents. Gregor reached for his bacon and eggs and started to cook. After about 15 minutes Eric's head popped out of his tent.

"Smells good," he whispered.

Gregor smiled. As he cooked up his tomatoes, onions, mushrooms, fried bread, eggs and bacon, he was glad that he had bought more rather than less. He filled his plate and on an impulse went and tapped on Eric's tent. A head appeared.

"Breakfast?"

Eric's surprised head appeared. "Are you sure? Yes please."

"I've only got one plate so eat up and I'll get some in for the other two," Gregor said.

He heard their spluttered stirrings in the other two tents. Soon, the two of them appeared, obviously slightly the worse for wear but with grins on their faces. The smiles widened as Gregor presented them with a plate to share while he ate out of the frying pan. Finally, when they surfaced, Gregor was packed up and ready for his hike up the hill.

"Are you three here tonight?" Gregor asked.

"Yep," Wayne answered.

Apart from Eric, neither of the two had been particularly effusive in their gratitude for the windfall of breakfast. They had grunted their hung-overed thanks, of course, but it was almost begrudging.

"Have a good walk," Eric said when he emerged from his tent and was running his hands through his hair and contemplating the walk to the shower block.

No reply from the other tents, just sleeping bags being unzipped and the scuffing of clothes as limbs were manipulated noisily within the confines of the tent as they got dressed. Gregor grabbed his walking pole and was off.

Visibility was fine as he ascended through the fields. He knew from previous experiences that there was a steep last step up to the top and then a flat continuation along the ridge until the descent on the other side on the way to the ugly whale of a hill that was called Whernside. Of course, Gregor was going no farther than the top and then retracing his steps. He was disappointed when he reached the peak because low cloud cover had obscured any potential views. Many people had passed him on his leisurely saunter. Some were in groups, obviously competing either with other teams or against the clock. There were married couples who were fit and middle-aged. There was the occasional family with teenagers who were either whining or exuberantly jumping from rock to rock.

"Strange," thought Gregor, "how the middle range of moods was often so foreign to the teenage years."

There were fewer people about as Gregor descended to the village. It was about 4:30 p.m. when he returned to his tent. He had had a sandwich and some trail mix for lunch, but he was hungry. Gregor had to admit that he was always hungry when he was on a camping trip. The family was not there, nor were Eric and his mates. Gregor brewed a cup of tea, pulled his sleeping bag and mattress from the tent and lay down for a read and a nap. Gregor awoke, cooked himself a dehydrated supper and resolved to have an early night, a laydown and a read in his tent. He heard the family come back but it wasn't until after 11:00 p.m. that he heard the motorbikes arrive and then only at the entrance to the campsite. They cut their engines and walked the bikes down through the grass. Gregor was learning not to generalize. His new friends were not the stereotypical macho men who cared not a jot for the world or what it thought. They were coming across as kind and considerate, albeit not very effusively thankful for the breakfast that he had made them.

Gregor was up bright and early, well rested and eager to get going on a beautiful day. He was not the first to arise, however, for Eric, Wayne and John all had their tents packed away and were ready to head home.

"Hope we didn't wake you when we got back last night, "Eric offered.

"I heard your bikes arrive but you were very quiet," Gregor responded.

"We're going for breakfast at the café. Do you want to come?" John asked.

"Love to," Gregor said. He had intended to cook but the expense of the bought breakfast notwithstanding, he would get going earlier if he did not have to clean up.

They found a table for four.

"Order what you want, you're not paying," said Wayne.

They had a wonderful feast made more memorable because Gregor heard about their adventures from the day before. They had been stopped by the police as they entered Hawes.

They were not surprised because the police were always suspicious of what they thought of as being their type. But they were surprised when the two policemen came over to talk to them. They had only put the sirens on when they had realized that the bikes were Harley Davidsons. One of the policemen was keen to buy one for himself and only wanted to look them over. John had offered to let him drive it as long as he could ride pillion. So they had headed north out of Hawes intending to travel only eight kilometres and return. They were only three kilometres out of the village when they heard a siren behind them and were pulled over by another policeman for speeding. The new cop, Geordie, realized that he was about to book one of his mates, didn't say a word, returned to his panda car and drove off. Harry, the bike enthusiast, apologized sheepishly to John and asked him if he would drive them back into Hawes, this time obeying the speed limit.

They finished up their breakfast. Gregor thanked them for their kindness and shook their hands. John thrust a package and a flask at Gregor.

"Packed lunch and some tea for you, my friend," he said.

"How do I get your flask back to you?" Gregor asked.

"You don't. We bought it for you," Eric said, looking embarrassed.

"That breakfast yesterday meant so much to us. We are not used to such acceptance from the likes of you. We don't forget."

They turned on their heels, walked out, cranked up their machines and, with a wave, were gone.

Gregor loaded his lunch into his pack, made it comfortable on his back and searched for the trail to Ingleborough. It wasn't long before he spotted the familiar but unusual limestone slabs that were to accompany him all the way to the top of the peak. Gregor loved the unusual terrain that led up to the foot of Ingelborough. Like the previous day, the top was shrouded in mist but this time it was that much colder than the top of Pen-y-ghent. He did find a nook in which to eat his lunch but was keen to keep moving. He backtracked down the path for a little bit before branching off to make his way to his final peak, that of Whernside. He had a cup of tea outside a farmer's house from an enterprising farmer's wife. He downed the flask at lunchtime, realizing that as he supped it there was not just sugar therein but something alcoholic that was heart warming.

The top of Whernside was packed with people. Gregor had forgotten that this was the middle peak of the traditional round. There were some clinging to the back side of a wall for shelter. Gregor did not hang about. He came off and down towards the Ribblehead Viaduct and onto the road that led back to Horton in Ribblesdale. He sunk his pride and hitched shamelessly along the road, soon being picked up by a delightful old couple in a Morris Woodie—so called because part of the framework was made of wood. They talked little on the way down to the campsite but smiled as they dropped him off.

It was Sunday night so the campsite had gone from "Woodstock" to empty field in a matter of hours. There were three other tents that Gregor could see but apart from that he was on his own.

He had the sleep of the innocent that night and set off early in the morning for the Lake District. He planned to camp at an interesting place called Boot for no other reason but that it had an interesting name. He also thought that it would be a good place to set off to conquer Scafell Pike, which at just over 3000 feet was the highest peak in England. The campsite at Boot was friendly. He was relieved to get there as he had just driven up what must have been the most hair-raising ascent of a road that he had ever driven. The Hardknott Pass single track route has the distinction of being the steepest road in Britain. He was relieved to get to the top without overheating. Indeed, he was amazed that it had made it at all. The ride down the other side to the west was much, much easier.

On the following day he set off the little knoll behind the campsite to walk towards Scafell. This was a mistake. He realized pretty soon that it would take him most of the day simply to get to the foot of the hill let alone to climb it. He returned and grabbed the car, drove out of the valley and round to Wasdale. He parked in the National Trust car park and set off up a very modern, newly-built trail. He was up and down the hill in four hours, praising himself that he simply had Ben Nevis to complete the three tallest peaks in the three countries. As he descended he had a quiet satisfaction but also an excitement and a wish to get over the border into his home and native land. He had not been back to Scotland in over fifteen years and he was very excited.

The drive to Gretna Green and the border was uneventful. He did not stop pope-like to kiss the ground as perhaps he should have done to mark the occasion. Instead, he headed for Dumfries where he wanted to spend time to honour his hero, Robert Burns.

Robbie Burns (1759–1796), the ploughman poet, had first risen into Gregor's consciousness when he used to visit his grandparents house in Nairn. As one climbed the stairs every night in that solidly built abode, one walked past two copies of two famous pictures. One was the meeting of Wellington and Blucher after the Battle of Waterloo in 1815, and the other was the death of Nelson at the Battle of Trafalgar in 1805. To Gregor, at a young age, these pictures were almost as old as the dinosaurs. It was only in later life that he realized that they were very close to his grandfather who was born in 1880. Indeed, his Grandpa had been twenty-one years of age when Queen Victoria died.

While these seized his imagination, there was a row of miniatures, cameo pictures that hung from the mantlepiece below the steady tick of the carriage clock and above the fireplace. One of those pictures was of Robbie Burns. The poet was born in the right place at the right time. He was born to a Scotland that, unlike many other countries at the time, had resolved to educate the common man. How ahead of its time, how enlightened this was, was driven home to Gregor when he came to study the Great War (1914–1918). It was possible to build up a picture of the social complications of the war by reading correspondence from the front lines. Thus did there come to be so many poignant writings and poetry from both the German and Allies sides but not so many from the Russians, simply because the average Russian peasant soldier was illiterate. The Romanov Dynasty had not taken it upon itself to teach the peasantry to read and write. Robert Burns, a hardscrabble peasant farmer, had taken his country and the world by storm with his simple observations on life from the perspective of the common man. His tributes to a mouse, a louse and a haggis, his socialistic comments on the rights of man as they related to princes and kings, his down-to-earth perceptive comments about "best laid schemes gang aft a gley" or "wad the power the giftie gie us to see oursels as ithers see us" has made their ways in various guises into the language. Now there are celebrations of his birthday from Australia to Canada to Russia. From a cottar in the rocky farmland of Lowland Scotland to the world had been this great man's journey.

Whenever Gregor entered Dumfries and wandered around the town centre, he watched and looked at the people, he saw their hustle and bustle and thought about the presence of the poet in the churchyard not far removed from the scene. If Gregor were to stop some of the locals in the street he wondered if they would know where the great man was buried. Would they be able to quote a few lines of his poetry? Would they be able to recognize some of the old Scots dialect as it was written and spoken? When the church bell tolls its call to congregate, would they recognize the words:

**"Now clinkumbell wi' rattlin' tow,
Begins to jow and croon."**

Surely this was more evocative than,

*"Now the church bell ringer with rattling rope,
Begins to swing and ring and murmur."*

Or would they be so engrossed in their phones and their texts and their shopping trolleys that such art would pass them by? Gregor didn't know but he did understand that one man's hero was another man's nobody.

He parked his car and walked down to the River Nith, which was wide and fast flowing. He walked over the new bridge, "puffed up wi' windy pride" as Burns would have it. He walked the riverbank to the museum and gave himself a tour around the building, reading and taking it in but not yet able to compare it to the magnificent museum at Ayr, which he would visit at a later date. He crossed the footbridge, visited the mausoleum in the churchyard and was impressed at how appropriate an honour this was for the great man. He was also impressed by the honour and respect paid to so many of Burns' contemporaries in the cemetery. He passed the statue of Jean Armour, Burns' wife, on the roadside and made his way to the house where the poet had breathed his last at the all too young age of thirty-seven. He was impressed by the longevity of his scratched signature on the windowpane of the room upstairs. He was awed by how much history had passed since the day of his death in 1796. This was but forty years removed from the Jacobite Rising that culminated in the Battle of Culloden in 1746. Burns was a contemporary of the French Revolution and a distant witness to the signing of the American Declaration of Independence in 1776. Burns was pre-Napoleonic Wars, pre-Victorian, in at the dawn of the Industrial Revolution, pre-American Civil War and all the tragic wars and wonderful white hot technology of the twentieth century. And yet, and yet, here was his authentic signature on an upstairs window all of those many years later. Gregor walked out of the house, back to his car and drove north.

On his way out of town he pulled up at some lights and spotted the public library. On a sudden impulse, he changed lanes and pulled into the library car park. He decided to check his emails, to catch up on the news of family and work. He was a little bit shocked and a lot disappointed when the first work email he opened was from his boss who explained that he was leaving for pastures new. He was going to be a headmaster at a school in California. Gregor had always got along well with his wise old owl of a head who was kindly, absent of educational jargon but full of common sense. So, while he was wishing him luck as he typed his message of congratulations, he was selfishly hoping that the school was not going to be burdened with some martinet, some innovator who would not leave well alone but had an educational bee in his bonnet that often meant the creation of work for others. Gregor sighed, signed-off and left the library, reflecting further on the words of Robbie Burns:

"There is no such uncertainty as a sure thing."

Gregor had been secure in his belief that he would be returning to his old job where his old boss would let him carry on as he had carried on before. He had to call on Robbie Burns again to remind him not to count his chickens.

He headed north to Glasgow, intending to stop south of the city, find himself a campsite for the night and head through the town after the rush hour had died down on the following day. Gregor found a campsite at Barnbrook in the Clyde Muirshiel Regional Park. Its facilities were basic but the price was right. Four pounds per night was enough for him. There was only one other tent in the park and it belonged to a man who was working at Prestwick Airport. It was only a low-to-the-ground single-person tent. It would be quite a hardship to crawl out of that every morning and present himself for work at the airport.

"It takes all sorts," muttered Gregor and then in a faux Yorkshire accent, "There's nowt sa queer as folk."

He buttoned his lip as he noted the man from the tent looking at him quizzically and realized that he had spotted Gregor talking to himself.

"Mustn't do that," Gregor said aloud and then put his hand to his mouth as he realized that he just had.

Gregor headed for the urban conurbation of Glasgow. He reflected that he liked the city not for his knowledge of it—he had been there rarely—but for his many contacts that he had had with Glaswegians over the years. Gregor had had a year or so working in the ski resort, the village of Aviemore, in the early 1970s. He had worked in a hotel there as a porter and lived in the staff block. There he had met a great number of Glaswegians who had abandoned their city because the work outlook was not good. They had come north. He respected their hardness and their humour, their gregariousness and their loyalties. He had known that he could never really be accepted by them because he had not experienced what they had experienced nor seen what they had seen, but he did jump at the chance to take up an invitation to go down to watch Rangers vs. Dynamo Kiev in a European Cup quarter final. He had been awestruck by the roar of the crowd, goose bumped by the aura of the stands and suborned by the whole sublime experience. He had seen the loyalty when John, the twenty-three-year-old waiter in the hotel, had taken the train home to Easterhouse to mete out a crude justice to the gang that had beaten up his brother. Apparently he had ambushed them singly and given them a good hiding. He had seen it from his room-mate Jimmy Culven who had returned one night in high dudgeon over something the waiter, Conn, had said to him. Gregor had quakingly persuaded him from taking out his razor blades to go and deliver a cutting justice to his "enemy." Indeed, his experience in Aviemore had reminded him of the old historical adage about Scotland that they fought each other much more often and with much more fervour than they did their real "enemies," that is, the English.

But on this occasion he was not stopping in the city but was eager to get up to the Loch Lomond side and explore the village of Luss on his way to Oban. Gregor was never really sure why he always seemed to find his way to Oban. It was a port and a train station, a Calmac ferry terminal, a gateway to the islands. It was the train journey to the city of Glasgow. Gregor believed that he was always attracted to cosy places, wee bays and coves that looked out on adventurous horizons. Either that or it was the smell of macaroni cheese that poured out of Mactavish's Kitchen, the café on the sea front. He also had a great affection for the fudge as well. Maybe it was just that moment that stuck in his memory when he was really hungry and the macaroni and fudge came together to be forever linked to his nostalgia. Nobody in his right mind ever visits a place because of its pasta and tablet, do they?

Gregor stopped at Luss for a cup of tea, slowed through Crianlarich and hastened through the tourist trap of Tyndrum. Gregor made a small stop at Black Mount near Rannoch Moor where he remembered that there was a plaque memorial to the author, soldier and adventurer Peter Fleming. He died of a heart attack while on a shooting expedition there in 1971. He was a famous man in his own right but his brother, Ian, was more famous because he had written the James Bond books. Indeed, his wife, Celia Johnson, would have been more recognizable at the time because she was a famous actor, once nominated for an Oscar.

Gregor carried on across Rannoch Moor and entered Glencoe just past the ski hill and with the "Big Shepherd" guarding its entrance, a magnificent Munro with its real name being the Buachaille Etive Mòr. It is a sentinel on double duty, guarding both Glencoe and Glen Etive. Gregor had often thought about climbing it but he had always been a cautious hiker and climber so had not wished to risk it on his own. He wound his way down through the glen to the little village of Glencoe and the Ballachulish Bridge. Gregor was old enough to remember having to take the ferry over on this western section of Loch Leven. As he continued his drive down to Oban he decided that he would have a couple of nights in that town then head back and have a couple of nights in the Glencoe campsite. He was excited that he was seeming to formulate a plan. He was no longer meandering and exploring aimlessly but was finding direction.

He drove down the hill to the town, through the centre, passed the ferry terminal and out towards the campsite, which he knew was on a promontory overlooking the Minch, that stretch of water that lay between the mainland and the islands. On his right as he drove was the island of Kerrera. Quaint little white-washed houses dotted the hillsides. The campsite was in a very large field, not deserted but with plenty of room. He parked and pitched his tent by a copse to the north. He knew that it would afford him a great deal of shelter from the elements.

He walked up to explore the facilities and noted a man in his late middle age coming towards him. He said, "Good Afternoon" and received a "Fine day," in return. The gentleman obviously wanted to pass the time of day so Gregor stopped. The man was from Dundee, that much Gregor established, also that he had lost his job due to Prime Minister Margaret Thatcher, that capital punishment should be meted out to westerners dealing drugs in foreign countries. These were snippets of a long diatribe in his broad Fife accent, very little of which Gregor could understand. Gregor listened and nodded politely but contributed very little to the conversation.

Gregor went back into the town that evening, explored a bookshop where he had an interesting encounter as he was examining the postcard rack and thinking about which of a couple of views of Buachaille Etive Mòr to buy.

"Have you been up it?" this voice piped-up beside him.

"Err, no, I haven't. Thought it might be too dangerous to do on my own," Gregor said.

"You'll be fine. Climb it and see the most spectacular of views. Do it. You'll never regret it."

"Yes, yes you've convinced me. I think that I will."

And he did. On the following day he drove back to Glencoe and settled in behind a hedge above the seashore in the campsite. He walked down to the littoral that evening and looked out to the small wooded island in the bay. The legend had it that the Macdonald Clan used to send its leaders out to that island when they couldn't make a decision. They were left there for as long as it took, a temporary exile until a compromise was reached. Gregor reflected on what a good idea that was and that it should be one that is imposed on teacher's staff meetings and national governments the world over. Particularly, when an island like that in the Highlands was bound to be infested with midges, an added incentive to reach a decision if ever there was one. Brexit negotiations between Britain and the EU could have done with a midge-ridden island to hasten things along.

It was a beautiful day when Gregor set off to conquer the Buachaille. There was a song in his heart as he drove up the glen. There was a handy off road car park about a kilometre from the foot of the peak. He warmed up nicely as he headed to the foot of what looked like a complicated scree slope. The map, however, told him that there was a path there so a path there must be. Sure enough as he got closer, the trail became obvious. It was steep but Gregor was fit for a fifty-six-year-old so, despite the sweat, which Gregor did when he did his shoelaces up in the morning, he was soon on the ridge. He headed east to the peak. It was probably the best view of Rannoch Moor anywhere in the world. He was not alone when he reached his goal. There were a couple of older gentlemen, recent retirees, who hailed from the Glasgow area. They were steadily conquering the Munros, picking them off on a good day here, a sunny one there. A *"Munro"* in Scotland is any peak over 3000 feet. There are 282 of them in the country. Gregor expressed admiration for the challenge and the relaxed way they were going about achieving it. They asked him where he was from and offered him a Mars bar, which he gratefully accepted. He told them the ten second version of his life, born in Aberdeen but living in Canada. As he left them to walk back along the ridge, he heard one explain to the other how it was an insult to call a Canadian an American and so forth.

Looking north as he walked back along the ridge, Gregor recognized a familiar sight in the near distance. It looked like he could reach out and touch Ben Nevis. The road from where he had parked at the head of the glen was a long drive to Fort William and Scotland's tallest mountain but as the crow flies it was very close.

Gregor decided to extend his walk so that he was not taking the same descent as ascent but walking farther along the ridge and going down into Glen Etive before heading back to his car. He did feel his knees as he came down the hill but the walk back through the heathery glen with the trickling burn for company was worth the pain. He was very satisfied with his day as he drove back down to the campsite.

He was sitting outside his tent having his supper when he looked up at the Pap of Glencoe. The Pap is a volcanic plug at the westernmost point of the valley. He was surprised at how strong he felt after his arduous hike so decided that if the weather was fine in the morning then he would walk up to the top of this peak. The Pap, so called for its resemblance to a breast, would make a nice bookend with the Buachaille, two interesting tomes to a shelf of infinite variety.

In 1692, Glencoe took its place in the history books when the Campbells abused the law of hospitality by spending the night being hosted by the MacDonalds and then murdering them in the morning. There was politics and money and power mongering involved as there always is with such tragic events. The event found its way into the history books. A memorial to the dead stands in the village and on the other side of the glen is a wonderful visitor centre. Gregor stopped off at the memorial on the following morning on his way to the foot of the trail that was to lead him upwards to the Pap. Yet again it was a steep ascent with a scramble up to the volcanic plug at the end. As he stood atop the basaltic rock he was suddenly transported back to the West Lion just north of Vancouver. Higher, steeper and longer that hike is if one ascends from Lions Bay and a long day indeed if one hikes out along the Howe Sound Crest trail with its many false summits, the cheating deceits of the hills. Just when you think you've reached the top, you are shown that there are more on the way. Yet again, there were panoramic views from the Pap as on the previous day, but this time they had the variation of an inland seascape rather the flatness of a moor. Gregor thought that all it really lacked was a lone piper to round off the day. As it was, he was sweating and a chill wind was coming in from the north so it was time for him to come down. Instead of turning right at the bottom of the hill he took a left and walked to the Clachaig Inn where he had himself a steak and kidney pie and chips to celebrate.

Pitching his tent at the Glen Nevis campsite where he had been many times before, Gregor noticed an older gentleman travelling on his own with a beautiful looking Alsatian. Having brewed a cup of tea he wandered over and offered him one. He accepted and told Gregor his story. He was on a long walk to raise money for cancer research. He was walking as far as Cape Wrath. He showed him his planned route on the map and Gregor noted that there were not many villages or towns en route. William from Birmingham explained that he had a mate who had arranged food stashes for him and Jerry the dog on the way. Gregor was fascinated by his story particularly as he knew the countryside through which he was travelling so well because this was his second time walking it. Gregor said that he was going to climb Ben Nevis on the following day and suggested that William come with him. He politely declined saying that he did not climb mountains, a fact that surprised Gregor greatly, considering his obvious love of the path and the outdoors.

Gregor was on the mountain side early on the next morning. He remembered the route well, the curve around the base and the eventual hop over the wee glen before the ascent up to the top plateau. Ben Nevis is not a pretty mountain, it is a bit of a slug slumped and slumbering over the glen and the shores of Loch Linnhe in the distance. Gregor had remembered the ruined observatory at the top from his last visit. He also smiled at the memory of the young man who had appeared out of the wind and rain, explaining that he had been camped up there for three days desperately wanting to get a picture of the dawn. Every day there had been no dawn, indeed there had been little light to speak of for the duration. Gregor had wondered at how anybody could wait for that one picture and, he had chuckled to himself, what if it had suddenly become a bright sunny morning, a beautiful red glow in the sky and he had slept in! That indeed would have been a poignant moment. Gregor was a bit ashamed at discovering that he was not totally exempt from schadenfreude.

Gregor again was surprised at his level of fitness. He guessed that he had developed a different idea of height and distance since he had lived in Western Canada. His Canadian wife reminded him frequently that there were no mountains in Britain, that even mighty Ben Nevis was a mere spot on the face of the Earth when one considered the many, many peaks that were often twice the size of these Scottish hills. He had, for example, hiked up the famed Grouse Grind near where he lived. It was a steep ascent from car park to near the peak of Grouse Mountain. It was 2800 feet of altitude gained, almost a Munro. Gregor was so practiced at it that he had covered that ground in just over an hour. His daughter, Jessie, was doing it in under 45 minutes. So Ben Nevis' might was shrinking towards the mundane. Jessie, in a later year, was to run up the highest mountains in England and Scotland as if she were simply on a training run. She added credence to Gregor's Canadian theory. So, Gregor skipped his way off the summit of the peak with a bounce in his step and a joy in his heart.

He arrived back in the campsite to find William sat down by his tent and aimlessly browsing through a magazine while occasionally reaching out and giving Jerry a stroke on the back.

"How was your ascent?" William asked.

"Pretty easy, really. Thanks for asking. Still plenty of hours in the day, would you like to come on a drive with me to Glenfinnan?" Gregor asked.

William thought for a second and said that he would love to. Jerry would stay with the tent as long as he had water in his bowl. So off they drove. They skirted the town and headed north across the top of Loch Linnhe.

The Glenfinnan Monument was raised in the 1800s to commemorate the departure of Charles Edward Stuart, having lost the war to win back the throne of Britain. He was the Young Pretender, a Stuart whose legacy had been the throne. He landed at Glenfinnan and departed eight months later with his tail between his legs after a devastating defeat in 1746 at the hands of Butcher Cumberland on Culloden Muir. The urban legend is that this was the last battle fought on British soil. One supposes that the Battle of Britain did not count, as it was fought in the air above. How instrumental this uprising was in devastating the language and culture of the Highland way of life is debatable. The kilt came back, the Gaelic language may have suffered irreversible damage. Round the corner they came, there were the tourist shops and café and there, a short walk from the road, was the tall column atop of which stood the unknown highlander. It says something about the mindset of Scotland that such a magnificent monument should be set up to celebrate a losing cause, rather like Robert Falcon Scott failing to get to the South Pole first but somehow usurping the fame and wisdom of Amundsen who did get there. It seemed that Britain preferred its heroes to be failures.

But there is a major success standing next to the road and that is the railway viaduct that has become a star of movie and calendar whether that be Harry Potter or older black and white movies. The irony of success on one side of the road and failure on the other was not lost on Gregor who mentioned it aloud to William.

"Princess Diana and Mother Teresa," he said, pursing his lips and nodding sagely.

The one was thirty-seven years old when she was killed after a lifetime of bulimia, anorexia, good causes, good looks and celebrity, the other having given of a long life to the poor and dying in India. Diana was always going to win a celebrity bake-off because she was glamorous and had died young. William reminded them both that the two women had died in the same week. Gregor and William had a cup of tea and a scone in the tourist café and drove back to

Glen Nevis gaining the welcome that only a faithful dog can give. Gregor and William had a bite and a deoch an doris in the local café that night. Gregor was sorry to say farewell to them on the following day as he headed north and William and Jerry were returning to the English Midlands.

In Gregor's opinion, the monument to the commando trainees at Spean Bridge is far more impressive than that at Glenfinnan. For one thing it is not as high. One can almost look the three commandos in the eye as they gaze their thousand-yard stare in three different directions. Gregor was about to take his leave when he noticed the memorial garden. This was impressive, too. Individual memorials to World War II soldiers who had trained in this area decorated the ground before him. Gregor took note as a gentleman bent down and picked up one of the photographs. Gregor was about to remonstrate with him at this unthinking sacrilegious act of vandalism when he noted the gentleman wrapping the photograph in a bouquet of heather and putting it back.

"Happy Birthday, Dad," he whispered.

Gregor looked over at the stranger. He glanced back.

"Yes," he said, "never met my dad. He was killed in action before I was born. I come up here every year from Troon to pay my respects on his birthday."

Gregor shook his hand but didn't speak. He reflected as he unlocked his car that he had just been a witness to history, that he had been in the presence of the tragedy and the character of the past. If ever he was asked to answer the question about whether history was worth teaching, he would tell this story. Indeed "the past is a foreign country; they do things differently there," as L.P. Hartley said. But foreign travel is good for the mind and the body.

Fort Augustus is on the Caledonian Canal. It is the southernmost tip of Loch Ness. It has a magnificent set of old buildings once owned by Lord Lovat but sold to the Benedictine Order in 1867. The monks turned it into a school. The village was originally called Kiliwhimin but had its name changed after the Jacobite rebellion of 1715. General Wade had a fort built there to quell future uprisings. The Bonnie Prince took it over shortly before his rout at the Battle of Culloden. The canal enables Scotland to be split into two. It is possible to boat from the Minch to the Moray Firth avoiding going over the top of the country.

Gregor walked along the side of the canal and up to the shores of the loch dodging between excited Japanese tourists happily snapping pictures of each other and no doubt hoping to catch a glimpse of the monster to take back home as a holiday snap. As Gregor casually tossed stones into the lapping waters of the loch, he had a decision to make. Was he going to drive up the west side of the loch through Drumnadrochit and past Urquhart Castle before going into Inverness or was he going on the road less travelled on the eastern side? Gregor shook his head. He knew that he had already made his decision. He would not be able to avoid the east. He would have to make the pilgrimage to Loch Ruthven.

"Nostalgia ain't what it was" as the saying goes but it was still a huge pull for Gregor. He realized that the loch was now a bird sanctuary and that he would be unable to have access to the southern end of the loch where he and his family used to pick up the rowing boat all of those long years ago. He knew that the loch was long and that they had never actually made it much beyond the halfway point in their fishing days, but he was happy enough to park at the north end and walk down to the shore. Gregor was glad to see that the loch was being preserved by the RSPB (Royal Society for the Protection of Birds) because he now realized how close he was to Inverness due to the new road. In the 1960s his father had had to drive south of Inverness and up over the hills to Loch Ashie and Loch Duntelchaig before calling at the farm for the key to unlock the boat. Now it was possible to skirt Inverness on the eastern side up the hill passed Raigmore Hospital and Culloden Moor. It was quicker and more convenient and, frankly, more encroaching. But Gregor had long since balanced the past with the present; it was the only way he could come to terms with the future. As he sat on the fence between the person that he had been all those years ago and the person that he now was, he did not fear stepping into tomorrow because the fence had given him enough confidence to accept the inevitable. Whether it had given him the strength to influence the inevitable was a different matter. Not for the first time, Gregor turned his thoughts and mind to Aberdeenshire but that was for another chapter.

"Mutato nomine de te fabula narrator." (Change only
the name and this story is about you.)
- Horace.

C H A P T E R   3 7

OF FAMILY
AND FRIENDS

Back in his Bunbury Youth Hostel days in 1981, there was an incident that was to affect Gregor for the rest of his life. At the time it was something of nothing, a "mote to trouble the mind's eye" as the Bard would have it. That it was to prove otherwise was unforeseen. It was a numinous nuance at the end of a normal day's work. Gregor liked youth hostels but he didn't like communal kitchens. He understood the idea of cooperation and community all too well, but when he was hungry he liked to cook and eat. He did not like reaching for the pan to find it gone, rummaging for the potato masher to find it unwashed in the sink and so on. Gregor, however, had resigned himself to the slow art of culinary chaos. So, he always turned up with something else to do. He could always write a letter, read his book or do the crossword in his newspaper, which was always at hand.

Gregor was tired and hungry. It had been a particularly hot day. The concrete had arrived at noon when the sun was high in the sky. So they had had to barrow it with unremitting vigour lest if harden before it was levelled off. Gregor arrived in the kitchen, grumpier and hungrier than usual. He prepared his meat and spaghetti for cooking, managed to get the pans he wanted, cranked up the cooker, set it on heat and sat down to watch and wait and stir. He searched in his top pocket for his pen. He turned around to reach for his newspaper that he knew he had brought in with him only to find that it wasn't there. He could remember deliberately picking it up, even turning it to the crossword page in preparation and putting it under his arm as he had come down the stairs after his shower. It was gone. Gregor was irritated.

As Gregor was stirring his pasta and ruminating on the lack of newspaper, he observed an attractive young woman enter the kitchen, find herself a seat and begin to peruse a newspaper. She casually flit through the pages until she reached the puzzles page and began to focus in on the crossword but not until Gregor had noticed the clues that were already answered and clearly noted that they were in his writing. That was Gregor's newspaper. He stood up and walked across to her. He loomed over her with definite intent. He tried but failed to keep the irritation out of his voice. His grumpiness was evident in his whole being. He forced a smile but knew that it was more grim than grin.

"Excuse me. That's my newspaper," he said.

"Sorry," was the blunt reply. And it was thrust in his direction.

Gregor noted the Canadian accent, which only made him more irritated, but as he tried to focus on his crossword, his eyes kept straying to the woman who was now eating her supper. He kept sneaking glances from beneath his beetled brows. Gregor could not keep his eyes off her. Gregor was smitten.

Some thirty-seven years later, Gregor is still smitten. He just doesn't admit to it too much. The crossword is still very much part of his life but nowadays it is a communal event. Gregor and Mae sit in their back garden in North Vancouver in the province of British Columbia in Canada. Occasionally they reflect on the fact that they have a thirty-four-year-old daughter and a thirty-two-year-old son, that they have been married for thirty-five years and that they should be content with the fact that they are both retired. They wear each other like comfortable old shoes. Their two children, Jessie and Ross, were both born in Lincoln during Gregor's Brampton School days. Mae had been an excellent wife and mother. She had been kindly and practical but forthright and clear when she needed to be. There was never a waffle or a waiver when it came to how she wanted to bring up her children. She wanted them to be liked and personable and acceptable to society at large. She had succeeded with the children, but Gregor was a work in progress. Both Gregor and Mae were proud of their children's character and resilience. Their lives had not been easy. Jessie had been diagnosed with Multiple Sclerosis in her late 20s. Ross had had Alport syndrome from birth. His kidneys failed in his early twenties. After two-and-a-half years of dialysis three times per week, he finally received a kidney transplant.

Mae had married Gregor because she thought that he would help him relax. Gregor had married Mae because she was the one; he ceased to have eyes for others and could not conceive of life with anyone else. So it was and so it is.

UNDER A SCOTTISH SKY AND AN ENGLISH HEAVEN?

It was late in the day when Gregor sat down and reflected on his life. As he pondered his wife, Mae, and their two children, as he thought about his forty-three years of teaching, he realized that it had been an ordinary life ordinarily lived. He thought back to his first teacher mentor who had liltingly explained that he would "never set the Thames alight." It produced a sharp intake of breath when he reiterated that saying. Ms. Thomas had been right. He had never really set anything or anybody alight with any smattering of charismatic energy. His strength had merely remained in the fact that he turned up to work every day that he could. When sickness spread through his three schools then Gregor wasn't. He had often been the first teacher standing in the morning and the last one there in the evening. There had always been an air of underdoggedness about Gregor that had had its advantages. On the few occasions he had raised his head above the parapet to be shot at he really had leapt off the fence upon which he normally sat and surprised a number of people in his ability to articulate his concerns. On these rare occasions he doggedly gripped the bone of contention.

When Gregor retired from teaching he could not preen himself on a life well-lived but he could credit himself on a life well-survived. He had heard plaudits about how he had inspired this student to that success. He had been awed by how a throwaway remark that befit an early morning mood had shaped a student to move positively forward. What he had not heard enough of was the negative statements he had thrown away, the scars that would resurface as a memory forty years later. The law of percentages said that they were there. Indeed, he had been present at a Professional Development when a fifty-year lady had shared. As a ten-year-old she had turned up in her party dress of which she was so proud and she was looking forward to attending a birthday party at the end of the day. Her teacher had said something like, "Why are you dressed like that?" in a disparaging, sarcastic manner and gone back to the calling of her homeroom thinking no more of it. But forty years on, her student still remembered it.

"Beware the anger of the patient man," had leapt off the page one day when Gregor was reading and he thought, with no false modesty, that that statement was a fair reflection of him. Always in the background, unnoticed and unheralded, always "watchful behind a fan" then it became a surprise when the wallpaper was peeled back and underneath was a hard brick wall, thrawn and immovable. On rare occasions Gregor could be that wall and when he spoke after he had forced himself forward from his hinterland, then he surprised enough of the people who knew him that they actually listened to him.

Gregor had accepted that he had been teased and bullied at school when he was a boy. He had coped with it. It would be wrong to say that he had risen above it but right to admit that he had slunk below it. He had seen the radar and slipped under it. He was happy to let others have the limelight and occasionally peer out from under his rock with curiosity. He was always aware of the happy shadow into which he could retreat. He had been the ugly duckling who suddenly found himself a swan, able to make friends, able to have respect and able to steady his mental and emotional ship so that everyday life began to hold no fear for him. He knew that he would never be a leader, knew that his confidence and self-esteem were only skin-deep but also knew that he could pretend and somehow keep a smile on his face.

Gregor had accepted that life was exciting, interesting and to be lived. When he had worked, he had found his relaxations with friends, sport, reading, writing, his family. He thought that his recreations were stress relieving and regenerating and, indeed, they substantially were.

But then he returned to the land of his birth in 2008. He set up his tent in Rothiemurchus where he had camped during the 1969 moon landing. The sun shone the following morning and he decided to walk up through the early stages of the Lairig Ghru, the "gloomy path," that eventually spilled out into Aberdeenshire and Deeside. The path was peaty, the heather was purple, the burn burbled and the Scots pines were the most beautiful trees he had ever seen. As he walked, a peace descended over him that he had not known for years. It was as if a curtain had been lifted before him and a world had been opened up to him which was a balm to his soul and a massage to his mind. It was like meeting with an old friend. He knew then what he had known all along: that wherever life had taken him, his womb, his place of foetal comfort would always be Scotland. He was Scottish, he sounded English. He was grateful to England for his upbringing, but for him there would always be a kilt in the closet.

CPSIA information can be obtained
at www.ICGtesting.com
Printed in the USA
LVHW101104120520
655427LV00006B/189